MOUNTAI

MOUNTAIN HOLIDAYS

By

JANET ADAM SMITH

'But for me, the Alps and their people were
alike beautiful in their snow, and their humanity.'

RUSKIN: *Praeterita*

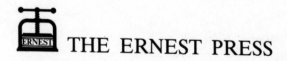 THE ERNEST PRESS

Published by The Ernest Press 1996
© Janet Adam Smith
First Published in 1946 by J M Dent & Sons Ltd

ISBN 0 948153 45 8

British Library Cataloguing-in-Publication Data
A catalogue record for this book is available from
the British Library

Typeset by Westec, North Connel
Graphic reproduction by Arneg, Glasgow
Printed and Bound by St Edmundsbury Press

FOREWORD

THIS book is an account, not primarily of climbs, but of climbing holidays in the Highlands and the Alps. It records no great feats of mountaineering, no striking new ascents—a few new routes there were, indeed, but some of these were made by accident. Our aim was not to establish records, but to enjoy ourselves; and the book too was written for pleasure, to recall the enjoyment of days on mountains as well known as the Matterhorn and Mont Blanc, as little known as the minor peaks of the Haute Maurienne or Wester Ross. But the enjoyment of a mountain holiday does not cease below the snow-line; and this book also attempts to recall the pleasures of inns and villages, glens and pastures, gossip and idleness—all the varied texture of holidays that included bog-myrtle and soldanelles, cows, haylofts, and *vin rouge*, as well as peaks, passes, and glaciers.

The lines quoted at the heads of the chapters come from poems by W. P. Ker, Gawain Douglas, James Hogg, R. M. Rilke, Michael Roberts, Lord Tennyson, and Thomas Traherne. The verse at the head of Chapter VI is from a French song.

CONTENTS

ILLUSTRATIONS

(at end of book)

I wish to thank the Victoria and Albert Museum for permission to reproduce the drawing by Francis Towne (20) in their collection (Crown copyright reserved); and to the Max Niehans Verlag, Zürich, for permission to reproduce the drawing by Jan Hackaert (21) from S. Stelling-Michaud's *Unbekannte schweizer Landschaften aus dem XVII Jahrh.* I also thank the following for allowing me to use photographs by them, or in their possession: St Andrews University Library (1, 2, 3); Mr. Hugh D Welsh (4b); Mr. Arthur Gardner (5, taken by the late Hugh Gardner); Mr. George Michie (9); Mrs. J. P. Butler (12a); Professor T. Graham Brown (13); Mr. J. Firth Burton (17); Lieut. David A. Robertson, U.S.N.R. (23); Captain George Patterson (31); and Andrew Roberts (32).

The Graian Alps

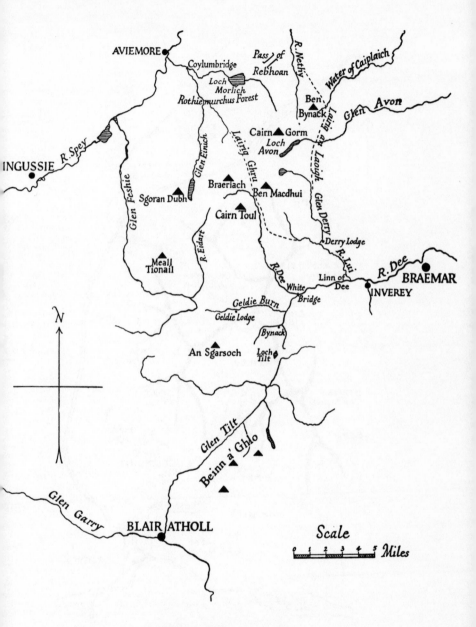

The Cairngorms

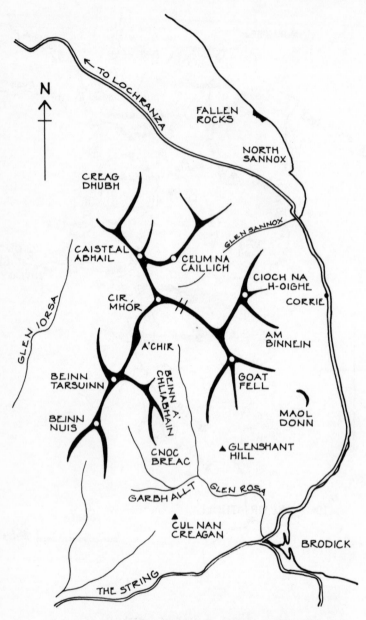

N

TO LOCHRANZA

FALLEN
ROCKS

NORTH
SANNOX

CREAG
DHUBH

GLEN SANNOX

CAISTEAL
ABHAIL

CEUM NA
CAILLICH

CIOCH NA
H-OIGHE

CORRIE

CIR
MHOR

AM
BINNEIN

A'CHIR

BEINN
TARSUINN

BEINN A'
CHLIABHAIN

GOAT
FELL

GLEN IORSA

BEINN
NUIS

MAOL
DONN

CNOC
BREAC

GLENSHANT
HILL

GARBH ALLT

GLEN ROSA

CUL NAN
CREAGAN

BRODICK

THE STRING

Arran – North half of the Island

CHAPTER I

THE APRIL ISLAND

There light is sown in mountain streams.

"RUN and ask Professor Ker if you can join the party for Ben Nuis," said my mother as we came down Glen Cloy in Arran after a picnic in April 1914. Professor Ker didn't speak for a minute or two after I had put my question: I wondered if he thought that eight years old was being too ambitious. Then "Yes", no more; and I fell back to my place beside my mother, feeling I was no longer a baby.

For years our family had gone to Arran at Easter, taking a house at Brodick, while W. P. Ker, with his party of nieces or god- children, stayed at the hotel. We joined forces for most things—for picnics in the Fairy Glen, for expeditions to Sannox and the Fallen Rocks, for jaunts by sea to Lamlash, Holy Island, and Whiting Bay, and even just for meeting the steamer at the pier; but especially for climbs, when the inevitable and undisputed leader was W. P.

Arran is a good place for family holidays when the family straggles over twenty years: the long legs and the short, the skilful rock-climbers and those who can hardly walk, can all enjoy themselves according to their powers, and yet not be completely divided. Picnics would be arranged in places which gave the younger ones a walk—and paddling, or dam-building, as on the lower crooks of the Rosa—while the elders, having flashed over the seven bens and seven glens and seven mountain moors, would come down like gods in time for tea. Once a year, on April 7th, we had a festival in Glen Sannox, to celebrate my mother's birthday. The parents, the food, and the babies went by Kaspar Ribbeck's horse-bus—or, if the party was huge, with contingents of Bartholomews, Barbours, and Wordies, by a special wagonette—and walked up the glen as far as the flat grassy stretch, with a line of beeches on one side and a heather bank on the other, that was traditionally

1

consecrated to the day. From there we would anxiously scan Cioch na h-Oighe for signs of the descending climbers. They were never quite punctual for this rendezvous, for it was always a lunch picnic (tea that day was in the Corrie Hotel, a beautiful feast given and presided over by W. P.'s sister, Miss Penelope), and the way over by Goatfell, the North Top, and Cioch is a good day's walk. Only the strongest were allowed to go by the hills that day.

So when, in Glen Cloy, I was told I could come to Ben Nuis, I knew I was no longer one of the paddlers, always destined for the picnic party, never for the tops. I dare say I was insufferably superior to my younger sister, but at three she had other compensations; I know I prayed for a fine day. And it was a fine day; but, oh, the wind! There wasn't a great deal on the road by the school house (where we always walked on the pink sandstone wall, though W. P. rather frowned on these capers at the beginning of a serious expedition); but it was blowing great guns down Glen Rosa, and by the time we had battled our way to the bridge over the Garbh Allt, I could hardly breathe. We had the usual pause by the bridge—for ginger-nuts, perhaps, or Velma—and I remember those subdued, withdrawn tones that grown-ups use when they are discussing something to do with children who aren't far away. My sister Maisie, almost a grown-up herself, seemed to be putting in a good word for me. But then my mother broke the news: W. P. did not think this would be a good day for my first climb. I expect I cried, for I cried easily; I certainly remember the sting of misery and rage as I watched the others stride up the steep brackeny slope that is the first stage towards Nuis, especially when my mother said: "The worst's over when they've got up there"; for quite soon they were up there, and I felt I might so easily have been with them. I don't suppose I gave a thought to her disappointment at missing the climb, but I couldn't help enjoying being blown down the glen again. There was another bad moment when the climbers got back in the evening, and I tried to look as if I didn't mind not being with them as they clumped up the pebbly path to Charters Towers with the content look of anybody who has reached his top, whether Meije or Nuis.

My consolation was to be Goatfell a few days later. But again the wind beat me, though not till we had reached the long shoulder that leads up to the final peak. By the time mother told me that we had better give up, I was too sick and tired of this tearing and buffeting to mind very much. And frightened too; this was something worse than thunder, for I couldn't just sit still and make myself be brave; I was just knocked over. It was no use saying 'I won't cry'; the wind whipped my hair, and the edge of my kilted skirt, into my eyes, and however much I wasn't crying, there were the tears. Up on the shoulder, my mother and I, we crouched behind the granite boulders, dashing from one to another whenever there seemed to be a lull. I remember Professor Terry and his wife, who had joined us at Brodick that Easter, also dodging from stone to stone, so it was not only eight-year-olds who found it stiff. Down by the burn again, the wind eased off; soon the rest of the party caught us up—they had not stayed long on the top that day—and it was in April sunlight, with no more than a breeze, that we skipped and danced down the stony path towards the rhododendrons and the primrosy Castle woods. For the first of many times, I knew that most exquisite mountain joy—the return to the valley and sunlight and flowers and running water, from the grand and terrifying world of bad weather on the tops. I held the two moments in my hand, and knew I had brought back something from my second mountain reverse.

Next Easter, nine years old succeeded where eight had failed, but these first climbs to the top of Goatfell and Nuis are not so clear in memory as the windy days of 1914. I remember the last few hundred feet of Goatfell, very misty, with my brother George giving just the sort of help and encouragement that my dignity allowed me to accept. I remember one incident on Nuis, a huge boulder slowly toppling loose on a scree gully, and again George, just above us, holding it back somehow without fuss, and grinning as we got level with him. Then down it went. But the remainder of that day merges into the traditional picture of our expeditions to Nuis—the halt at the Garbh Allt, the plod across the high moor, the lunch by the rowan pool of the upper burn, the long curved shoulder up to the top, and, if the day were fine and the party strong, the return by Tarsuinn, the Bowman's Pass, and A'Chliabhain. Climbing with W. P., the days took on a natural order and rhythm. One reason, perhaps, was that our parties, of such widely different ages and capacities, could obviously not be allowed to go helter-skelter across the hills as they pleased. There are straightforward ways up nearly all the Arran hills, but there are plenty of rocks, and heather ledges ending in sudden drops, to make any ignorant straying silly and dangerous. But this ceremonial approach was more than a practical necessity, it was part of W. P.'s attitude to the hills themselves. They were beautiful, they gave us our finest holiday pleasures; we must behave among them with dignity and respect. One of the ways of achieving this right relation was to establish a proper rhythm and pattern for our days: always the lunch by the rowan pool; or, on Goatfell, by the pathway just under the shoulder, 'with the tinned sardiney smell'; always the steady stride over the ridges, with no sudden fancies to climb this or that pinnacle; always, if we came off the hills at Corrie or Sannox, the placid trudge round to Brodick by the coast road, with no sudden impulses to ring up for a car. In 1915, indeed, there were no cars on the island; but any kind of lift would have broken this last movement of the day when the body, for many hours alert and responsive to every change from track to heather, snow to rock, ridge to slope, at last relaxes, the legs do their last lap willingly and mechanically, and the mind is free to follow its disconnected sequence of fancy, memory, speculation, and somnolence.

Does this discipline, this order, sound oppressive? I don't think we ever felt oppressed. There were mild rebellions, of course. We lingered behind so as to climb over all the monkeys—those great stacks of granite blocks—on the ridge from Goatfell to Cioch na h-Oighe. We took short cuts home through the Castle woods, dancing down in jiggety-jigs. Coming off Goatfell on the Glen Rosa side, we would slant round the hillside, so as to run down full tilt to the burn unseen by W. P. as he stepped steadily down at his hillman's pace. After a crossing of the Saddle, Alick would sweep Kathleen and me ahead down Glen Sannox, to make an ambush and a sortie. Once, greatly defiant, Kathleen went for a climb in shoes, saying she hated boots. W. P.'s silence was enough; next day, the boots were on.

But these were the grace-notes, the exuberant decorations in the margin; they did not affect the essential pattern of the day,

and with that pattern we were very well content, sometimes up-
holding W. P.'s standards with a fierceness and intolerance that he
had never shown towards us. I remember a cocky and talkative
stranger, imported by one of the Barbours, who told us one evening
on the sands of Brodick that he could run up to the top of
Goatfell in gym shoes. We told him then what we thought of
him, and the next day when he did go up Goatfell (but not
running), not a hole in the gym shoes, not a stumble on the
unfortunate's descent down the rocky path, escaped our withering
comment.

If W. P. disapproved of personal idiosyncrasies in routes or
footgear, it was because he was doing more than give the best of
holidays to a dozen boys and girls. He was teaching them a skilled
craft; and he knew that if they, in their turn, were to find in
mountain holidays a never-failing source of energy and happiness,
then they must learn the right mountain way. Of course Goatfell
could be romped up in gym shoes; but the person who did it
would have blisters the next day and would probably, next holidays,
have a craze for motor-bicycles or roller-skates, and never think
of the hills again. But the April children (as, we learned long
afterwards, he used to call us) must have that freedom and delight
that come from the mastery of a physical skill. And so, without
consciously realizing it, with hardly a word spoken, we learnt to
climb slowly and steadily; not to ask for 'rests'; not to drink at
every burn; to keep an eye on those in front and behind, and
not to jostle too close; to be careful about loose stones, and never
to throw one down deliberately; to save time on a rocky step by
noticing what hand- and footholds the person in front used; to
come downhill at a springy, steady step, and not in a series of
bone-rattling, liver-shaking rushes. 'Chi va piano va sano,' was one
of his few explicit teachings; 'chi va sano va lontano.' We learnt
that you could chatter going home down the glen—I remember
a long talk with him on Hakluyt one afternoon by the Rosa—but
that it was silly to waste your breath and spoil your rhythm by
talking on the way up. We learnt to obey at once the occasional
word of command, and not to bother the leader by asking him
if he were on the right path. As we watched him scanning the
weather on the Saddle between Cir Mhor and Goatfell, with mists

boiling up from Glen Sannox, we learnt that decisions to go on or turn back are not taken light-heartedly; as he relaxed into conversation on the coast road home we realized perhaps something of the energy and concentration needed to guide a large party through a long mountain day.

When any of the company had mastered the craft, then W. P. would set them off on their further explorations with a cheer. He always saluted real enterprise, and independence based on skill, as when my elder brothers George and Beppo, with Tom Lindsay or Ian Bartholomew or James Wordie, went off with a rope to try a new climb on the face of Cir Mhor, or a variation on the A' Chir Ridge. He was proud and pleased when George came in quietly one evening, having climbed all the great Arran peaks that day, by himself. W. P. too liked an adventure, when the conditions were right. Sometimes, when it was no weather for taking a large party over the tops, or when departures had thinned the ranks towards the end of the holidays, he would go off with two or three on a special ploy—to find a new way off Goatfell by the North Top and Am Binnein; a new route from the Fallen Rocks over the top of the island to Loch Ranza; an exploration of the waterfalls at the head of Glen Cloy; a direct descent from the Castles to Glen Sannox. I remember one of these days in 1921. We were a fairly big party that year, not altogether harmonious: for some were new to the island and could not help unconsciously violating a number of our unwritten and unspoken rules. (I remember one innocent remark, spoken on the lonely North Sannox road, that made me absurdly angry: 'Is it safe to leave a coat on the bridge till we come back?' As if Arran were Hampstead Heath!) So it was with a sense of escape that Kathleen, Olivia Horner, and I went with W. P. for a last climb on Cir Mhor. He led us up a gully that started from the Saddle, new to us and exciting all the way. Half way up, the rain still held off, and there were the Cumbraes, fifteen miles across the Firth but clear enough to pick out the lighthouse and the white farms, with a black sky almost touching them. Five minutes later we could hardly see each other for the rain.

All my feeling for mountains is coloured by W. P., and yet I cannot remember his talking much about them. Over baps and sardines, or over tea at Corrie Hotel—when he would refuse jam with his bread and country butter, saying 'I am an epicure'—he would talk about *The Hunting of Arran*, the poem that describes St. Patrick's landing on the island, or about the peregrine falcons on A'Chliabhain. We hardly realized all that he was giving us; but we knew that the Arran holidays were the best of all. The ruddy brown tweed jacket; the brass ring round the tie; the jerk of the shoulder as the rucksack was heaved on after lunch; the figure on the boulder by the burn, smoking a peaceful pipe after the glen had been reached, while the younger and hardier dipped in cold green April pools; the lift and sweep of the hand in the direction of a peak; the gallant flourish of the hat on the last stretch home, as the non-climbers came out to meet us—these are the pictures that come when I try to remember how W. P. showed us the way to the hills.

Chapter II

TO THE ALPS

Whilk to behold was pleasaunce and half wonder.

FOR many years my horizon was limited to Scottish hills, with an occasional glance at the Lakes. We still went to Arran most Aprils, and from our home in Aberdeen there were expeditions, by train and bicycle, to Benachie, to Morrone and Mount Keen and Clochnaben. I was only vaguely interested in the Alps; if I had put my feelings about them into words, I should have said that they were another world altogether from the hills on which we were at home, and that only outstanding climbers could go there at all. Father had climbed from Zermatt for several summers in the eighties, and his ice-axes hung on the study wall at Chanonry; but the climbs seemed to belong to the legendary period of family history, and the axes themselves were like the honoured trophies of a far-off heroic battle in which we had no part. We knew, of course, that W. P. went each summer to the Alps (he traversed the Zinalrothorn and the Matterhorn when he was sixty-five); but he was so much beyond us in mountain wisdom that we never supposed ourselves able to do what he did when climbing with his equals. There had been talk of George going out to the Alps in the summer of 1914 (his last climb was in Arran after all); but George, too, was a prince of climbers.

And so, I am ashamed to think, my first feeling on being told that my mother and younger sister and I would spend the summer of 1923 at La Grave in the Dauphiné, was annoyance because I would miss the local Highland games and balls where I had hoped to put in my first grown-up appearance. I was so ignorant that I didn't know that the Dauphiné mountains were part of the Alps; I had certainly never heard of the Meije.

Ten days before we started, the worst blow came from the Alps themselves. W. P. had died at Macugnaga. With three goddaughters, Olivia Horner, Freya Stark, and Poldores MacCunn, he had started for the Pizzo Bianco. 'We put out the lantern at Rosareccia; it was a most beautiful clear morning, and as we came into the corrie above the Alpe, where the stream was shallow through grass, and one can look out on the ring of Monte Rosa and see all the hills of Val Anzasca, he said: "I thought this was the most beautiful spot in the world, and now I know it." ' A few minutes later his heart stopped; he was buried in the churchyard at Macugnaga, under the lime-trees.

It was under the shadow of this loss that we drove up the valley from Bourg d'Oisans, past banks of wild lavender, into air that was sharp and clean; suddenly the Meije came in sight. So this was his world. But his death—so harmonious an ending for him, however desolating for us—made the Alps seem even more an enchanted country, forbidden to all but the initiates. From La Grave there were splendid expeditions, with the Sorleys and the Somervells, to the Plateau de Paris, the Lac Bleu, the Chalet de l'Alpe, the Col du Galibier (walking up all the short cuts between the zigzags of the road); but it never entered my head that I could do a real climb. For one reason Alpine climbing seemed to be prohibitively expensive (a man down from the Meije told us that it had cost him £10 plus champagne); but my lack of imagination and enterprise were also to blame, for when my mother suggested that perhaps I might go with a guide to the Brèche de la Meije, I wasn't enthusiastic. We often looked through the telescope at parties on the Meije, and went through sympathetic agonies when once a man lost his nerve coming off the rocks on to the glacier and would neither go on nor go back; but I never thought that some day I might be there myself. Instead, I played bad tennis on a shocking court with a French boy who cheated (I expect he thought that I did), or hung about waiting for the post to bring long letters from school friends describing tennis tournaments and summer dances. But I loved the holiday at La Grave, and later at Pralognan, and enjoyed for the first time many of the pleasures of the Alps below the snow-line—the cow bells on the high pastures, the rush and colour of glacier-streams, the taste of good tangy *vin ordinaire*, the glissades down the steep hillsides where hay had been cut, the smell of wild lavender, the reflections of snow on a blue mountain lake.

My second visit to the Alps was made in a less ignorant and more enterprising frame of mind. In the six years since La Grave I had climbed a good deal in Arran and the Cairngorms, no longer in large family parties following a leader, but with one or two companions, of about the same skill and experience as myself, sharing the responsibility of a climb, deciding whether it was safe to go down from Braeriach to the Garbh Coire in a mist, or whether there was time to do the Castles as well as Cir Mhor. These experiences bred self-confidence, and a first reading of *The Playground of Europe* gave colour and body to my growing hopes about the Alps.

There was a special tingle of excitement about this holiday, for we were going to the Riffel Alp—almost holy ground to our family, for it was there that Father and Mother had met and, after five days, decided to marry. Now, after forty years, they were going back; Margaret and I felt like pilgrims to a sacred shrine. And, going with my father in this way to the mountains he had climbed when he was young, the last shred of the hesitancy and doubt with which I had faced the Alps vanished. When the train from Visp to Zermatt stopped a minute or two at St. Niklaus, there was Josef Imboden, a ruddy, cheerful man, to greet Father and say a word or two about their days together in the eighties. All the way up the valley Father gave the shining mountains their names—Weisshorn, Dent Blanche, Dom, Täschhorn, and, round the last corner before Zermatt, the Matterhorn itself. By the time we got to the Riffel, I knew I had found the link with the Alps—with these Alps, at any rate. I had no more doubts about wanting to climb them; I was only eager to do it properly.

There could have been no better place for a novice than the Riffel that year. The first evening we met some old friends, the Kenneth Leyses; they at once introduced us to Professor Wilberforce and Mr. F. N. Ellis. As soon as they heard I wanted to start climbing they were all encouragement. Mrs. Leys had been up the Dent Blanche a year or so before and spoke of it as quite a possibility; Mr. Ellis at once offered to lend me his spare ice-axe; Professor Wilberforce suggested a good young guide. Father had already given us a handsome start by offering us each, in London, a pair of Carter's boots. Margaret went to be fitted, but I already had some that I had been using in the Cairngorms, and could not bring myself to accept a new pair at £4. 15s. That refusal exasperates me still, almost as much as the missed chances at La Grave. Margaret, whose career as an Alpinist was not very long, still has hers in excellent condition, but three sizes too small to be of any use to me.

The first day at the Riffel was cloudless, and we just looked at the peaks. The second was grey, with a smirr of rain. Professor Wilberforce set me along the path by the cricket ground; after he had left me I went up and had some charming scrambles on good rock until I realized that they must be the Riffelhorn which I had promised Father not to climb alone. I plodded up to the Gornergrat instead, on to the Hohthäligrat, and down by the back-stairs path to the Findelen valley and home. The next day Professor Wilberforce and the Ellises took me across the Gorner glacier; then at last, on the fourth day, came the first real climb with a guide, and Margaret to share it. It was only the Riffelhorn by the Skyline couloir, and the climb was over in three hours from leaving the hotel; but it still leaves a very gay memory. It was lovely rock, it was perfectly easy though always amusing; it no longer seemed presumptuous to think of bigger things. Father suggested the Breithorn next; he had escorted Mother up it in 1889, when it was considered the most suitable mountain for a lady, being all snow. But Moritz Dirren, the good young guide, was emphatic that the Rimpfischhorn would be far better fun.

The Rimpfischhorn it was, and I don't think he could have made a better choice for a beginner, with its mixture of snow and rock, its view into another valley, and its easy descent. I was seen off by the kind and helpful Riffel Alp friends with as much enthusiasm and encouragement as if I had been bound for the Zmutt ridge of the Matterhorn. Offers of goggles, glacier cream, puttees, and extra sweaters made me feel important. My own family walked with me as far as the Findelen; as Moritz and I crossed the glacier, in not too hopeful weather, I prayed desperately that my return mightn't be an anticlimax.

After he had persuaded the hostess's daughter at the Fluh Alp to sleep in the hay, so that I might have her bed, Moritz disappeared to hobnob with other guides, and I was left rather shyly to acquaint

myself with hut life. There were about a dozen climbers—a party
of Swiss, a couple of Frenchmen, a civil engineer on leave from
India, and three Canadian girls. The Swiss were rather silent, two
of the Canadians lively and friendly, the Englishman interested
and encouraging; altogether supper was very jolly, except for the
weather, which was rain and mist. In the hostess's daughter's room
I fussed round getting everything just right for the morning—the
little pile of spare woollens for Moritz's sack, the lumps of sugar
in the breeches pocket—and then read by candlelight to make me
sleepy (*Mrs. Dalloway*, in a Tauchnitz edition). I woke at midnight
and listened; no sound of rain. I went to the window; a clear
and starry night. Happily I snuggled down again on the rustling
straw mattress, and slept till the expected knock at 2.15.

What I chiefly remember about my first midnight breakfast is
the cherry jam—black, luscious, plentiful. For the first time I
knew the delicately balanced sensations of a start in the dark.
One impulse draws you towards the climb, the top, the snow, the
sun; another pulls you back, away from the cold and dark, into
the fuggy warmth and lamplight of the hut. You shiver as you
sling on your rucksack at the door of the hut, and the cold feeling
in your stomach, the backward pull, does not quite leave you until
you climb to the sunlight and are caught up into the full swing
and beauty of the day.

This first morning, though, I had no sack to sling on; Moritz
shoved my extra sweaters into his enormous Swiss guide's holdall.
We were the fifth party to start, and the lanterns of those ahead
jerked up the first slopes; in the starlight we could just see the
outline of the hills. I wondered if climbing the Rimpfischhorn
was going to be an entirely different business from climbing Cir
Mhor in snow; if some quite new skill would be demanded, some
undreamt-of exertion; anyway, at the moment, I had better concentrate on not stumbling in the dark. For the Rimpfischhorn,
you cross two snowy slopes separated by bands of rock. These
rocks were perfectly easy; the snow was a bit of a plod, but no
more; and with the help of a good deal of poetry I managed not
to let the rope between me and the briskly stepping Moritz get
too taut. I expect I said Keats's *Odes* to myself and *Kubla Khan*,
Lycidas, *L'Allegro*, and a few of Shakespeare's sonnets, for these

are my usual stand-by for upward plods, far better than counting steps; but half way across the first snow slope it was lines from *Romeo and Juliet* that rushed into my mind. I looked up, and saw the dawn on Monte Rosa:

> Night's candles are burnt out, and jocund day
> Stands tip-toe on the misty mountain-tops.

Here on the Alps I felt that same breathless catch at the heart, that same purity of joy, that I had sometimes known listening to Mozart, or looking at Piero's 'Nativity' or Leonardo's 'Virgin of the Rocks.'

Back to the plod, and for the last steep snow slope *The Stag at Eve* was the right rhythm; then the last rocks, a delightful scramble, the sun, the top itself. The rocks had been easier than some routes we had made up the top rocks of Benachie; the snow plod was not more tiring than the heather slopes of Nuis, and the time, just inside five hours, probably rather less than Macdhui from Coylum bridge. My respect for the Alps was terrific, I knew that I knew nothing about glaciers, I had never cut a step in ice; but the Alps no longer seemed to offer a different order of experience from the hills of home, they were an extension and amplification of things already known. This, in time, might be my country as Arran was.

We spent three quarters of an hour on top, with the Englishman and his guide and one of the Canadians. Though mist hid the near valleys, we saw down to blue Como and Maggiore, and all the circle of Alps, from Monte Rosa near us round to Mont Blanc and the Oberland. I munched bread and sardines and chocolate, and felt that utter satisfaction of the top reached, the day fine, the body satisfied, and the glories of the world for the eye to look at.

We romped down cheerfully, with a ski-ing motion on the melting snow, and were back at the Fluh Alp soon after eleven for a sleep in the sun and a full view of the Matterhorn every time I opened my eyes. The only jarring note was struck by one of the Canadian girls, who said: 'I suppose you'll be making the Matterhorn next'. I was shocked that she should imagine that on the strength of the Rimpfischhorn (which she knew to be my first Alp) I should consider myself fit for the Matterhorn. I knew enough by this time, from the talk at the Riffel and Mortiz's gossip, to realize that any one sound in wind and limb could be taken up the Matterhorn by a couple of guides. But I had no wish to go up except as a fully competent member of the rope, as far as the actual climbing went; and I certainly didn't mean to grab the Matterhorn greedily, or casually. Of course it was the greatest mountain of the Valais; all the more, it should be approached with respect. Already, since the morning, I had planned to do all the peaks round—Monte Rosa, Breithorn, Dent Blanche, Gabelhorn, Rothorn, Weisshorn, Dom—and then, some day, the Matterhorn as a solemn climax.

In the meantime there were plenty of possibilities. One sunny morning I spent with Moritz and a man on leave from West Africa on the glacier face of the Riffelhorn, where we danced across the rocks in rubbers, took turns to lead, and came down a pitch to go up again in a slightly different way. The Zinalrothorn, Moritz's next suggestion, did not now seem too ambitious. Father agreed; but he couldn't remember much about his own climb on it, and said I must have a porter too. Feeling a little like Gertrude Bell, I commissioned Moritz to engage a Biener for the climb. The day we should have gone up to the Trift Hotel was not at all promising, so instead I went with some others from the Riffel to the Staffel Alp, and up to the Schwarzsee. There I telephoned across to the Riffel, and heard that Moritz had already started for the Trift. Leaving the others to a decent descent, and pancakes and cherry jam at the Hermitage, I lolloped down to Zermatt in three quarters of an hour, and up to the Trift in another hour and a quarter.

The Rimpfischhorn had given the perfect pattern of a successful Alpine day; the Zinalrothorn gave the compensating pleasures that can be snatched out of a reverse. I woke at half-past one, heard noises, dressed, and went down; Moritz said the weather was bad and sent me back to bed, but I noticed with some envy that some young Germans were starting. At seven it seemed worse—mist and rain—and Moritz announced with a grin that the Germans had given up after an hour, and would now be back in Zermatt. However, after talk of the Untergabelhorn while we drank our coffee, the mist cleared a bit, and Moritz thought we might have a look at the Rothorn. The Canadian girl who had spoken of 'making the Matterhorn' (last night she had grumbled about guides not climbing on Sundays) started just before us with two Lochmatters. We caught up with them at the foot of the curtain of rock that separates the mountain proper from the Rothorn Glacier; for five minutes Moritz and the Lochmatters discussed whether to go on. Not knowing German, I felt again like one of the children, shut out from the grown-up plannings. The decision was reached, and interpreted. The wind would be too strong on the arête, the slabs too wet. But would we like to do the Zniebelenhorn? Now this point, which I have never seen marked on any map, and which no one I have ever asked has heard of, is only a bump on the Rothorn glacier, and I do not suppose that it can have given any of the guides any pleasure to prolong their trudge on this dismal day. But Moritz, at any rate, knew how disappointed I must be about the Rothorn, and knew that I should like to go back with some top reached. And even though the Zniebelenhorn remained a great joke to the sceptics at the Riffel—the Snifflehorn, it became, reached by the Whisker glacier—by that time I had so enjoyed my day that I didn't care. We glissaded all the way down the snow slopes from the horn, cantered down the moraine, and reached the Trift in watery sunlight—all the more pleased, I fear, because the Canadian girl was miles behind. Our high spirits took us down in a bound to Zermatt, Alphonse Biener cutting it the finest as we jumped and short-cutted through the Trift gorge. It was the time that stout gentlemen work off their good table d'hôte by a walk uphill; they looked startled to see us hurtling by, and I amused myself by imagining that I impaled them as I passed on the point of my ice-axe, and wondering how many would be sticking to it by the time we got down.

Two days later, in the Simplon-Calais express, I settled down to dinner and *Running Water*, and didn't even regret the failure on the Rothorn. The Alps were all before me, a whole heaven of possibilities. At the Riffel I had been given the best possible send-off to my explorations; Professor Wilberforce had even added a couplet on the Snifflehorn to his celebrated *Riffel Alp Mountaineer's Progress*. No more doubts and hesitations, no more fear of a world to which I did not belong; the only thing that bothered me was, how on earth to get Highlands *and* Alps within the compass of a three weeks' annual holiday.

The Alps, I found on coming home, were not only a world of mountains, but of books. The *Alpine Journals* in the hall bookcase at Chanonry were no longer just part of the furniture of home, like *The Head-hunters of Borneo, The Island of Stone Money,* the Works of Martin Lightfoot, and other familiar and unopened volumes. On my next visit to Aberdeen I spent hours on the floor beside them, picking out, of course, all those which referred to the Rimpfischhorn and the Zinalrothorn; it became a habit, every time I went back to London, to take a handful with me to fill in the pictures of the mountains I had already seen, and to give a solid basis for the plans I was always making. Then there were the books, Whymper, Tyndall, and Leslie Stephen; to read them in their early editions, presents to Father from his climbing friends of the eighties, was to feel another direct link with the great age of Alpine adventure. Books written since that day I began to discover for myself—Mummery's *Climbs* (found among George's books), Conway's *Alps from End to End,* Geoffrey Young's *On High Hills,* Gertrude Bell's letters, and David Pye's memoir of George Mallory.

The holiday of 1929 had been one which included climbs; 1931 was planned as a climbing holiday. It began in the Dolomites, with Elizabeth and John Monroe, on a marvellous day that started with snow and rowan berries in the Arlberg, and ended with painted houses, carved galleries, scarlet geraniums, and gilt onion domes on the Italian side of the Brenner. We spent the first night in the Val Gardena, under the Langkofel, staggered by the nakedness and abruptness of this colossal rock. The Dolomites never ceased to give me delicious shudders. Keep your eyes level, and you see villages, fields, churches, woods, a normal pattern of human life; swivel them up thirty degrees, and you see shocks and freaks of crude pink stone, whose shape, proportion, and colour bear no relation to the valleys from which they spring. In the western Alps there is a harmony between the different elements; the snow mountains pick up the rhythm where the trees leave off; even a mountain that is mainly rock, like the Matterhorn, sweeps up in lines which recapitulate familiar forms, the shape of a pinetree, or of a steep pitched roof. Even where the peaks are vertical and abrupt, like the Chamonix Aiguilles, they are usually only incidents in a greater mountain whole, and the eye is drawn beyond them to the harmonious mass of Mont Blanc, the Verte, or the Grandes Jorasses. But these terrific Dolomite fingers pushed up through the pretty landscape and held one with the same baleful fascination as Suilven, uncannily vertical on the undulating Sutherland moors.

The climbing, though, was tremendous fun, however odd it might be to do climbs that could be started, if you liked, after lunch. That happened with the Stabelerturm, which we did from the Vaiolet hut on such a cold day that we had to let the rocks get a morning's sunlight before we tackled them. It all seemed so lighthearted—no starts in the dark, no heavy packs, no sober trudging across crevassed glaciers, no puttees, no five-pound boots. Up the tower we scampered in *kletterschuhe*, behind Virginio Derzulian, reaching the top in one burst of energy and delight. Father's comment, when I showed him a postcard of the Vaiolet Towers—'That climb can't be as difficult as it looks'—was too true. We had two spectacular *rappels* on the way down—spectacular because they were my first, though Elizabeth, who made me envious by having a job in Geneva and getting to Aiguilles at week-ends, was sophisticated and expert. Next morning, on the Rosengarten-spitze, we were so far above ourselves as to wish we hadn't bothered with a guide, it all seemed so easy.

The weather stayed fine for Venice and Padua, Canaletto and Giotto, but crossing the Simplon we ran into rain; and installed at the Wengern Alp, I guessed that the lovely programme I was now drawing up with Hans Graf of Wengen was a parlour game rather than a practicable plan. Most of the days I spent in solitary misty rambles, along the ridge of Baedeker's 'precipitous Tschuggen,' round the lower part of the Eiger Glacier, over to the Männlichen for a drink of apple wine. When Hans and I finally got up to the Jungfraujoch (by train), our first attempt at the Mönch stopped at the Mönchjoch, in a heavy fall of snow; we had already had to turn back once to the Jungfraujoch for skis, after trying to break a trail. Next day was better, and (again on ski to the Mönchjoch) we got to the top without much bother, though Hans had to knock off some chunks of cornice on the right of the ridge. The pears, tea, and brandy on top were delicious, the view was splendid, and we had an amusing afternoon's ski-ing practice before taking the train down. All the same, I had little of the exhilaration that I had felt on the Rimpfischhorn two years before. I missed, as I had missed in the Dolomites, the long rhythm of the climb which begins by lanternlight at three in the morning; and, puritanically, I felt that to gain half your height in a train was no way to climb a mountain. I had not felt these scruples about the Gornergrat railway—I had seldom used it, but that was mainly to save francs—nor do I feel it about the line to the Montanvert. Perhaps it is because on both those lines there is not the least difficulty about tacking up the path beside. But to reach the Jungfraujoch on foot would mean at least a day's exacting climbing; by taking the train you are not only saving your legs and breath, you are getting to a place that perhaps you would not be able to reach otherwise. So I could not really feel I had earned the Mönch.

But the next fine day brought a climb that I could enjoy from start to finish with no puristic scruples. Another fall of snow had put the big hills out of reach for a day or two, so we made for the Lobhörner, a cluster of rocky spikes on the hillside above the Saus Thal, on the west side of the Lauterbrunnen valley. It was a light-hearted day, like the Stabelerturm, with luggage and boots left at the foot of the rock; we traversed the four main points, fitting in as many rock pitches as possible. Running down to Isenfluh for enormous glasses of milk, everything seemed set for the Eiger the next day, Hans Graf only regretting that the snow put the Mittelegi ridge out of the question. I didn't worry, the usual way up the Eiger seemed about my proper desert; but these hopes were knocked on the head when I woke at 4.30 and—since the start was to have been two hours earlier—realized that there were to be no more peaks these holidays.

CHAPTER III

CAIRNGORM CROSSINGS AND NORTHERN MONSTERS

Out owre yon moory mountain,
And down the craigy glen.

THE answer to my doubts and scruples on the Mönch was found in the Highlands. I wanted to extend my skill, so that on my next Alpine climb I should be less of a passenger and more of a partner, and it seemed sensible to get new experience by some climbs on my own, in country that I knew fairly well already. Fairly, not very, for I wanted practice in finding the way; it must be in places easier to get lost in than Arran. I knew the Cairngorms in a general way, and had climbed most of the tops in company; but I had never crossed any of the passes. Now my plan was, on short autumn and Easter holidays, to go home from London across the hills. I would send off my suit-case to Aberdeen, and myself take the night train to Speyside, walk through the hills, sleep at Inverey or Braemar, and arrive home the day after my luggage. It was always a good joke to end the journey from London by clattering up the Chanonry in climbing boots. My arrangement with myself was that, if the weather were good, I was to take in a peak as well; but whatever the weather, I was to get through.

As it turned out, the four great passes gave me two tops, and two struggles. The Lairig Ghru was first, taken on a day in early October. The expedition did not really conform to the general pattern, for I arrived the night before, slept at a cottage at Coylum Bridge and was able to make an almost Alpine start at 7.30. It was drizzling, and resolution was soon tested as I stood on the footbridge a little after eight o'clock and wondered about going on. But I had deliberately chosen the Lairig Ghru for my first crossing, as I knew it was almost impossible to miss the way, so there was really little doubt. I still had an unsuppressed hope of getting up Macdhui on the way. When I left the wood it started to snow, and began to get very cold; by the time the hills closed

in on me I could not see more than fifty yards ahead. The snowy
flanks of Braeriach, seen uncertainly through mist, and the lowing
of unseen deer, were frightening—solitude and mist and snow have
always found me vulnerable. In mist alone you can look at stones
and roots and know that you are still attached to earth; in snow
alone you can see the landscape; but to be cut off above, beneath,
and round about from the familiar solidity of hills, to walk in a
muffled, silent, sightless world, is to feel too near to ghosts. But
here in the long pass there could be no difficulty about the way,
so long as I did not climb up either side, and the small cairns
stood up well in the snow. At the top of the Lairig, three hours
from starting, I had to give up my flickering hope of Macdhui—perhaps on such a day memories of the Long Grey Man once seen
by Professor Collie on the summit plateau reinforced what was
obviously the only sensible decision. Over the watershed the wind
dropped a little, the snow turned to rain; but the relief did not
last long, for I twisted my ankle, and cursed the pain. The mist
cleared down by the Dee; and the ankle was easier over the
stretch to Luibeg. Derry Lodge looked dank and desolate as usual.
I always find it fascinating, if unmannerly, to look in at the
windows of empty Highland shooting-lodges, and see the dust-covers,
the mattresses stacked against the wall, with the twelve-pointers'
heads aloofly looking down—a picture complementary to the gay
house-party photographs in last September's *Tatler*.

At the Linn of Dee the ankle was just tiresome enough to
make me think of cadging a lift. After a couple of miles with no
car I decided it would be more dignified to complete the walk
on my own feet, and reached Braemar just under nine hours from
the start at Coylum Bridge. It had never stopped snowing or
raining. I oozed and dripped, and the really bad moment of the
day came when I knocked at the door of Lui Cottage and, instead
of the friendly Miss McIntosh, out came a supercilious Aberdeen
parlourmaid. The cottage was let, but Miss McIntosh was in her
own little house at the foot of the garden, and in a few minutes
I was in bed with two hot-water bottles while my clothes dripped
and steamed at the kitchen fire.

It was October again for the next crossing, by Glen Tilt, but
this time there were no steaming clothes at the end of the day.

The minute I woke in the train, in the Pass of Killiecrankie, I could see that it would be fine: there was sunlight on the tawny bracken, and a nip in the air. After a breakfast of porridge, eggs, and oatcakes at Blair Atholl I felt it wasn't rash to take the farm road by Loch Moraig instead of the direct road up the Tilt. The morning was so fine, the air so keen, that Beinn a' Ghlo was not in doubt. I went straight up Carn Liath, then, with the blue hills of home spread out on either hand, swung along the magnificent ridge to the Braigh Coire top, a series of curves, swoops, and turns that carry you on in one unbroken movement from top to top. The sun was hot now, and there was a haze over the far hills, but as I ate my jammy baps and ginger-nuts I could look my fill at Ben Alder and plan half a dozen ways of climbing it; and then, turning round to the north-west, look at the wild country over by Carn an Fhidhleir and An Sgarsoch, the last stride in a great winter walk that George had made in 1911, from Glasgow to Braemar, joined on this final stage by Beppo and James Wordie.

Very reluctantly I decided that there was no time to go on to the Carn nan Gabhar top if I wanted a bed that night: but it didn't take long to run down to the Tilt and find consolation in a pool under the wooden bridge by the flat green place where the A' Fheannach burn comes in. Never was anything more splendid —glacier-cold water, with wind and sun for drying. At 3.15 I had to remind myself that the day's work had now to begin, for I was still a long way from the watershed. But the day kept up its enchantment as I walked up the bridle-path—the birk stems were white, the birk leaves brown and gold, and the waters of the Tilt gold and tawny in the sunlight.

> Sweet the laverock's note and long
> Lilting wildly up the glen—

it is always this stretch of Glen Tilt that comes to mind.

But after all, it was the twenty-fifth of October, and the mood of the day had changed as I came up to Loch Tilt. At 5.30 the light was fading, the wind swishing in the reeds, moor-fowl and whaups crying desolately, and the deer, as all day, roaring and bellowing in a sad fury. The empty boat jobbling up and down made the scene as melancholy and romantic as an eighteenth-century engraving. Back I went to the bridle-path, not so easy to spot in the fading light, over this level waste between the two burns. At 6.15 I had my last strained look at the map (I had forgotten to bring matches); soon after, a dark clump of trees, a sudden light, and an imagined voice, which reason said was Bynack shieling, but which I felt as much too sinister to investigate. Now steadily, and rather wearily, I plodded down the burn—Allt an t' Seilich, water of the willows—often losing the track, until at length it reached the Geldie and joined the full-sized shooting road from Geldie Lodge. It was a bit hard on the feet, but there was no need now to think, as it took me down to the White Bridge and the Linn of Dee. It was a soft clear night, though moonless; the stags were still sadly roaring. I considered sleeping out in the heather at the roadside, beneath the firs—but decided I was too hungry to forgo supper. For the last mile to the Linn it was very dark under the firs, my footsteps very noisy in this tunnel of trees, my boot-nails striking out sparks on the stony road. In the open I had kept myself awake by singing, but I could not sing here. Now the Linn, and a light in the cottage—but after I had passed it I wondered if there really was a cottage here—and a girding up for the last mile and a half to Inverey. The lights of the first cottage there were certainly no mirage; I knocked, and a kind old man advised me to try Maggie Gruer down the road—if she couldn't take me, I was to come back, and his wife would manage something. I stumbled over the bridge, and knocked at Thistle Cottage—it was only 8.15, though I seemed to have been walking for hours in the dark. Maggie Gruer took me in with no fuss, and gave me oatcakes of her own baking, scones, butter, cranberry jam, and two fresh eggs. 'Into flat unspringy bed', ends my diary, 'delicious, exquisite aches all over. O Lord, what a good day.'

Five months later I did the third crossing, by Glen Feshie. Again, when I woke in the train and looked out—this time straight up Loch Ericht to snowy Ben Alder—I knew that the weather would be all right; but it wasn't so clear as last time what particular top I could allow myself as bonus, for there are no great peaks dominating Glen Feshie as Beinn a' Ghlo dominates Glen Tilt. A mile out of Kingussie men were ploughing the tilted fields, with the gulls wheeling over their heads; away beyond them the hills were white. Loosening my legs up the glen, I thought that the decent-looking mass on the other side of the burn must be my top, though the name, Meall Tionail, was new to me; so, just by the lodge (and the last human being, a man on a bicycle), I crossed the Feshie and made up by the side of a burn, to baps and ginger-nuts in the sunshine at about two thousand feet, where the snow began, and to the top of the Meall an hour later. Here I was on the edge of the big Cairngorm plateau, that stretches over to Loch Einich, Braeriach, and Cairn Toul. It was clear enough, but on the wide flat waste I couldn't see far for the dazzle of the snow. It looked big, but not terrifying; there was no noise except for the occasional rustle of shifting snow and the crunch of my own footsteps as I walked easily and dry-footed along the top till I could see the water of Eidart. Down I went in a rush, striking the burn about a mile higher than its junction with the Feshie. There did not seem to be an obvious crossing-place; when I waded through, the green water was high up my leg, and the current strong enough to make me wish I had brought an ice-axe for support. As I trotted down to join the main track again, with legs now prickling and tingling, I saw a great herd of deer on the grassy flat between the sharp elbow of the Feshie and the head-waters of the Geldie. I counted a hundred and watched them for some time before they saw me; after the roaring and belling all that autumn day by the Tilt it was odd to see them so still and dumb.

Suddenly the stretch to Geldie Lodge seemed excessively long and dreary, and my body slipped over into tiredness. I plugged on without thinking of anything at all; and there, far sooner than I had expected, was the dreary grey barracks of the shooting-lodge. If necessary, I could break in and sleep, I told myself; and that sort of knowledge makes you good for another ten miles. Immensely tired but perfectly cheerful I reached the junction with the track from the Tilt, just as the light went, and the rest of the progress was almost mechanical—though I managed to notice again the sparks struck from my boot-nails on the stony road under the trees on the last mile to the Linn of Dee. 'Noctu ambulant per silvas, et loca periculosa, neminem timent'—these words swam up, their message was bracing, but their sound did nothing to lessen the haunting stillness of the place and time. I remembered a night walk of my father's through woods. He had arrived at Visp in the evening, and wishing to sleep at St. Niklaus, engaged a young fresh-faced porter to carry his bag. The porter walked ahead, singing; in the dark my father lost the path, and could not hear the voice; then he struck it again and once more heard the song. Nearer and nearer he came to it, till he saw the porter waiting for him in a clearing; he turned; and there in the moonlight my father saw no fresh-faced boy, but an old, old man with a silver beard. The rational explanation—that the young porter had met the old man coming down, had suggested changing loads so that each could set his face for home, and had missed Father in the interval when he was off the path—did nothing to cheer me. All the imagination could grasp was this awful metamorphosis of youth into age in the moonlit clearing.

But here, hurrah, was the Linn; and yes, it was a real light in the cottage. There was a moon as well, making the fields at Inverey as white as the high snows of the Cairngorms, as I came over the bridge and knocked at Maggie Gruer's door.

Over a lazy breakfast next day Maggie gave me the clash of the countryside. This walk was in March 1932, and the Christmas before had seen the most strenuous efforts made to keep sterling in Britain by a Winter Sports at Home campaign. Braemar was to be the British Mürren. Splendid plans were made, and many of them put into action. The hotels were to be centrally heated, Swiss guides were to be engaged, the fields flooded for skating, ski-ing championships arranged. Now Maggie, along with every other inhabitant of Braemar, knew perfectly well that while it is possible and likely to get snow good enough for ski-ing at Braemar some time during a winter, it is quite impossible to say precisely when. There is no particular probability of a fall during the Christmas holidays; and there was not one this year. The fields, though flooded, were not frozen, the Swiss guides had nothing to do, the naive skiers from the south cursed the pound sterling and telegraphed for their golf clubs. Maggie had greatly enjoyed the comedy. One day the shepherd had burst in on her: 'Hey, Maggie, come and look, there's a naked man rinnin' doun the road!' — a disappointed skier taking exercise in a singlet and running shorts. And on the one slightly snowy day a car appeared at Inverey towing a skier; the shepherd was so startled that 'he took up his doggie and jumpit over the dyke. That wis the wye.'

Thistle Cottage is built on the usual pattern for a Deeside village, two rooms downstairs, two rooms above them, with a tiny slip of a third between; but Maggie had never been known to turn any walkers away. When the beds were full—and she would give up her own blithely, and sleep in her chair at the kitchen fire—there was always room in the barn. At whatever hour you arrived (and I never gave her any notice), whatever the wetness of your clothes, Maggie would show no surprise. She would set you down at once by the fire—if necessary ordering 'twa chappies frae Dundee,' themselves now dry, to make room for the new-comer—pour you out a strong black brew from the teapot simmering on the range, and crack a couple of eggs on the frying-pan which, in Thistle Cottage, was seldom off the fire. No fuss, no excitement, no bother about 'seeing your room'—you were warmed inside and out before you had time to realize that the walk was over. Then, with the kettle on again for the hot-water bottles (and this evening there had to be one for the shepherd who was sleeping in the barn—'he has a wifie most nights'), Maggie would let the talk play over the doings of the countryside.

One evening, I forget after which of these walks, there was a long and splendid saga concerning an attempt to stop some Inverey tenants from taking summer visitors. To be docked of this extra source of income would have meant considerable hardship; Maggie, as an independent householder, was in a good position to lead the resistance. Like almost all the natives of the valley, she was a Catholic, but she was sister to Jenny Geddes as, with fierce blue eyes and iron-grey hair, she recited the iniquities of those in high places, and spoke contemptuously of 'chappies wha put up the boardies wi' them screedies "Not to look at the grouse"' (the last words in a devastating mock-English accent). She made it a wonderful story. There was something about a niece of Charlie's writing a letter six times, as she had the best hand, and it being printed in a Dundee paper, and read out in the House of Commons, moving to the magnificent and surprising climax, 'and when the

King heard of it he fairly danced, and said Maggie could have all the visitors she wanted, and Balmoral was to be opened two days in the week.' 'I held my head fu' high,' she said, as she spoke of a meeting with the chief antagonist; 'I was aye proud.' Then Jenny Geddes melted away in Maggie's sudden grin: 'But we're chief now, and it's "Good morning, Maggie", and "How are you to-day, Miss Gruer?"—and the car sent up for me at the election to vote for the Tories. I take the car, but . . .'

The last of my Cairngorm crossings was the hardest, the Lairig an Laoigh on a wet October day. The evening before I had looked out of my office window in London to note what time the dark came; I woke at Blair Atholl to misty hills, and could see no Ben Alder up Loch Ericht. Breakfast at Aviemore, and a warm by the fire, made the day look a little better, though it was undeniably rainy; there was no temptation to linger along the road by Loch Morlich and through the Pass of Ryvoan. At the Green Loch I struck over to the Nethy, and found a footbridge, and a bothy to shelter in while I ate my baps. Someone had left an old *Bulletin* there, and I was amused to see staring up at me the face of a girl whom I had played tennis with a fortnight before in a garden in Kent. The grubby picture seemed somehow to bring to a point the contrast which had always been a big part of my enjoyment of these Cairngorm journeys. To be settled very happily in a sociable towny life, with work one liked; to spend the lunch hours eating with friends, or munching a bun at the National Gallery; to have a game of squash, or look in at a party on the way home from the office—to do this till 7.30 one evening, and then break it off abruptly as the night train left Euston, and within fifteen hours find oneself alone on the great, and occasionally cruel, Cairngorm hills, was for me the perfect way of beginning a holiday. Even if, as on this occasion, my romantic impulses had landed me for the moment in a dark and smelly bothy.

When I put my head out it seemed mistier, but there was a track for the next stretch, round the flanks of Ben Bynack. In the other three passes you go up one glen and down another, with only a short stretch between; and in the Lairig Ghru this watershed is so held between steep hills that you would have great difficulty in losing yourself. But in the Lairig an Laoigh you are in no containing glen till the very end; all the first half of the way you are cutting across the line of the waters falling away from the eastern slopes of Bynack, A' Choinneach, and Mheadhoin, and in between each crossing there is a rather featureless stretch, sometimes in a shallow trough between rounded hills, sometimes on the hill-slope itself. There is a track, but when I got to the 1750-foot level there was snow on the ground, and soon after it began to fall. Down at the bothy there had been a smirr of rain, but I could see a mile or so; up here, my world contracted to a quarter of a mile, two hundred yards, a hundred, and then not more than fifty, and then not more than ten. At the first high, level place, where I had to start work seriously with map and compass, I stopped and went through the customary debate whether it was possible, wise, and necessary to go on. I was walking well, I said; I was up to time; it should be difficult to mistake the way, and the wind was behind me. Then I let the devil's advocate speak up: he said the weather was filthy, I was walking blind, and it was impossible to see the path. Why look for the path ? I snorted, and went on. Actually, I did not so much decide this consciously as find myself going on because I so much wanted to. For one thing, it completed the pattern: Lairig Ghru bad, Glen Tilt fine, Glen Feshie fine—a struggle through the Lairig an Laoigh would round it off. Further, I had set myself this test, and if I was now being tried for route-finding and resolution as well as for legs and lungs, that was nothing to grumble at.

In fact, the Cairngorm Club had marked the track so well with cairns that there was never any real difficulty. I could not see from one cairn to another, but I could steer towards it by compass, and I usually hit it off. A slight clearing of the air, and snow half turning to rain, and I was at the Water of Caiplach; if necessary, here was a way down to Tomintoul. As with Geldie Lodge, the knowledge of such a possibility made it quite unnecessary, and I walked confidently on, in rather clearer weather, across the Glas Ath, by the tiny Lochan a Bhainne, and along the Allt Dearg till it joins the steep water from high Loch Avon and swings east down to Inchrory and an easy step over to the Don. But there was no need to worry now about possible back doors of escape,

for the big hills had closed in on the pass. All the way from the
bothy it had been down to the burns, and up again between them;
the last pull up from the Dubh Loch seemed long and dreary,
but here at last was Glen Derry, and the way home quite clear.
From the last rise I could see the glen below the snow-line, and
pick out trees and stones quite black and plain, not white and
indifferent like everything in the country behind me.

My only bother now was time—would the daylight see me
down? When I stopped for a ginger-nut at the footbridge, I could
just read my watch, and down among the trees I kept on losing
the path. I tried following the burn, but got impatient with its
twists. Derry Lodge at last, but it was too dark to peer in at the
windows; on the road to the Linn, the rain stopped and though
half the sky was cloudy, half was bright with stars. Across the
Dee I could begin to see hills, for the first time that day—very
friendly and secure they looked in the starlight, after my snowy
isolation by the Barns of Bynack. Very dark under the big trees
on the last stretch of road to the Linn; sparks struck off the
stony road; the pungent smell of pine-needles, as reviving as a
long drink; the light in the cottage at the Linn; and there was
the moon, to whiten the fields of Inverey as I came over the
bridge to Maggie Gruer's.

In between these last two Cairngorm crossings there had been
a holiday in the north-west, leisurely motoring with Margaret Monroe
from Loch Maree to Loch Assynt, with an unforgettable camp on
Gruinard Hill, where we watched the sun set near midnight over
the long line of Lewis. A little later the clouds lost their rosiness
and themselves looked like islands, a cloud archipelago set in a
still sea, as still as the real Minch and Hebrides. This holiday
was not primarily a climbing one, but there was a misty ascent
of Slioch, a magnificent day on the Teallach, scrupulously following
the ridge from Bidean a' Ghlas Thuill to Sail Liath, up and down
the great stacks of weathered sandstone; and, to end the holiday,
three full days alone on the Assynt tops—'Not man's hills', as
Dorothy Wordsworth said of other mountains, 'but all for themselves,
the sky, and the clouds.' On the first, I traversed Quinag, going
up from Kylesku to the Barrel Buttress, and finding a gully that
gave a very scrabbly climb; the views back up Loch Glendhu and

across to the heights of Reay Forest made up a little for the loose
stones. Next day on Ben More of Assynt I began in steady, windless
rain, and ended in a sun hot enough to send me diving into the
green and lily-covered waters of Loch nam Cuara, and to warm
the slabs of gneiss where I stretched to dry. On the third day I
nerved myself to climb Suilven. For two years, since my first
sight of it, I had been haunted by the mountain—an astonishing
pillar, seen endways from the Oykell road; from the shores of
Loch Assynt, a crouching monster. 'The Hielan, hills, the Hielan,
hills, I never see them but they gar me grew,' said Bailie Nicol
Jarvie as he came into Rob Roy's country; when I look at Suilven,
I know what he meant. Even to-day, every time I open the Scottish
Mountaineering Club's Guide to the Northern Highlands, I turn
to the photographs of Suilven with a shiver of terror and delight.

This day, to put off the moment of seeing it face to face, I
chose to climb first the easy Canisp, which blocks the view; then,
grasping the summit cairn firmly, I turned to look at Suilven
across the gash of Glen Dorcha. A monster indeed, but at the
moment passive. I started up its gentle slopes at the south-east
end in sun; but once embarked on the long ridge, down came
the mist. Suilven is made up of three humped masses connected
by very narrow *bealachs*; as I came over the top of Meall Bheag,
the first hump, I could dimly see the slopes of Meall Meadhonach,
the second, but I could not see down to the *bealach* in between;
when I had groped my way down I found that it consisted of
one rock, across which you could straddle—a nice place, and by
some freak of wind the mist cleared to the south-west as I sat
there a minute, and though I could not see the top I had left
five minutes ago, I could see the hills of Skye forty miles away.
On the second and broader *bealach*, connecting Meall Meadhonach
with Caisteal Liath, the highest, I met a party of three coming
back from the top, and realized from their sad and dripping
mackintoshes just how wet I must be myself. An easy forty minutes
took me to the top of Caisteal Liath—the Grey Castle that faces
the sea, more majestic and less terrifying than the monster seen
from Canisp or the spike from the road to Lairg. But I could
not see the sea, or Lochinver, or the little lochans starring the
moor all round the base of Suilven; and I was beginning to tire

of walking along the wet spine of the monster enclosed in mist. How dull it would be, I told myself, to retrace my steps to the *bealach* where I had met the other party, and take the usual route down the gully. When my other voice remarked that the dull thing was the only sensible thing on a day like this, I dismissed it as the devil's guile. Quite wrongly; the devil in fact was busy at my elbow as I peered over the edge of the castle ramparts, pointing out to me that there was green nearly all the way down, and suggesting that I should save time and energy by descending straight to the string of lochans on Suilven's northern base.

Gaily I started down. In a quarter of an hour I realised three things. First, that this north face of the Grey Castle is made up of continuous rock bands, ten to fifteen feet high, with grassy terraces between (from above, of course, only the terraces are visible); second, that these terraces slope outwards; third, that it would be difficult and lengthy to retrace my steps because I had zigzagged down a good deal, finding the weak place in each rock band. Although I knew now which voice had been the devil's, this last consideration made me decide to go on, scrambling somehow down the rock band, then prowling along the grass terrace to find the best place to attack the next band. This worked all right for a dozen rounds or so; then came an unfairly high band, perhaps twenty feet, with no visible cracks, and wet tufts of grass the only apparent holds. I scouted along the terrace, and finally saw a small ledge about seven feet down, and a possible foothold about six feet lower. I swung cautiously on to the ledge, did a complicated doubling-up to shoot my feet down to the hold—it was wet and slimy; I had to make up my mind quickly, and I did so by praying hard and jumping for the grass terrace below. I landed square, and everything would have been perfectly all right but for my rucksack, which I had entirely forgotten, and which now swung outwards and twitched me down over the next band. It was a moderate one, only about twelve feet, and the terrace below was flatter than most. So I stopped after one bound, and for two minutes sat and laughed in a loud and silly way at my extremely humiliating but very funny situation. 'Here is one calling herself a mountaineer', I mocked, 'fancying her judgement, her eye for a good route, her caution on rock, reduced to falling off a mountain to get down it!' My stockings were ripped, my legs bloody, and my body all bumps, but there seemed to be nothing really wrong as I picked my way as soberly as possible down the rest of the castle wall. Down in the heather I ate an orange, and looked back in clearing weather at Caisteal Liath. From below, of course, the grassy terraces were invisible and the rock bands looked like an uninterrupted face. As I plodded over the weary boggy moorland to reach the road at Little Assynt, I felt I had been let off lightly by the monster.

In the mountains themselves there is seldom any particular moment when you know you have mastered a lesson. The immediate action absorbs all your energies; it is only weeks afterwards, perhaps in the middle of a concert in the Queen's Hall, or sitting in a bus in the Strand, that you are suddenly conscious that your scope has been extended, and that the plans you have been making for your next holiday are more exacting than last year's. Turning over these Highland days at such moments, I counted the gains. They had taught me to sum up possibilities and take firm decisions; to treat each expedition as a new situation, not necessarily to be met by applying the methods that had answered yesterday; to go on mechanically at the end of a long day, not letting the mind brood upon the body's aches and tiredness. If I had been fussy over times, it was because it seemed important to know what rate I could keep up for a long day, and how fast, at a pinch, I could go. On the waste land between Tilt and Geldie, among the snowflakes on the Barns of Bynack, I had learnt in some measure to be proof against the sudden desolation that comes upon the solitary climber confronted with the warning that he must depend upon his own exertions—and discovered, too, what practical aids to courage a map and compass can be. I had new pleasures, too, to turn over; chief among them was the pleasure of making a real mountain journey, crossing a great range in order to get home.

CHAPTER IV

NEW WAYS IN SAVOY

Exposed on the high hills of the heart.

THE next summer in the Alps, 1934, began on a new note, with Michael Roberts greeting me on the platform at Bourg Saint-Maurice by a horrified 'What on earth are you going to do with those suit-cases?' Climbing from the Riffel, or from the Wengern Alp, I had enjoyed the luxuries of a settled base—booked rooms, a wardrobe for the off-day cotton dresses, a shelf for all the books one had brought because one might possibly be in the mood for them. (To Zermatt I had lugged, among others, the one-volume *War and Peace,* and the Clarendon Press Shelley, not realizing that they weighed about as much as a pair of crampons or a dozen tins of sardines.) Michael's experience of the Alps had begun ten years before when, with a grant from the Donald Robertson fund, he had spent a long vacation walking across France and Switzerland to the Great St. Bernard and back by way of Lyons and the Loire, sleeping mostly in the open and living on ten francs a day. Since then he had walked by himself across most of the passes of the Tarentaise and Maurienne; once or twice he had been over the Col du Bonhomme and round Mont Blanc, and he had climbed a few easy peaks. His idea of luggage was one sack for a whole summer; of lodging, a bed (or tent) in a different valley each night. His view of guides was that you had to be pretty good to do the sort of climbs for which you needed one; whereas I believed that you had to be pretty good to venture on anything without one. Climbing in the Cairngorms the summer before—I led him up the Bachelors' Buttress of Sgoran Dubh, he led me up the Central Buttress of Coire Bhrochain, and we both slithered and failed in slimy Castlegates Gully above Loch Avon—we had discovered that our pace on the hills fitted in well, and our ideas on what made a good mountain day. Now, as I saw him sunburnt and rather villainous-looking—breeches which an English country tailor had made incongruously horsy and tight at the knee, topped by a red spotted handkerchief and enormous black hat—balefully surveying my tidy coat and skirt and two shameful suit-cases, I realized that we should need to make further adjustments. To make it worse I had a friend with me, Ann Moorsom, in no better plight. A suit-case each was jettisoned straight away, at Bourg Saint-Maurice; the others, after a quick change and repack, thirty kilometres up the valley, at Val d'Isère. But by that time we had seen, from the bus, Mont Pourri throwing down its long glacier fingers almost to the valley, the beautiful gleaming sickle of the Sassière's frontier ridge, and the Tsanteleina brooding behind. We had seen La Gurra perched on its ledge under Mont Pourri, the meadows at Tignes with the waterfalls cascading through the pinewoods—and I didn't mind what books or bedroom slippers were to be sacrificed to exploring these peaks and valleys whose names I had never heard before.

This first afternoon, we dawdled up through the pinewoods and scented pastures to the Col de l'Iseran and the new chalet-hotel—a massive stone building with crow-stepped gables, rather like a gaunt Highland shooting-lodge. Michael and Ann looked surprised at my entry in the register; but I follow Principal Forbes in thinking that there are practical as well as patriotic reasons for signing *Écossais*—'*Anglais*,' as he remarked, 'being too generally associated abroad with pride, wealth, and extravagance.' That was in 1839, but Michael was now certainly helping to perpetuate two-thirds of the legend; I was startled and delighted to find on the table with our *thé au citron* a huge open fruit tart, decorated in pastry with my name, the letters C.A.F., and an ice-axe twined with rope. He had been that way a few days before, and thought we should celebrate my début in the French mountains and in the Club Alpin Français: a few words with the guardian, Pierre Rond, had arranged the matter, and no doubt stamped him for ever as characteristically wealthy and extravagant. After supper we stood on the col and looked across another new valley at other new mountains—the pointed Albaron, the dark mass of the Charbonnel, and the tent-shaped Ciamarella, startlingly white above the darkening valley of the Arc.

Next day we crossed the limestone gullies of the *pays désert* and the gently sloping snowfield to scramble up the easy rocks of the Aiguille Pers, where we ate a wonderful cold omelette given us by Pierre Rond, and the rest of my Alpine tart. We lazed in the sun and looked at hills from Mont Blanc to Monte Viso; then we went down the rocks again and turned off to the glacier on the far side until a leisurely walk through high pastures bright with campion and yellow poppies brought us to the Carro hut under the Western Levanna. This was my first experience of a C.A.F. hut—the chalet-hotel on the col, though technically a hut, had hot and cold water in the bedrooms—and it was an unfortunate sample. A mule tethered to a post by the little lake made us hope that fresh provisions had arrived from the valley; but there was no sign of them in the dinner of stringy goat and sodden lentils. The sloppy young man who was guardian talked a great deal about his difficulties, and the cigarette in the corner of his mouth dropped ash into the saucepan of hot milk for the coffee. There were other things equally hard for Ann and myself to stomach; but the company was pleasant. Over dinner we chatted to a little Dutchwoman of about sixty sunburnt summers; she had climbed in the Lakes, was very spirited and spry, but rather bothered at the difficulty of securing guides in this district—'they're all too busy haymaking.' Then in came a French family of father, three daughters, and attendant young man, who did some wonderful cooking on their tiny spirit lamp and were very merry and noisy. 'Story of La Gouvernante,' says my diary; but there is no amplification, and tease my memory as I will, this promising anecdote remains forgotten.

Next day Michael and I left Ann to botany and *Moby Dick*, and started, rather late, for the Central Levanna. The three Levannas are all on the frontier chain; we crossed a spur that runs west from the western peak, descended towards the Glacier des Sources de l'Arc, and then made our way up a vague buttress on the south-west face of our peak. The rocks were no less brittle, and no more difficult, than some of the Cairngorm gullies we had scrabbled up the year before, and we did not rope till we reached the summit ridge. Then we prospected for the top (the rocks were worse than ever), and when we found it sat in the sun eating our lunch, straddling the ridge, and spitting our prune-stones down to Italy. The day was very fine and I expect the far views were very good, but I can remember only the Val d'Orco at our feet, the milky green of the river in the trees, the white houses of Ceresole, the richness and softness of the whole chestnut valley. We promised ourselves to go down next year.

Though it was 21st August they had not yet cut the hay on the slopes above the Arc, and the air was very sweet next morning as we walked down to the Pont Saint-Clair above the hamlet of L'Écot. We rested in the shadow of a big stone, watching French artillerymen at work—we could hear the guns all day—and then zigzagged up to the C.A.F. chalet-hotel des Évettes, where they managed to squeeze us in, though crowded already by boy scouts, priests, and scout girls.

I was beginning to grasp the general pattern of this countryside, which was in some points rather different from the other Alpine districts that I knew. In the Tarentaise and Maurienne the main feature is a grassy plateau between 2,000 and 2,500 metres, with here and there rock ridges capped with snow rising from it, and a few deep valleys—the Val d'Isère, the Val d'Arc, the Pralognan valley—carved out of it down to a level of 1,500 to 1,800 metres. In tackling a mountain or a pass from the valley, the first thing that you have to do—as we had just done, in heat that made each successive zigzag increasingly unwelcome—is to climb up 600 or 800 metres to the level of the plateau (where most of the climbing huts are placed); then you go over more or less level ground to the foot of the actual peak or col. But if you choose not to go down into the deep valleys, you can walk for days round high grassy passes, at the level of the gentian or the soldanelle, without either descending into a deep valley or climbing very high.

For the Ciamarella next day Michael and I started out at 4.30, the morning cloudy but not actually raining. The usual route goes some distance up the Glacier des Évettes, and then to the left, over the Col Tonini, to approach the west ridge from the north; but as we walked up the lower part of the glacier Michael decided that, with the snow in good condition, it would be more interesting to follow the glacier to its head, and then cut straight up the steep slope to which your eye is drawn as you look up the four-kilometre-long stretch from the hut. (Ball's *Guide* said that the topography of the frontier ridge was badly given on the maps; his corrections puzzled us more; and it was not till we could see the country for ourselves from the Col de Chalanson that we realized that our route wasn't one of the regular ways up.)   The glacier was easy right up to the great enclosed bay at its head; there were a few big crevasses, but these were easily circumvented. Now we were faced by the steep snow slope, but the snow was firm and crisp, and we stepped up in crampons without special difficulty; as I peered into the greeny-blue crevasses, or followed Michael up a thin tongue of ice between great gashes, I reflected that I was tackling, without a guide, a slope considerably steeper than any I had done with one.   Towards the top the angle increased, and here and there the snow gave place to ice, so that Michael had to cut a few steps.   Up at the Col de Chalanson, we were on a ridge that runs straight along to the Ciamarella, but the Piccolo Ciamarella was between us and our peak, and we decided to turn it on the Italian side.   The schisty traverse was easy, but we soon saw it would take us too long, so we glissaded down to the glacier on the Italian side and crossed to the south-west ridge of our mountain, filling our water-bottle from a trickle of melted ice that attracted us by its tinkle on the rocks. After the pleasantly exciting snow slope it was an anticlimax to find a sort of track up this last shaly stretch; all the same, I made heavy weather of the zigzags.   We ate our lunch on top, and had occasional glimpses into the Italian valleys; but the mists were rolling round, and we could never see very far. We wrote our names on the wrapping-paper of a slab of Kendal Mint-cake, left them with the visiting cards—mostly Italian—in the little box shrine dedicated to Madonna della Consolazione, and found a quick way directly down the scree to the Ciamarella glacier.   There were a few minutes' haggling, niggling, and boggling over the step from glacier to rock on the short rise back up to the Col de Chalanson, for the schist flakes were brittle, and sloped the wrong way; but I led up eventually, and Michael followed.   I was glad I could score a point on rock, for I had my doubts about that snow slope.   And rightly; the sun, which met us on the col, had been hard at work, and the whole slope shimmered and slithered.   I was obsessed by the fear of slipping, and though we came down the whole way one at a time, I did my spells clumsily enough, and was slow over the business of driving my axe in deep and belaying the rope round it when it was Michael's turn to move. He seemed to be enjoying himself, and 'I could hold an elephant,' he said cheerfully as he urged me to get a move on. I had no reason to be pleased with my performance, when we had taken off the rope on the lower Évettes glacier and it was possible to think again of something beyond the next step. But I had found something all the same. The Alps were no longer a different kind of mountain from the hills of home. There were problems here, of course, that one did not have to face in the Highlands; the scale was greater, and the penalties more severe, but one could learn the right way of walking on them as one had learned the right way in Arran or in Wester Ross. Guides had not suddenly become superfluous, but a guide would be valued now because he was a better climber, and could teach one a hundred necessary things, and not because he possessed some magic power which made guided parties safe and guideless rash. New possibilities suddenly appeared: I stooped on the moraine, picked up a green pebble veined with black, and thought that perhaps one could learn to walk through the Alps as lightly and confidently—and inexpensively—as through the Cairngorms.

Though we did no more peaks in the Tarentaise, there was plenty of excitement before we got back to Bourg Saint-Maurice. Too much sock-washing in the Arc, too good a *déjeuner* at the C.A.F. hotel at Bonneval, too long an idle in the woods, made us disgracefully late in starting up the zigzags to the Col de l'Iseran. We took the short cuts up the first slope, but had not the energy for the still steeper tracks that cut corners off the short cuts. We stopped several times in the upper valley, where the new road to the col looked out of scale with the summer chalets squatting under their big roofs that touch the hillside at the back. We passed the barracks of the Italian workmen, who were now on the last and steepest bit of the road, where it is carried above the gorge up to the final slopes. It all reminded me of Corrieyairack, which I had crossed the summer before, and I thought that the stretch above Garbhamore must have looked like this when Wade built huts for his men, great bonfires of whin and heather burned through the night so that work on the Devil's Staircase need not

pause, and the great red gash crept on steadily up the pass to
end the old order in the Highlands. With its grass-grown track
and moss-grown broken bridges, Corrieyairack now has all the romantic
sadness of something that has been deserted; but the Highlander in
1731 hated it and kept to the old drove-road beside. He knew that
it was the enemy of his way of life; and in the same way this
unfinished road over the Col de l'Iseran was making changes in the
valleys. Bonneval was already beginning to be rather more of a
holiday centre, and rather less of an Alpine village. Wade had made
it easy to bring soldiers into the heart of the Highlands, but the
invaders on this road were the busfuls of tourists.

In a milder way, for it only touched our holidays and not our
livings, we hated the road as we glumly plodded up the gorge
below it; one more channel for charabancs, one less pass to enjoy
without the smell of petrol. The Highlander had done his best
to destroy the Corrieyairack road by rolling down great stones on
the new-made stretches; with us, the situation was reversed, and
the road now did its best to destroy its critics. We were keeping
to the foot of the gorge, well below the road, when suddenly there
was a great cry from a file of workmen above, going back to
barracks: 'Les mines! les mines!' It took us a minute to grasp
what was happening, then an explosion close at hand told us
everything. The men above shouted and waved to us to take cover,
up on the right, under some big boulders. But the lunch and
the late start had been too much, and I remember thinking that
'fear lends wings' is not always true; nothing could have made
my leaden legs move any faster. Out of the hillside above us,
though mercifully not directly above, boulders came whanging and
hurling, spattering us with earth. We crouched under our rock
for some minutes after the last explosion, then went up to the
road where the Italians, under their umbrellas, had been watching
the show. They were excited and concerned, but said the way
would be clear now up to the col. Round the next corner, however,
we met a straggler, who was less encouraging. 'I *think* all the
charges have gone off,' he said, 'but sometimes one fuse burns
more slowly than the others, and you may get it popping off long
after the big bang.' We walked along the next stretch of jagged
road as quickly and delicately as if we had been crossing a crevassed

glacier after a snowfall. Nothing happened; and we stumbled up to the col in the dark and found the anxious Ann at the door of the hut. She had wisely done her climb earlier in the day and had seen, from far above, the hillside exploding over our path.

Up at the col all was bustle and excitement; there was to be a great review of troops the next day, with *déjeuner* for over a hundred officers. Together with a few travellers like ourselves, we were huddled at one end of a table, for already the places were being laid for next day with intricately folded napkins, but the dinner (which included asparagus) was splendid and elaborate—a rehearsal for the military feast. By breakfast time many officers and their girl friends had arrived, three times a messenger appeared to warn the chef that there would be *encore douze chasseurs,* and nobody was particularly interested in giving us a bill. We learnt more about the ceremony: the garrison at Bourg Saint-Maurice was being relieved, and was handing over the colours to the new troops on the col. This was one of the big occasions of the year in the district, and as we went down to Val d'Isère we met, not only the troops, but half the population of the valley, and a fair number of summer visitors. They were easily distinguishable; the visitors wore miscellaneous and untidy clothes, 'good enough for the mountains,' but the natives were in Sunday best—the old ladies striding freely under their big black gathered skirts, and the girls not so happy in smart black chiffon and high heels. Most of the older women had the handsome black Tarentaise head-dress, *la frontière*—a sort of black mutch coming to a sharp point on the brow, and embroidered in bright colours. Often a party of girls would stop us to ask how far it was to the col, and if we thought they could manage the walk; but the old ladies smiled cheerfully, and strode up like Meg Merrilies. Far the most striking figure was M. Florian, mayor of Tignes—a giant of a man, in his dark thick peasant clothes and his black broad-brimmed hat over the keen dark eyes, the strong face, and the great mane of black hair hanging down to his thick neck, the very picture of a French revolutionary. When M. Florian stopped for a friendly word with Michael, Ann looked at Michael with a new respect, as if Churchill had stopped in the street to clap him on the back.

Everything was very gay and friendly, and there was a homely note not usually associated with military displays—a general ambling up on a small donkey; a detachment of colonial soldiers brewing a drink in a little glen just under the tree-line. Half way down we were stopped by more questions, asked rather crossly by three English schoolmasters in shorts. Why was there all this racket? Would it spoil their chance of rooms at the col, or should they have booked? What a rotten bus service there was up the valley! and why didn't the French speak more English? Ann and I tried hard to be polite; Michael, whose hat matched the mayor of Tignes's in blackness and width, withdrew to a rock and would only speak French.[1]

Late that afternoon we came up to the Little St. Bernard, by bus (ourselves now making use of Alpine roads), with a horrid moment on one of the turns near the top; the hand brake slipped, the gear had to be kicked into position, and we stared like anxious goats at the abyss over which our back wheels were hanging. At the frontier we changed out of the padded springy P.L.M. monster into a more austere Italian machine, with body perched high above the wheels. As we swung back to the left after a turn I saw a great dazzling white wall in front, filling the sky. 'Le gros Mont Blanc,' said Michael as I held my breath in amazement. We rattled into the cobbled street of Courmayeur; there was a shout and a rush, and a gay sunburnt face at the window, yelling something about 'Robert le Diable,' and snatching out of Michael's hands a scarlet teddy bear that we had bought at Bourg Saint-Maurice. This was Othon Bron, the guide we were to climb with, and the bear was for his son Horace. After dinner that night we walked a little way out of the town, along the lane that leads towards Entrèves, and, happier than we could say, looked up at the light in the Torino hut on the Col du Géant, and Mont Blanc itself. 'And visited all night by troops of stars'—luckier than Coleridge, we could see our Alps at first hand, and not from a German lady's poem.

---

[1] 'Our guide said, with surprise, "They are your countrymen, and you have not spoken to them—what queer people you are!" I excused our reluctance to make the acquaintance of our countrymen abroad, from our ignorance of their characters at home, and from our conviction, that many of them pass their time at liberty, out of England, whose peregrinations at home would be confined to the wards of a prison, either upon the felon's or the debtor's Side.'—WILLIAM BROCKEDON, *Excursions in the Alps* (1833).

Courmayeur is the best of Alpine towns—small, clean, and the main street so narrow that a motor-car will brush its mudguards on the walls at each side if it tries to go beyond the post office. And under the stone arches there are shops with all the colour and variety of southern Europe. Bourg Saint-Maurice is still the north with, at the best, a team of tight-rope walkers in the square on a summer's evening, but at Courmayeur people sit on the doorstep at dusk and play guitars. Still, even one day's shopping, repacking, postcard-writing, strolling, and coffee-drinking was too much to stand, with the snows shining above; and I was heartily envious of Othon and Michael as they set off late that afternoon to sleep at the Pavillon du Mont Fréty and climb the Aiguille de la Brenva the next day. Othon, jumping on to the bus the evening before, in his rather dashing town suit, had looked comically unlike the Swiss guides I had known, with their felt hats, neat tweed breeches, and jackets of many pockets. As he swung up the road now with Michael, everything about Othon's clothes and equipment showed the mountaineer, but there was a panache about his short neat chamois jacket—'peau de diable,' he said—his all-leather reddish-brown rucksack, his little green hat set cockily on one side of his head. He walked towards the mountains with zest and gaiety, not as a professional going to do a job and collect a fee, but as a man returning to the world where he is most himself and most at home.

Ann and I stayed behind at the Albergo di Savoia, for we had a rendezvous there that day with my cousin Jock Butler. We had given him up, and gone to bed, when in he walked; he had come from upper Austria, by the Brenner, and the meeting had that excited happy note you get when the parties have come from different directions across high mountain ranges to the appointed place. Jock arrived the proper Tyrolean, in leather shorts and hat with curling feather; next morning we had to fit him out with clothes for higher levels. Othon's wife helped us to shop in Italian; Othon himself was practically bilingual, Mme Bron spoke French with some hesitation, her brother Octave Ollier (the guide whom Jock now engaged) had only a few words of it.

We walked up to the Pavillon du Mont Fréty that afternoon in a drizzle, with the peaks misty—I imagined Michael and Othon having a slippery time on the Aiguille de la Brenva. But at the Pavillon they told us that *ce grand Anglais* was in bed, and opened a door on the two soundly sleeping climbers. An early start, a battle with bad weather, we sympathetically supposed; then the two heroes woke up to inform us that, on hearing heavy rain in the early morning, they had turned over to sleep, and had continued to do so all day except for meal times. A sound plan, we conceded, as we ordered a second round of zambaglione at supper. This melting delicacy inspired Othon to describe his first ascent of the Grépon, soon after he had qualified as a guide. As a Courmayeur man, he was anxious to avoid the accusations of the Chamonix guides that he had simply followed them, or accepted their shouted advice. So he started first, and ordered his client, an Italian who knew no French, to keep mum, whatever happened; then he knocked down a few stones himself, and with imprecations of 'Sale client!' 'Charrette!' 'Quelle charognerie!' and so on, yelled warnings to the Frenchmen below to keep a good distance away from this clumsy traveller whom he had the misfortune to guide. It worked.

Valley tempers were getting strained. We disagreed over the kind of poker we were playing. I suggested the childish 'donkey' in the interests of peace, but even then Ann (rightly) accused Michael of 'not even trying.' And we were all glad to be out early next day on a fine morning. Jock and Ann zigzagged straight up to the Torino hut—she was anxious to see a high glacier before going back to Courmayeur and over the Great St. Bernard—while Othon, Michael, and I struck west to the Glacier d'Entrèves and the Aiguille de la Brenva, which after all I was not going to miss. Michael, having at last decided he was good enough to take a guide, had done the Tour Ronde and the Dent du Géant with Othon the year before; today would show me if I could fit in with them, or if I would clearly be a nuisance. Brenva was a name of disturbingly ambitious associations to a voracious reader of Alpine literature, and the couloir up from the glacier was depressing: everything was loose—rock, shale, and snow—but somehow icy too. But round the corner, on the Brenva glacier side, we came on to a climber's paradise of sound rock, and I forgot to be self-conscious in the pleasure of slab, ledge, and chimney,

an hour from the little col and all too short. There was mist
everywhere, and we could not, from the top of the Aiguille, see
down to the glacier. It was still white and thick when, after
lunch on the rocks, we wandered up the Glacier de la Toule. We
could hear the *choucas* croaking, but could see nothing more than
five yards away. Through the crevasses, and between the séracs,
stopping once or twice to sniff his bearings, Othon led us straight
up to the little col between the Aiguille de Toule and the Grand
Flambeau. I was hazy about the map here, and it was astonishing
and delightful to find that we were looking on to a vast snowfield,
entirely free from mist, with great spires of yellow rock sticking
out. It was a good way of seeing the Chamonix Aiguilles for the
first time.

At the Torino hut we found Ann, on the point of starting
down to Courmayeur, and Jock, very impressed by his first near
sight of the high Alps. Next day he started for the Tour Ronde
with Octave Ollier (whose father had travelled with the Duke of
the Abruzzi, and been one of the first party to climb Mount
Kenya). We set off for the Dent du Géant, and had a pleasant
hour and a quarter's gymnastics in the sun, up to the surprising
aluminium virgin on the top. There was one very good moment
when I put my left leg over an arête, straddled it, and then saw
nothing between my foot and the snow five hundred metres below;
and one most uncomfortable moment when I got winded half way
up the last fixed rope. But the gap between the twin summits
was easy, and so was the descent back to the little platform at
the foot of the Grande Plaque. As we sat there eating our lunch,
we discussed the fixed ropes. Othon defended them. He pointed
out that the other big centres were well supplied with minor
peaks—such as the Petits Charmoz and the Aiguille de l'M at
Chamonix, or the Riffelhorn and Untergabelhorn at Zermatt—suitable for less expert climbers, or for less good weather. Courmayeur
had none of these, and if the high peaks were out of condition,
the guides were out of work. But by putting fixed ropes on the
Dent du Géant they had brought a very good rock climb within
the possibilities of the climber who was not yet able to tackle the
Grandes Jorasses or anything on the south side of Mont Blanc;
and as the Géant was mainly rock, it could be climbed on many

days when conditions made the big snow climbs impossible. It provided, as it were, a small fixed income for the Courmayeur guides, and made them less dependent on the hazards of the *grandes courses* of Mont Blanc and the Jorasses.

The snow was soft on the way back to the col, and it would have been easy to glissade down the first slopes; but Othon made us walk down, for practice and discipline. At the hut, we found Jock already back from the Tour Ronde, which he had enjoyed and, according to Ollier, done with ease and confidence; so we were all in a mood to sit on the sun-warmed blocks of granite, smoke, drink *vin rouge* mixed with lemonade, and pity the travellers sweating up the last thousand metres of rocky zigzag to the hut.

It was a beautiful night, clear and starry, and there was no need of a lantern as we all set out for the Aiguille du Midi next morning. Othon set a great pace down the crisp snow from the col to the trough between the Vierge and the Gros Rognon, and I was dismayed to find that he hardly slackened as we pulled up again the other side of the Allée Blanche. *Kubla Khan*, the *Ode to a Nightingale*, *Ode to a Grecian Urn*, *L'Allegro*, *Il Penseroso*—I got through them all, and still we weren't up; so I had to beg for a gentler pace—very ignominious, as the novice Jock was walking very well indeed. Five minutes at a pace too fast for you can entirely alter your feelings towards the other members of the rope. They are no longer your friends and companions; they are callous, selfish monsters; you hate them for going at all, and for going so easily; you centre on them all the discomforts of the day. You want to tell them what pigs they are, but you have no breath; their steps in the snow do not match your stride; when you lift your head, their back views spell indifference to your agony. You are obsessed by your grievances, and blind to everything else about the climb—on this morning I barely noticed a lurid smoky dawn coming up in streaks of red and green behind rows of black Aiguilles—and you share the child's bitterness: 'They'll be sorry when I'm dead.' Then the hated monsters turn; suggest a breather; offer dried prunes or barley-sugar—and behold, they are your friends again!

There was nothing remarkable about the final rock climb on the Midi except that I entirely forgot to look down on Chamonix from the summit. Four hours and a half after leaving the hut we were back, and Othon's pace justified, for the weather turned bad almost immediately, with rain and high wind.

This only created a new problem—killing time in the hut; and a heavy fall of snow that afternoon confined us for two days more. We slept, looked through the visitors' book, gossiped, ate, looked at maps, practised knots with spare bootlaces, slept, argued about God, and washed shirts which froze stiff as soon as they were hung on the line outside and dried in the wind without ever melting. (To see if they were dry all we had to do was to feel if they had softened.) We practised our Italian on the C.A.l. notices on the wall. There were exhortations signed by the president, Manaresi:

'Sons of Italy! Lift your eyes and dominate your mountains!' These meant little to us; we were more concerned with other notices, relating to stoves, w.c.s, etc., which bore the appropriate signature—Frizingheli, secretary. Then we read the visitors' book again, spinning it out with only a few pages at a time, and found the benches got harder and harder. A familiar pattern for hut-bound parties. But if during these three days we were occasionally bored, it was infinitely worse for the Italian frontier guards. In weather like this there were not many travellers crossing the col with papers to be examined. The younger guard was sensibly using his spell of duty up here in learning to ski, and he was out in the col whenever it cleared. But the other was what Othon, always contemptuously, called *un type méridional*; he obviously hated the height, the snow, the view, the hut, the cold, and was pathetically glad of any diversion. We provided one, by teaching him spillikins with matches; he found a much better one for himself, in a flirtation with the solid wife of a solid Swiss doctor. It had to be carried on publicly in the salle, but the rest of us co-operated with a will, holding the doctor in conversation at one end, while at the other his nice plain wife and the swarthy mustachioed *carabiniere* talked what we presumed was the language of love, as they had none other in common.

There were some departures, and a few new arrivals; Jock and Ollier crossed the col the first day, but Othon, Michael, and I were waiting for better weather, so as to do the Requin on the way down to Chamonix. The guide Georges Cachat came in with

a party from the Montanvert; Michael had skied with him at
Tignes that spring, and he and Othon were old acquaintances. A
young German, starting off with his girl friend in a snowstorm
for the Géant, united the hut against him by refusing to listen
to any advice from the guides (who felt it all too likely that
they would be called out later to look for him), and insisting that
he was going to lead up the North Face. 'Ça, c'est marcher à
l'allemande,' said Othon with contempt; two hours later they were
back, not even having reached the foot of the rocks. We spent
an agreeable afternoon chattering in French to an Italian boy and
girl, aged eleven and thirteen, who had done the 2,200 metres
from Courmayeur in one stretch that morning. They knew English,
too, and had read *The Daisy Chain, Little Lord Fauntleroy, Bimbi*,
and *Misunderstood*—the last they considered 'a beautiful book.' I
could have done with it myself; by this third day of confinement
my chief cravings were for plum cake and a nice book. Othon
was not good at sitting still. He would dart out to help in the
kitchen, or mend the water-pipe outside, or chat with another
guide in the doorway, looking out at the mist and the *choucas*.
Up in the guides' dormitory there was talk and tobacco smoke,
tobacco smoke and talk. 'What do you all talk about?' I asked
Othon. 'La montagne,' he said, 'toujours la montagne.' Politics
were barred; with guides of three nationalities, and climbers of a
dozen, it would have been too tricky.

At last, on the fourth morning, Michael woke me at 5.30 with
news of good weather. There was a wintry greenish light over
the glaciers of the Ruitor and the Gran Paradiso, and new snow
everywhere, including the hut. An hour later we were off for
Chamonix, the first party to cross the Glacier du Géant after the
big snowfall. Making his way between the masked crevasses, Othon
was all concentration and quick decision; watching him was as
absorbing as watching a sheep-dog bring his flock down a fellside.
There was the same absolute mastery, the same quick co-ordination
of decision and action. Always, as he stepped forwards on to
the spot already prodded by his ice-axe, Othon kept his body
in balance, ready to shift the weight on to the back foot if the
snow should give. Down among the miniature Alps of the
Géant séracs—where you feel like a print of de Saussure ascending

Mont Blanc—we met a party coming up the glacier, and Othon had withering things to say about a guide (a Chamonix *type*, of course) who let his clients come down a sérac on their *derrières*.

As we came under the Requin our faint hopes of climbing it faded as we saw the new snow white on every ledge and couloir. Othon was perhaps the most disappointed; he always liked to do his climbs on the way from one place to another, and the crossing from Chamonix to Courmayeur, which he did a dozen times each season, was hardly complete for him unless some peak had been taken on the way. Beyond the junction with the Talèfre glacier, I looked back and had the odd feeling I had been here before. I knew I hadn't, but the feeling persisted, and puzzled me inter-mittently for the rest of the holiday. Home in London, the explanation was found in a drawing by Francis Towne, which I had bought just before coming out. I had only seen it for a few minutes, and had bought it thinking it was of the Argentière glacier, also unknown to me. Now, as I looked at it again, I could see in Towne's beautiful small handwriting: 'L'Aiguille la Moine, le Charmoz, le Géant' (this marking the point we call Mont Mallet); his careful notes: 'Glacière running down white,' 'dirty colour of snow,' 'gravel thrown up by the glacière,' and, on the back: 'Glacière taken from Montanvert looking towards Mount Blanc Septr. 16th 1781.' I had been standing in the middle of my picture.

We rushed down to Chamonix, with a deliciously elaborate lunch at the Montanvert on the way. Tea at several pastry-cooks' (where they had everything but plum cake), baths and dinner at the Hôtel Suisse et de Chamonix, Othon's usual port of call, and coffee and Cointreau at a café next to an undoubted English *milord* complete with his cloak, his brandy, his toady, and his cigar—city life had its charms.

Out of the window next morning we saw a perfect J. R. Cozens landscape—the Bossons glacier trailing down between the pinewoods, mist rising from the Aiguilles. The weather was far from settled, and nobody was energetic. Othon went off for a walk with some friends; Michael and I inspected Chamonix (observing a notice chalked up at the bus station: AUJOURD' HUI—15 fr.—CIRCUIT

BALMAT ET CHRIST—ROI THÉ COMPLET), and dragged ourselves a
couple of kilometres down the valley to eat a lunch, sleep in the
grass, and look up at the Bossons and the Midi. Othon came
back grumbling at his walk: 'Traîner dans les prés comme une
vache....'; it was time to go up again.

Next morning was cold and clear; we took train to the Montanvert,
dumped our rucksacks, and were off for the first time along the
path to the Nantillons glacier. Fifty yards from the hotel, two
middle-aged French ladies sitting at the side of the path stopped
us, and pointing to the gentle blaeberry slopes above, asked anxiously: 'Y a-t-il du danger là?' By now it was warm in the sun,
but when we got to the sheltered couloir leading up to the north
of the Petits Charmoz everything was cold as death. We went up
a couloir and came to a great smooth flake, perhaps twenty-five
feet high, up the edge of which Othon had to go. It was glazed,
and the first ten feet were almost vertical, with no visible holds
at all. Othon stopped and slowly filled his pipe, lit it, and then
went steadily up the first ten or twelve feet. After that he stopped
from time to time to blow his fingers, the rocks were so painful;
and he asked our pardon for being slow. I think he expected us
to feel as impatient as he would have done behind someone else.
At last, after some delicate and strenuous work with an ice-axe
jammed in a crack for a foothold, he was up; I followed clumsily,
with a heave from Michael below, and shouts from the invisible
Othon above: 'Venez donc, Jeannette! Je ne comprends pas ce
que vous faites!' After the wait under the flake, and the scramble
up, my fingers were exquisitely painful; I unfroze them while
Michael came up (to the tune of more 'Je ne comprends pas,'
rather unfairly, for Michael had the party's rucksack to manipulate,
and no one to give him a shoulder); and then had to go through
the whole agonising process again in sympathy with him.

Nice rocks took us into the sun, and on to the summit, where
we ate our lunch and watched two Dutchmen slowly make their
trail up the perpendicular-looking slopes of the Blaitière opposite.
As we munched, Othon propounded one of his proportion sums.
The couloir of the Petits Charmoz, in winter conditions such as
we had found it, was as hard as anything on the Grands Charmoz.
Some time before he had told us that the Grands Charmoz was

as good a course as the Matterhorn by the ordinary route.[1] There-
fore, we calculated, we had just done the equivalent of the Matterhorn. It was not at all convincing, but it made us feel slightly
better about the way we had come up that ice-defended rock.

There was still too much snow for a *grande course* next day, so
we took a holiday from the rope and inspected the new hut over
at the Couvercle; but by evening the Aiguilles were blacker, the
Mer de Glace more grey than white, and next morning we started
for the Grands Charmoz. The path by lantern light was
tricky—stones lying across it where it was being widened, blaeberry
bushes pushing from the side: all one's energies were focused on
the small lit circle in front of one's feet. Stopping for a moment
before the zigzags up to the glacier, one's world was suddenly
extended; there below was Chamonix, its lights making a cross in
the valley. On the Charmoz itself all was delight: rocks just within
one's scope, and not freezingly cold, and one nice back-and-knee
passage, off which Othon had to chip a lot of ice. Very soon,
it seemed, we were looking over the ridge to the Mer de Glace,
and Othon was saying we had come up well. He said there was
a rather easier way, and we need not have taken the back-and-knee
chimney; but 'il faut toujours faire le plus difficile' was his motto
for us that year, and if he didn't always hold us to it, at any
rate he gave us a few difficult variations on routes simple enough
in themselves. Accidents, he maintained, happened in the easy
places.

The first step along the ridge was a step indeed, a slab about
fifteen feet high, with no apparent holds. Othon took the spare
rope to lasso the top of the block, and then climb up with it as
hand-hold. He tried several times, but the high wind made it
difficult. At last it seemed to stick; Othon must have slackened
his hold, thinking the rope well hitched, for when suddenly it
slipped back it ran through his cold fingers, and down on the
Mer de Glace side. Without a second rope, for this step up and
for the *rappel* down the other side of the summit, we could hardly

---

[1]The Matterhorn is a favourite standard of comparison; when my father climbed
the Grosse Wendenstock, near the Titlis, in 1885, he was assured by his guide, one
of the few men to have climbed both Matterhorn and Wendenstock, that the latter
was the harder climb.

go on. The situation looked black: fine weather, probably our
last climbing day this holiday, the trudge all over, a delightful
climb just before us—and now all lost, because of a spare rope
slithering through cold fingers! I tried to be philosophical, and
we had to reassure Othon, who was dumbfounded. 'C'est la seule
fois que j'ai fait une telle chose'—this was obviously something
he would have jeered at in another guide, especially a Chamoniard,
and here he was doing it himself.

But after the drink which we made him take, he peered over
the edge and saw the rope, not on the little hanging Glacier de
la Thendia, as we had feared, but caught in the rocks about eighty
feet below us. In spite of our dissuasions, Othon insisted on
going down; I was taken off the climbing rope, so that Michael
could let Othon out on its full length. Michael stood on the
Nantillons side of the ridge, paying out the rope, belayed round
a rock; I straddled the ridge, receiving and shouting messages to
Othon. He had a complicated plan of untying himself from the
climbing rope, tying the spare rope on to it, so that we could
haul it up and then let them both down again, so that he could
tie on one and use the other as a hand-hold—there had been few
of these, we gathered, on his descent. The roar of the wind
through the gap made it difficult to grasp all this; by some freak
I could hear the train at Montanvert, 1,200 metres below, and
from time to time the sound of an aeroplane above us, but Othon's
words only came up in gusty fragments. 'This mountain is too
damned noisy,' said Michael angrily. 'I can't hear myself think.'
When we did at last grasp Othon's idea we disapproved, as this
north face of the Charmoz seemed no place to leave a man without
a rope, even for a minute, and we might well be much longer
getting the ropes down to him again with this wind sending their
ends flying. But he won, and the plan worked out all right;
Othon came back to the ridge with both ropes at ten o'clock, just
an hour after the disaster. He was vexed and gloomy; he muttered
about the incomprehensibility of the whole affair, and worried
because it was now too late to lead us over the Grépon too, as
he had intended. But after an hour and a half on beautiful rocks
to the summit we felt entirely content; there was a nice *rappel*
down the other side of the top, and we ate a lazy lunch perched

in the sun with the Grépon just across the gap. There patriotism, often sluggish in response to flags and anthems and processions, suddenly stirred and tingled as Othon talked to us of the great crack across the way—'la Moomerie' it became on his lips—and of the skill and enterprise of the Englishman who had first climbed it.

It was pleasant to have a first-class view of one of the classic Alpine passages, so often read about in Mummery's own account; it was equally pleasant to relax and doze, to float in airy detachment—a luxury we certainly shouldn't have enjoyed without a guide. We should have been thinking about how we were to get down. Even with a guide we were not very neat that afternoon on the avalanchy snow of the Charmoz-Grépon couloir. We used the spare rope, hitched round knobs and spikes, as a hand-hold nearly all the way down. Once Michael and I managed to tangle it a bit; Othon was very fierce, addressing us as Monsieur and Mademoiselle. The snow was abominably slippery; as we slithered along we felt like a couple of pigs or sheep being driven along by an impatient herdsman. But we were forgiven by the time we reached the rocky rognon, and stopped to munch oranges and bread; and as we left the rocks to cross under the toppling séracs, Othon grinned: 'Ils tombent souvent. Alors, c'est fini!'

Content and exultant, we walked back by the blaeberry path to beer and lemonade at the Montanvert. At dinner we celebrated our best climbing day by ordering something not on the menu. An omelette arrived, so enormous and sustaining that we could hardly face the next course, *tournedos*. Othon, as usual playing the clown after a good day, insisted that the only thing to do with this dish was really to turn your back, and did so, eating off the windowsill, to the scandal of the two Frenchwomen of the blaeberry path—shocked enough anyway by the spectacle of a guide eating with his clients—and to the amusement of the waitresses. Then, over coffee, he unfolded the Episode of the Thunderstruck Trousers. He had arrived one day at the Montanvert from the Col du Géant, soaked through by a thunderstorm; so he had given the girl his coat and breeches to dry. When he went to reclaim them that evening, the girl was full of lamentations and apologies. 'Le pantalon est grillé, m'sieur.' 'Comment, grillé?' 'Oui, m'sieur, il est grillé.' Toasted they were, to that brittle consistency at which cloth needs only one touch to crumble into soot. Very delicately, Othon wore them down to dinner; and then retired stiffly. Next morning he made an early start before any one could see them. Before long the toasted trousers disintegrated, but no other party saw them until Othon and his client were returning down the Nantillons glacier. A Chamonix man eyed the singed tatters with surprise. 'Lightning on the Grépon,' Othon had glibly explained. 'It struck me on the Râteau de Chèvre, knocked me silly for a second, and left my breeches like this.' Telling the story to us now, he was still surprised at the effect of this happy invention. 'You should have seen his face! And do you know, there are still people down at Chamonix who believe I was struck by lightning on the Grépon!'

Next morning we came down late to breakfast and discovered Othon, sitting out on the terrace, typing out the day's menus—having taken this work out of the hands of the senior waitress, just as he had also taken over the duty of sweeping out the terrace after the last of the day tourists had gone down by train. He liked tidiness, and he hated having nothing to do. We were going back to Courmayeur, over the Col du Géant. Othon led us at a good pace up to the Requin hut, unroped; in the maze of crevasses where the Mer de Glace bends round to the right he had a fancy for walking on thin tongues of ice poised above blue depths. Once, Michael was going to follow him. Othon, who always knew exactly what was going on behind him, turned round and eyed him critically. 'Faites comme vous voulez,' with a shrug, 'mais si vous glissez, c'est fini!' No nerves could stand that, and Michael walked round. It was midday, and insufferably hot as we toiled up the airless trough above the séracs of the Géant glacier. Yesterday's harmony seemed lost; we roped, but each was concerned with his own special preoccupation or grievance; here was effort without enjoyment. All my energy was concentrated on keeping up with Othon's reasonable pace; every time a foot failed me, by slipping even ever so slightly, I would pull a bit on the rope; every time I looked up into the dazzle, the dancing snow slopes had no limit. I became morose and self-centred, angry at losing by this unhandiness the credit I had won on yesterday's rocks.

But the slope unbelievably eased off: here was the col, and here was Othon, surprisingly saying that we had gone very well, that the two hours and a half from the Requin hut was good time in soft snow, and that we might yet make mountaineers. In delighted relaxation we sat on the tiny terrace of the Torino hut drinking the sourish red wine and eating plain chocolate, while Othon, the guardian, the guardian's wife and wife's sister, exchanged the gossip of Courmayeur and Chamonix.

We started down the path from the hut a minute or two before Othon; the swinging movement down the short zigzags was exhilarating, and I went faster and faster, though not exactly running, and not taking the short cuts because I heard Othon shouting and thought he was telling me not to. The intoxication grew; faster and faster I spun down the zigzags—half an hour down to the *cabane* where they stable the mules which bring provisions to the foot of the rocks below the Torino, another twenty minutes to the Pavillon du Mont Fréty, then a rattle down through the woods into the fields of autumn crocuses at Entrèves—2,000 metres down in an hour and a half: a good ending, I felt, to a holiday. I had only a few minutes to be pleased. Michael arrived, saying there was trouble; and here was Othon in a fury, shot like a thunderbolt down a scree gully. The worst thing for my muscles, he said, and my balance, and my feet, and my mountaineering generally. I should never be able to climb the next day. But there was no next day for me, I retorted. Othon pointed out that though it might be the end of my holiday, it was not the end of his working season; I had made him come down at an absurd, jarring pace, because he was responsible for me, and could not let me go helter-skelter down any way I liked. I knew he was right—as right as W. P. was in his insistence on the proper ways of climbing up and down a mountain—but I couldn't bring myself to admit it. I remembered a pebble in my boot that I had felt above the Mont Fréty, but had not bothered to stop and take out; now I had the boot on again in no time, for the skin had come off the sole of my foot in great strips, and I could not let Othon see how right he had been. We marched into Courmayeur a comically disgruntled procession, I trying not to hobble. Michael did his best to be conciliatory; I turned my guilty bad temper on him. 'Fumez la pipe,' said Othon quietly, understanding the feminine temperament. In Courmayeur, Othon went straight home, but as we sat after dinner in a café, there he was with a couple of friends, cheerful and hilarious about our ten days' doings, and all was well. We walked through the village again to see the lights up at the Torino, and the high snows; coming back to the hotel we passed the café, and heard a voice: 'Alors, tout de suite je descends! . . .' The saga of the Charmoz rope was in the making.

At the Albergo di Savoia Michael offered to help plaster up my feet; I had to reveal the full horror, and he was duly appalled. Certainly I was thankful next morning that I could put on gym shoes without arousing suspicion, when we called at the Droguerie Bron—where Othon, or more often his wife, sold Palmolive soap, crunchy sweets wrapped in gay papers, and other necessaries and delicacies. We drank vermouth and wrote in Othon's guide's book; noticing that almost his first engagement as a young porter just after the war had been with a party of G. L. Mallory's. They had planned to do some climbs on the south side of Mont Blanc, but the weather had turned bad. They had let Othon do a good deal of leading and step-cutting to give him practice, and spoke well of the way he had done it, also of his handiness in the Gamba hut.

There seemed to be no bus up the Italian side of the Little St. Bernard, so in a last fit of extravagance we got a taxi. Othon came up to the pass with us, and carried our sacks across the frontier. A last gay smile, 'à la prochaine année,' and off he went, leaving us to an enormous picnic lunch and a bottle of wine from the Maison Bron, before we took a French bus down to Bourg Saint-Maurice. There again were the Sassière, the Pourri, the lovely Tsanteleina, the tiny villages under the long-tongued glaciers—this year's new countryside of peaks and pastures that already touched the heart with something of the spell of the familiar hills of home.

CHAPTER V

THE ALPS WITHOUT A SUIT-CASE

Living at our full compass, we were one
With the four elements, and knew the rock,
And the sweet smell of earth,
And ice and fire.

ARRIVING at Bourg Saint-Maurice next July (luggage, one ruck-sack), I found that the spell still held. On the P.L.M. bus up the valley I tilted my head back to see the shining glaciers of Mont Pourri, and picked out a route, up one of the long green ridges, that should take us on to the upper glacier. But a lot of other things had to be done first. Michael had brought out a party of sixteen schoolboys and four masters, and we nearly filled the new chalet-hotel that Pierre Rond, guardian of the hut on the col, had just opened at Val d'Isère.

I had been brought up on the principle that you begin a mountain holiday gently, working up from mild rambles to genuine climbs. Michael's methods with school parties were more direct. He believed in giving them good value for their £10 ten days' holiday; loafing in the valley would be better tempered if it came after a summit; and, once in sight of the mountains, he was never happy himself till he had gone high. So he always took the boys up some kind of peak the very first day. Within thirty-six hours of leaving Victoria, fourteen of the sixteen achieved the Aiguille Pers—the only casualty being a thirteen-year-old, well versed in Alpine literature, who insisted that he was suffering from 'glacier lassitude'—and next day five of them were still strong enough for the Grande Motte. We took a rope-load each; I remembered Othon driving his two sheep down from the Charmoz-Grépon couloir and now, coming last down the snow slope from the 3,656-metre summit, I was critical and firm with No. 3, who walked gingerly and slithered, and with No. 2, who muddled

the rope. Two days later we had the whole party on the Grande
Sassière—higher than the Motte, but easier; half of the party went
up the evening before to the Chalet de la Clitaz; the rest of us
started breakfastless from Val d'Isère and, in spite of one man's
evil attempt to spoil our sleepy tramp down the road by community
singing, we were up at the Clitaz for coffee and bread by 5.50.
The Sassière was good fun, and not too exacting for such a
caravan. We mustered five ropes this time, but discipline was
rather weakened when one master, who had asked to drop out
before the final pyramid, suddenly turned up in the middle of
our meal on the summit, alone and unroped. Three days later
we were back at the Clitaz, a more select party, bound for the
Tsanteleina. It was not a regular climbing-hut, only a stone
summer chalet with a hay loft where a few climbers could sleep.
The family's main concern was with cows and cheeses, but
Madame, a bright-faced old lady in a frilled black dress, seemed
to enjoy a little conversation as a change from her duties with
vats and presses. She produced a good *vin rosé* to go with the
sardines and bread that we had brought up for supper, and
later she made beautiful coffee; when we praised it, she said
she liked coffee herself, and so always made it carefully: 'Always
grind it freshly—and no chicory.' Great cheeses stood on the
shelves; and in the box-bed at the end of the table one of her
sons was already asleep, the shutter open a few inches for air.

To walk up the flowery Sassière glen on a fine early morning
is pure delight: a high valley, defended from roads and buses by
steep grass slopes down which its lower waters leap in great cascades;
on the left, the dark rocks of the Sassière, with white threads of
snow suggesting cracks and gullies on which the fancy agreeably
plays; and, closing the view, the graceful, brooding Tsanteleina.

For this day we had taken two of the local guides—Gunié,
short and gap-toothed, from the hamlet of La Daille, and Max
Costa, big and debonair, who spent his winters as an electrician
at the Odéon Theatre in Paris. As soon as we roped, they
started up in their patois what sounded to us like the angriest
quarrel—'A man is always suspicious of what is saying in an
unknown tongue,' as Boswell observed when, storm-tossed with
Johnson off Mull, he listened to the sailors shouting to each

other in Erse. But it turned out that our two were just exchanging friendly memories of previous crossings of the Santel glacier. Black streaks running down the snow-filled gullies and stretching far out across the glacier warned us to mind our way, and we turned off the glacier and up the rocks to the left just as the sun touched the ridge in front. Within a matter of seconds the stonefalls began. We were in shade till the very top, when the sun and the view greeted us together. Monte Viso, shimmering in the south, we admired purely for its beauty; we scanned the nearer Gran Paradiso and Grivola more practically, looking for the good way up; on the great south face of Mont Blanc we picked out the Innominata, Brouillard, and Péteret, ridges to revere and not, as yet, consider. Over food there was another brisk outburst of patois; later, Costa and Gunié told us they had been discussing their first day's guiding twenty-five years ago, and how much the glaciers had receded since then. Gunié thought they took up about a fifth less space now. They had been easier too—smugglers had used the Col de la Goletta constantly, and cattle were driven over. Even in September it was perfectly smooth and safe; now there were holes big enough to sink a cow. At this point I started rummaging about to find a suitable boulder under which to hide my sardine tin. Costa took it from me, added a little orange peel of his own, stood by the top cairn, and flung it over the Italian side, shouting gaily: 'Ca pour Mussolini!' Now they talked to us about climbing in Italy; they said that for the last ten years French guides had been subtly discouraged by the Italians from doing the obvious passes and traverses that would bring them down on the Italian side. If they went over the Col de la Galise, or the Col de Rhêmes, the first Italian gendarme they saw would send them to get their passports stamped at Ceresole, or some other village down a valley or over a hill, thus making them waste at least one climbing day.

The four boys in the party came down the steep and softening Glacier du Quarre Dessus with assurance and style; it was a good last day for them. That evening, we saw the party off from Bourg Saint-Maurice; coming back up the valley under the Pourri, our real holiday began. We started with an easy, ambling day over to the Carro hut, one of those days when there never seems to be any strong reason of route or weather why you should not idle for ten minutes in the flowers. High up on the Glacier des Sources de l'Isère the crevasses were masked with new snow, and we had to jerk ourselves into a more purposeful mood. There was compensation on the other side of the Grande Aiguille Rousse, in a snow slope defended by a great cornice, but perfect for a glissade. Thinking there might be a bergschrund at the bottom, we kept on the rope, but came down fast, and with surprising harmony.

Outside the Carro hut the mule tethered to the post by the little lake repeated last year's picture; but inside there were great changes. There was a new and efficient guardian, and in the *salle* there were bowls of gentians, daisies, and forget-me-nots. A late start at eight ensured a long hot day over the glaciers to the Évettes. When we got to the top of the rocks dividing the Glacier des Sources de l'Arc from the Glacier du Mulinet, we discovered that the snow slope above was, in fact, ice. 'Hardly worth putting on crampons,' we agreed. Michael started cutting steps, and we kept on thinking that two minutes would see us on to the level glacier. The axe whanged, the ice tinkled, a glacier stream fussed and chattered, I stood in my steps, or moved up foot by foot—for two hours! An absurd episode, in view of the crampons clanking on our rucksacks, but no doubt good practice. Further over, on the Glacier du Grand Méan, a wind suddenly blew up, breaking the thin crust of ice on the top of the glacier streams, and sending the pieces skimming along like a flock of silver birds. Across the Évettes glacier was the Albaron, with its long white shelf of snow resting on a band of black rock; we discussed possible ways up to the shelf, and later at the Évettes hut tried to harmonize the wisdom of Ball, the information of natives, and the evidence of our own eyes.

At dinner we sat with two young Frenchmen, also bound for the Albaron next day, and their non-climbing girl friends, and talked about sporting priests. Two had gone up the Albaron that morning, saying mass at 2.45 before they started, and removing their soutanes on the glacier. These were the years of a new kind of record—'première ascension avec messe'—and our jokes ran on possibilities of gaining renown by 'première ascension, pieds nus.' Eight hours later it was obviously not a good morning, but we thought we would 'have a look' at the Albaron; so did the two Frenchmen. In a misty drizzle we missed the tricky little path up the side of the moraine, and spent a cold wet hour in and above a rock gully up from the glacier before we picked it up again. On the edge of the upper glacier, the long white shelf we had looked at the afternoon before, I was now the devil's advocate, urging caution in bad weather, and not speaking of my own laziness; Michael was determined to go on 'just a quarter of an hour, to see what this glacier's like.' I thought honour was satisfied; it seemed no weather for pulling people out of crevasses. He said we should kick ourselves if we didn't go on, as it was obviously going to clear. So it did—but not till we were well on the farther side of the Albaron, looking down to the valley of Averole. Michael had led us unhesitatingly over the new mountain, whose subsidiary ridges made it a moderately complicated problem in thick mist, and I was glad to eat my words. The rain came on again heavily as we walked down the hillside. Wherever we expected a path on these flowery pastures, splashed blue with harebells, there was a neat little runlet drained off from the main stream, and ingenious devices led these right through the summer chalets. These, with their roofs of stone slabs overgrown with russet lichens, touching the hillside at the back, seemed as natural and necessary a part of the landscape as the rocks and cows.

The Averole hut, perched annoyingly on the top of a hillock about two hundred metres high (you nearly always begin your climbs from there demoralizingly, by going down), was clean, and empty but for a French honeymoon couple. The first half of their *tour de noces*, they told us, had been an affair of best clothes and smart hotels in Algeria; this was the part they were enjoying most. We had eaten our last gobbet of dry mutton from Val d'Isère on coming off the glacier from the Albaron; and we were disappointed to find that the Averole hut was nearly out of supplies. The *gardienne* did her best with some more cold gobbets, and the French couple had spent part of this rainy day in picking and mixing a beautiful dandelion salad which they allowed us to share. Tomorrow they hoped to do the Charbonnel with Pierre Blanc le Pape of Bonneval. He did not turn up; but Michael, in spite of another drizzly dawn, decided once more 'to have a look,' also at the Charbonnel. Again I was the devil's advocate, pointing out that 8.45 was no time to start for a mountain; I had woken up with a painfully swollen lip and there was a considerable dash of bad temper in my argument. Michael had the confidence of having pulled off the Albaron the day before; but this time it was difficult to pretend that it might clear in an hour or two, and at eleven we turned back again down the Vallon de la Lombarde without much discussion. In the Cabane des Bergers where we ate our bread and sardines the shepherds had carved their names, with PATRE after each, on the stone walls.

The way down to the main valley took us now through the Combe d'Averole, a gloomy gash in the hills. On the east the Albaron and the cliffs of the Bessanese, on the south the steep grass and shale leading up to the Arbeyron and Croce Rossa, on the west the great scree slopes of the Charbonnel, falling to cliffs above the gorge, hem it in and shut off the sun's rays for half the year. There is only a narrow strip of hummocky pasture on each side of the torrent, which often rushes twenty or thirty feet below the level of its rocky banks. A gloomy place, and we were glad to come across a cheerful St. Grat, a square, bearded little wooden figure standing in a box shrine in a stone alcove by the path. Travellers—especially British travellers—are sometimes superior about what they imagine to be the superstition implied in the building of these shrines. But any one coming over a deserted pass in bad weather—when unreasonable as well as reasonable fears are apt to invade the mind—finds himself cheered at the sight of these reminders of human workmanship and human piety and the ways of everyday life. I know that I should have welcomed a St. Mungo, for instance, at the head of Glen Tilt in the gloaming of that October day when the deer were roaring.

When we reached the main road we stopped to look at the emblems on the twelve crosses on the stretch down to Bessans. On one was a carpenter's tools, on another a smith's—'all trades, their gear and tackle and trim'—and the countrywomen, stiff in their black dresses on the backs of mules, bobbed as they passed. On the slopes across the Arc they were just finishing the laying of a wire cable up the hillside, to bring the hay down from the highest patches: the first bundles were now tied to the cable, and came shooting down. We squeezed into a bus already full of people and hens in baskets—one old woman in Maurienne dress gaily sitting on a young workman's knee, and cracking jokes about it—and swayed down to Lanslebourg and civilized life at the Hôtel Valloire. We dined exquisitely at a table under a plaque in the wall which records that Maréchal Pétain, 'en tournée d'inspection dans les Alpes,' had once stopped here.

Next morning was far too hot to make the plod up the hillside to La Turra an undiluted pleasure, but the two kilos of peaches from the Sunday morning market at Lanslebourg sweetened the way, and I had evolved a new and helpful variation of my old stand-by,

> The stag at eve had drunk his fill, drunk his fill, drunk his fill,
> The stag at eve had drunk his fill, and so say all of us,

to a tune from *Petrouchka*. Towards the top of this first pull up from the valley there were a lot of long red strings lying here and there on the hillside, of the kind that ski-ing parties carry on avalanchy slopes, so that if the snow does break away the rescuers will have some indication where to look. It was difficult to realize that there could be any danger so near these pleasant chalets; but almost every spring we used to read of some party of Chasseurs Alpins, on their way to the military post at the Col de la Vanoise, being overwhelmed at this point. We went on leisurely over the hill and down to the chalets of Entre deux Eaux, then up by the steep zigzags, with the barbed wire, notices, and concrete emplacements of the military zone, to the Col de la Vanoise.

The rain caught us in this mile-long trough. At last, drenched and chilled, we came in sight of the Réfuge Félix-Faure. 'Dinner,' said Michael. 'A second helping of good hot thick soup; there ought to be cutlets; and after all, they're only an hour and a half from Pralognan—there *might* be meringues.' We opened the door, expecting cordiality and a red-hot stove. A tall, lanky young man with a vacant expression, wearing the uniform of a French sea scout, pushed his face at us. 'Have you got an altimeter?' he demanded. Michael thought this one not worth answering, and countered with: 'Have you any hot drinks?' The sea scout, making strange noises, gave no sign of understanding; and it took some time to find the guardian. When we did, we were told that the kitchen stove had gone out. The Refuge Félix-Faure has a fine situation, at the foot of the Aiguille de la Vanoise and facing the Grande Casse; and in other years Michael had found it a friendly and cosy hut. But this season it had fallen into the hands of a guardian who was more interested in making quick money by selling postcards and tea to day trippers from Pralognan than in looking after the climbers, with whose money, after all, the hut had been built. There was a large rubbish heap at the front door; the *salle* was dingy and dirty, the *dortoir* unswept. The sea scout, and an equally menacing friend of his, were the only other people in the hut, and they seemed to be incapable of withdrawing their minds from their distressing lack of an altimeter. The only sympathetic spirit in the neighbourhood was an unhappy mule, who from time to time nuzzled at the door. Unnerved by all these encounters, and by the black lentils served for supper, we rushed to bed and oblivion.

Ever since the Albaron I had staked out my claim for a rest day, and had fancied the Félix-Faure would provide the right background for lazing in the sun with a slab of chocolate and a new Arsène Lupin. Now, not a word was said on the subject, and if it had been snowing next morning, I think we would still have climbed something to get away from the hut. Actually it was fine, and the great glacier of the Grande Casse clear from top to bottom. I led up the *grande pente*, an easy business in crampons on firm snow, and a great zig-zag-zig took us up to the Col des Grands Couloirs in four hours from the hut. But by now the world had shrunk again, and we could see neither the summit of the Casse nor the Pointe Mathews to our right. Very gingerly we fumbled our way along the top snow ridge, sometimes walking just below and using the ridge itself as a handrail. Once, by a queer break in the mist, Michael saw Mont Blanc; otherwise we were muffled and isolated, and the ten metres of snow slope we could see to our right disappeared downhill at an alarming angle. A photograph taken from six feet away shows me a picture of disagreeable misery by the summit cairn, cold and huddled, a white blob of unmelted glacier cream giving me an inappropriate clown's nose. Coming down the *grande pente* again was a sort of test. Was I better on steepish snow than I had been last year coming down from the Ciamerella, or in the Charmoz-Grépon couloir? The snow seemed easier, anyway; a light crust, through which one's boot broke to find good footholds in the firmer layer below. At first, in the mist, we followed our uphill tracks, but soon we began to see more and more of the slope stretching out below, and could pick our own line. Then a hailstorm started, and soon there were quick little runnels of hail pelting down the slope, and bringing some stones with them. We were quite pleased with ourselves when we unroped on the edge of the glacier, and the sun had come out; we discussed what we should drink at the Félix-Faure to crown the climb. I fancied fresh *citronnade*; Michael was for beer and lemonade. We got to the hut, and found a mob of Pralognan excursionists. Michael disappeared to get the drinks, and came back breathing fire. Not a *citron*, not a bottle of beer or lemonade!—the tourists had cleaned the place out. Then and there we decided not to spend another night; packed up, haggled twenty-five francs off the extortionate bill, and in very British mood tramped back along the Col de la Vanoise. There a thunderstorm broke; we pelted down the zigzags—*le chemin à sept lacets*—to the bridge, and arrived, dripping, at Entre deux Eaux.

Here all was welcome; of course they could take us in, we must have our clothes dried, and what would we like for supper? It was a whitewashed stone chalet, rather like a farmhouse in the Lakes, long and low, rising at one end to a second storey. It was not a C.A.F. hut (being anyway, at two thousand metres, rather low for most of the climbs near), but for years the Richard family, who came up with the cows every summer, had put up climbers or walkers. Entre deux Eaux stands at an Alpine cross-roads. Down from the north-east winds the stony, barren Vallon de la Leisse, and the path from the Lac de Tignes; to the east is the green Rocheure glen, at the head of which a pass leads down to Val d'Isère; to the west rises the steep bank down which we had just come from the Col de la Vanoise; and the southward track leads through a gorge to Termignon and the Arc valley. The houses stand on a grassy promontory between the Rocheure and the Leisse, and well above them; the Grande Casse and the

Rocher du Col are set back so that the summits can be seen, and the way to the south lies wide open, letting the sun in at all seasons. Madame Richard told us that she usually had two or three parties every night; this year she had also a *pensionnaire,* an elderly woman whom we had seen out in the thunderstorm with her tiny dog, and who had come to Entre deux Eaux 'pour la solitude.' Our other companions were a Frenchman on a walking tour with his two children; they passed the time before dinner playing Celebrities, and the ten-year-old girl scored with Ishmael for I. The dinner was delicious: broth, bacon and eggs, French beans, salad, *crème fraîche* and quince jam, and an admirable *vin rosé.* When she gave us her short, moderate bill next morning, Madame Richard wanted to know all about the Félix-Faure. It was hideously expensive, wasn't it; did dinners really cost twenty francs each, *vin non compris?* We painted it in the blackest colours.

A cloudy, lazy day took us back to Val d'Isère by the Rocheure glen, the Pointe de la Sana, and the Glacier de la Barme de l'Ours. On the way down the pastures by the Pisset we saw two marmots, heard their shrill whistle, and felt at one with the early Alpine travellers who seemed to hear it all day long. At Le Goray a hundred cows, tethered in rows, were being milked by six men. At Val d'Isère there was the customary unsurprised welcome from Pierre Rond, while Madame, as usual deep in her armchair, looked up from her novelette to ask about our trip. They said a telegram had come while we were away. I ran to the post office, fearing disaster. The message I got was 'SHOULD LICE COME WELCOME TANKS RIDING'; we worked this out (correctly) as an invitation from Laura Riding to visit her and Robert Graves in Majorca to discuss an anthology which Michael was compiling.

But we were not quit of poets and anthologies. A review copy of Auden and Garratt's *Poet's Tongue,* that had pursued Michael across France, and could not by this time be decently refused, at last gave me my rest day, and one over. Sometimes we sat on the flat roof of the Galise, till the girls bringing out sheets to dry made us move; sometimes in the Hôtel Parisien, where some children were being firmly set to holiday tasks at the shiny café tables; most often on the terrace of the friendly rambling Hôtel des Glaciers, with its huddle of carts, outhouses, washing, hens, timber, and children, beside the grey glacier stream. We took set photographs of each other with a beer bottle and the *Petite Anthologie Surréaliste* as stage properties; we read *Les Dents du Tigre*, and *La Demoiselle aux Yeux Verts;* and somehow the book was reviewed.

Gone entirely were the days of three-pound volumes of Shelley. This year my staple reading was the *Chartreuse de Parme* (in the one-volume Nelson edition about 6 in. by 4 in.); Michael was faithful to the lighter Maurice Leblanc. Choosing a new one at the Gare de Lyon each year was a recognisable stage in the start of the holiday. But we had heavier, necessary literature: Commandant Gaillard's excellent *Alpes de Savoie* (though so far the volumes on the frontier chain were unobtainable), which in careful, unemotional detail take you clearly up every possible route to your top; Ball's *Guide to the Western Alps* which, for the frontier mountains not covered by our Gaillards, was useful though brief; and Beet's *Guide to the Sky*. This latter was not an aid to early morning starts, but a cover only, used to enfold the relevant pages of Ball for any expedition, and save carrying the whole volume.

Ball, more personal than Gaillard, affected our language and outlook; we found ourselves talking of 'the Calebourdane glen,' reckoned that 'six and a half hours of fast walking' would take us up the Pourri, and wondered if we should ever make 'practised icemen.' Two figures in his pages specially intrigued us: the Rev. W. A. B. Coolidge and Miss Brevoort, frequently cited as having climbed such and such a peak in the district in the 'seventies. Memory and fancy, unchecked by any possibility of getting at the facts, placed Coolidge as a venerable Alpine Club figure and Oxford don; from there it was an easy jump to suppose that Miss Brevoort must be the lady that he would have liked to marry, but could not, on pain of losing his fellowship. Obviously, the best place they could enjoy each other's company, without the slander of gossiping Oxford tongues, would be the Alps; on the shaly south ridge of the Mont Pourri they could be united at last, though harsh academic necessity parted them for the rest of the year. As we made our way towards the Mont Pourri on a steamy afternoon, we fondly pictured this romance—the sympathetic guides, the lovers barely noticing the discomforts of the haylofts and bivouacs of those early, hutless days. Severe readjustments had to be made a few weeks later, in England, on discovering a reference to Mr. Coolidge as 'the American who climbed with his aunt and his dog.'

Our objective that evening was the Granges Martin, a cheese-maker's chalet an hour's walk up from Les Brevières, the next village to Tignes down the valley. It was a large and new building, with a big cattle byre, beside a small murky lake on which a boy was sailing a raft. The front room was full of cauldrons with cheese. Two men were stirring with long black wooden ladles; they barely looked up when we asked if we could sleep in the hay, but nodded assent. In the back room there were three wooden beds for the two men and two boys; their belongings were neatly hung on hooks at the bed-heads, or ranged tidily on shelves, and a table was laid with wooden platters, tin mugs, and spoons. In a few minutes, when one stage in the mystery had been completed, one of the cheesemakers came over to us with a great pail of new milk; we ate our supper, then cleared out to make room for our hosts, and to reconnoitre the first part of next day's route. We took the path round the hillside till we could see, across a torrent, the Croupe de Caroley—one of those long fingers of grass and rock that we used to scrutinise from the bus, stretching up between the descending glacier tongues. Down the Croupe now came a helter-skelter of sheep, mustered by one small boy, with no dog to help him. He had to get them on to the one bridge across the torrent; first they overshot it and disappeared behind a fold of ground; he vanished too, and then they dramatically reappeared, a broad white stream, suddenly narrowing as they squeezed on to the narrow bridge, then fanning out again on the near side. The boy jumped here and there, shouted, threw stones in the direction they should go; near the Granges Martin the boy who had been paddling the raft came out to meet him, and they got their flock into the pen as quickly and neatly as two old sheepdogs. The little shepherd came into the chalet dead beat; a few mouthfuls of soup and bites at the great disk of hard, brown bread, and he was asleep on the bench.

It was still light, so I produced my *Chartreuse de Parme;* but Michael, whose tastes become more elementary the higher he goes, preferred to read all about the Tour de France in the Petit Dauphinois in which the butter had been wrapped. 'The striking thing about Stendhal . . .' I said. 'The Belgians seem to be doing better this year,' answered Michael, turning over to see what hat Mrs. Baldwin had worn when opening the flower show at Aix-les-Bains. But I still maintain that Stendhal and Henry James can be read with least distraction, and with added appreciation of their civilised refinements, in the intervals of a mountain holiday. *Roderick Hudson* will always be associated for me with waiting for fine weather at the Jungfraujoch, and my copy of *The Golden Bowl* still bears the marks of my drenching and battering on Suilven.

Next morning the rain drove us back from the Croupe de Caroley, and by midday we were back at Val d'Isère for another day and a half of Stendhal and Leblanc, drinking vermouth at the Hôtel des Glaciers, coffee at the Parisien, coffee at the Glaciers, tea at the Parisien, beer at the Glaciers, inspecting the barometer, and sleeping.   The pull up to the Granges Martin the second time, on a hot afternoon, was happily none the harder for these orgies. The head cheesemaker prophesied good weather for the next day; they liked it themselves, he added, for it made the time go more quickly.   An occasional visitor helped too, but they seldom had more than a dozen every year, *en route* for the Pourri. ('Neuf mois d'hiver et trois mois d'enfer' is a local saying about a peasant's life in the Val d'Isère; during their three months at the chalets the men work an eighteen-hour day, seven days a week.   The only times they rest are between twelve and four in the night, and two and four in the afternoon.)   We were well asleep in the hay when another party clattered up the ladder into the loft—a guide and two young men.   This was at nine o'clock, and they woke us again when they clattered down soon after midnight. Absurdly early it seemed; we slept on till three.   I led along the path and went too low; there was a bad-tempered interval of separate gropings for the path with our tiny torchlights, and shout-ings in the dark.   We found ourselves at last by the torrent, but a good way below the bridge.   It was a starry night, with shooting stars too, light clouds over Mont Pourri, and black clouds massed over Mont Blanc.   Plodding up the Croupe, I began to see daisies and saxifrage; Michael slowly became more than a blur ahead. On the glacier, the day no longer looked so good; the black clouds

had spread to the summit of the Pourri, there were long grey
clouds to the east, showing red underneath. We hit the tracks
of the party who had left the Granges so early; then we saw them
coming down the glacier. We hardly thought they could have
been to the top and back; nor had they. The guide said they
had hoped to see the dawn from the summit, but it would not
now be worth while, as there would be no view. We did not
want to underestimate local judgement, but it did not seem rash
to go up as far as the Brèche Puiseux anyway; so we climbed
on. (Later, at the Granges Martin, we learned that the guide had
really turned back because he wanted to get in his hay.)

Over the bergschrund by a delicate snow bridge, and we were
breakfasting on the rocks in fitful sunlight. We left one sack,
and one ice-axe, and climbed up a face of loose rock and shale,
over a small, steep field of névé where some steps had to be cut,
to the main arête just above the Brèche, where we left the other
axe. Two hours' scramble took us to the top, the mountain justifying
its name at every step—'solid slabs of bad rock' I feelingly noted
that night in my diary. There was no climbing difficulty at all,
but attention could never be relaxed. All the same it was pleasant
work winding in and out of those tottering pillars and turrets,
with the glacier rushing down on our right to the Val d'Isère,
and on the left the shaly slopes leading to the still unexplored
Peisey valley, with the horse-shaped Aliet rearing up beyond. On
the snow patch on the top the sun was quite strong, and the mist
kept moving, showing us now Mont Blanc, or the Grivola, or a
horizon of Dauphiné peaks. We certainly had been right about
the day—and so had the old guide, now happily getting his hay
in dry two thousand metres lower down. We were rather slower
down the ridge than up; but when we picked up the first ice-axe
we thought the climb as good as over. Not a bit of it. On the
shaly face below the steep little patch of névé, we were attracted
by an apparently easy traverse, and by the time we realized we
were on the wrong route it hardly seemed worth while to look
for the right one. Michael suggested making horizontally for the
glacier, then going straight down it to the breakfast rocks. I,
more confident on rock, however crumbly, made some objections,
but agreed. From the point we stepped on to the glacier we

could see the sack, and the iceaxe we had left that morning, absurdly near; but it was afternoon, the snow was vilely soft over hard ice, and we had only one axe between us. I behaved badly, slithering, and asking why we hadn't stuck to the rocks. Eventually we crossed back to the very edge, where rock and glacier meet. 'It doesn't go down to hell, you know,' shouted Michael, as I looked distastefully at the black crack separating rock from ice. That was just what I was sure it did.   These hundred metres down to the sack took us as long as the mile-long ridge, and I felt very silly.   The delicate snow bridge over the bergschrund had not improved; and so, to distribute our weight, we sat down and slid delicately over it.   The rest of the glacier we took at a run, and got off it as the rain began; we rattled and bumped down the Croupe in three quarters of an hour, rather like the descent from the Col du Géant, but this time there was the excuse of lateness and the fear of losing our bus and our dinner.   We crossed the bridge over the torrent just after the evening procession of sheep, and as we came to the Granges Martin, the shepherd-boy, the sheep, and the Dôme de Val d'Isère stood out black against a lurid sky.   We picked up our sacks and raced for the valley, hoping the Paris train had been late at Bourg Saint-Maurice.   No luck; the autobus had passed.   But the day had been good enough to make us reckless, and we telephoned to Tignes for a taxi and drank half a dozen *cafés filtres* at Les Brevières while waiting for it.   Though it was 9.15 when we got back to Val d'Isère, Pierre Rond smiled, and gave us an excellent dinner to wind up a grand day.

At the end of last year Othon had asked us to do a job for him. He had admired Michael's sleeping-bag, and decided that only in England could an equally downy quilt be made.   So we were to order a *duvet*, six feet square, and bring it out.   This involved us, rather shamefacedly, in the only smuggling either of us had ever deliberately undertaken above the level of a Tauchnitz; though, indeed, to this day I am not certain if the monstrous quilt were dutiable or not.   However, Othon seemed to think yes; so we sewed it up in a couple of old sheets, and tied it to one of the sacks with string, hoping it would pass for camping equipment. The day was wet when we went over from Bourg Saint-Maurice

to Courmayeur, and the bus far from full up the Little St. Bernard;
the other passengers had plenty of scope to turn round and examine
the enormous unconvincing sleeping-bag. But they seemed profoundly uninterested, as were the Customs officials at the pass.
Sponge-bags were their quarry that day, and our toothbrushes and
sponges were squeezed and prodded—for cocaine? An hour and
a half later the bundle was pushed over the counter of the Droguerie
Bron: Othon, enchanted, nipped it out of its sheets, and shouted
for Madame Bron to come and admire the thirty-six square feet
of royal blue cosiness. He had something in return: new climbing
boots, which he had had made for me in the Dolomites, short
in the leg, square, dark red. And he had a new prize of his
own to display: a book of mountaineering drawings by Samivel,
Sous l'œil des choucas. We went into the back room and he showed
us all his favourites—'Pourvu que ça dure!'; 'Pendant que nous
montons, le glacier descend!'—and identified himself with the enormous hairy guide who values his clients according to their lightness,
and us with the knock-kneed clients themselves.

We had arrived in Courmayeur on 14th August, so we had to
wait over the next day, which was the Feast of the Innocents,
and also the traditional feast of the guides. As we pottered about
the town, Othon would sometimes flash by with a shout and a
laugh at the heart of all the day's doings. When we saw him
in a café in the evening he was a trifle apologetic; he had his
Fascist uniform on, for some party official had to be taken round
something, but he seemed to disclaim it—*peau de diable* and corduroy
breeches were for him the only proper uniform.

Our plan was to take the High Level route to Zermatt from
the Great St. Bernard, climbing as many peaks as the weather
would allow on the way. Othon had an idea that it would be
cheaper for us to hire a car over the pass than take the bus. He
always made these arrangements sound reasonable. It certainly
wasn't cheaper, but it was quicker and pleasanter, and it gave a
girl friend of Othon's a nice afternoon's outing. At Aosta, where
we stopped to get money and eat water-ices in the *place*, attention
was equally divided between Roman antiquity and prison reminis-
cences. At the end of his walk in 1924 across France to the
Great St. Bernard Michael had fallen into trouble, by producing

a large curved knife (useful for cutting wood) at the Italian customs, and asking if it was all right. Immediately he was arrested for the unlawful possession of weapons, and put into the guard-house at Etroubles. All ended well three days later before a reasonable judge at Aosta—though he never got back the knife—but there had been an eventful half-hour at Etroubles, with a scuffle in the cell when remarks had been made derogatory to Italy's present regime. Michael was carrying an *Oxford Book of English Verse* in his pack, and beside 'Stone walls do not a prison make' is still pencilled: 'In prison at Etroubles, Italy, 20th July 1924; "Les Anglais sont des gens tranquils" ' (a remark made by a fellow prisoner who appreciated the extent of the provocation). His other arrest had been a friendlier affair. He was seized one night as he was walking into a village in central France; when he asked what it was all about, the gendarmes announced that they were looking for a short murderer with a wooden leg. It looked well in the records if they put someone in jug for the night, and he would be let out tomorrow morning.

We could not drive fast up to the Great St. Bernard, for troops were coming down at the end of manoeuvres, chattering and straggling over the road. We were a convenient target for jests, but Othon could hardly be bothered to pay them back with his usually lively tongue: 'ces types méridionaux' was his term for the cheerful, untidy little soldiers. 'Je ne suis pas Italien—je suis Valdôtain,' he said once; and, when provoked by inefficiency at Courmayeur or Chamonix, 'Il faut tuer tous les Italiens' came as readily as 'Il faut tuer tous les Français.' He was the local Fascist secretary, and accepted the regime in good faith. In his view it had abolished some unnecessary distinctions—titles, he said, no longer counted for anything—and it had tidied up a good deal of the world he knew. When we had been flabbergasted by the bill at the Montanvert, he had been quick to point out that in Italy you could have no such unpleasant surprises, for the prices of each kind of hotel were fixed by decree. But in broader political issues he was not interested—or found it wiser not to be. When Mussolini invaded Abyssinia later that year, Michael wrote to Othon that the differences between our governments would never affect our relations with him. He wrote back rather angrily, saying that between friends like us there must never be any talk of politics. (But we were glad that the imposition of sanctions did not prevent the sending of a yellow monkey to Courmayeur for Horace's Christmas present.) All Othon's enthusiasms were for the mountains. In war, of course, he would serve his country, but in peacetime the links between him and his fellow guides at Chamonix were stronger than those that bound him to these *types méridionaux* now straggling down from the Great St. Bernard.

Behind us, across the Val d'Aosta, dazzled the Grivola, as white on this side as we were used to seeing it black from the mountains of the Tarentaise; and where the road turns west at Gignod, we looked right up the Valpelline to the Matterhorn. We left the girl friend at the frontier, to await the car's return, and ourselves dropped down to Bourg Saint-Pierre and the Hôtel du Déjeuner de Napoléon I.

Stocked up with about four days' food, we started off next morning for the Valsorey hut: the sacks were heavier than I had had to carry before, and I was glad to stop at the highest chalets and drink milk out of bowls, while Othon told us what real sackfuls were like. For a week that summer he had guided a party of thirteen Swiss climbers from the St. Gall section of the Swiss Alpine Club, and his first action had been to make them jettison fifty-five kilos of luggage. We talked too of Dolly, the elephant whom an American had led over the Alps that summer, in the supposed tracks of Hannibal. She became our standing joke that season; we followed her progress (some months behind the times) by hunting up old newspapers wherever we went. We were particularly touched when we learned that she had developed corns on the Route Napoléon, and had had to perform the next stage of her journey by lorry.

The Valsorey hut has no permanent attendant; the guardian lives at Bourg Saint-Pierre, and goes up from time to time to put things in order. In the hut book we found many records of his visits, and his comments—'Cabane très sale et la vaisselle pas lavée. Affreux de ce guide de Haudères de faire cela'—made us extra careful about our own hut manners. There was a tariff nailed up—so much for members of the Swiss Alpine Club and other affiliated clubs, two francs for a bundle of firewood, and so on—and a box to put the money in. Although rather chilly outside, it was nice to stroll out, look across at the Vélan, spot parties descending from the Combin or toiling up the last zigzags from the valley. The Valsorey is perched on top of a considerable spur of the Combin, and you are directly below it a long time before you reach it. When Michael and I went to our mattresses, Othon was well embarked on some of his lurid stories to an audience of two mild gentlemen from Lausanne: they were good gapers, and produced the proper 'Ohs' and 'Ahs' at the story of the Saint-Gervais guide who missed the Torino hut in a snowstorm, and so spent three days in a hole in the snow with his party, within 150 metres of the hut. Just as we were dozing off, in clattered a party of week-end climbers from Geneva, who laughed and sang and clashed plates till nearly eleven. The whole weekend was a holiday for them, and it did not particularly matter if they missed a night's sleep; but we listened to the racket with all the outraged feelings of the family breadwinner when his daughters rollick in from a dance at 3 a.m.

We let them go off in the dark next morning, while we waited for the daylight to start up the Grand Combin. It was a fairish morning: clouds over the Mont Blanc massif, which looked white until the top of Mont Blanc itself appeared rising far whiter above them. The snow was crisp and hard; we did not put on the rope until we left our sacks on the other side of the Glacier de Meitin, but I felt quite happy. On our way up the Arête de Meitin—but we were as much on the shaly face as on the arête—we kept wondering when the difficulties would begin. It was Michael's first 4,000-metre peak in Switzerland, and he had expected something more exacting than this alternation of scree, good snow, and easy rock, which brought us to the top of the Combin de Valsorey in three hours and a quarter from the hut. The only snag was the mist, which made us agree with Othon's suggestion that it was hardly worth plodding on to the slightly higher Graffeneire top. In view of the weather later on, he was probably right, but we have regretted that missed summit ever since. Some way below the top we met two of the noisy Genevese, who had started before us, up a ridge further to the west: that did not go well, so they had traversed to ours, but now the mist decided them to turn back. We came into the sun again on the Plateau du Couloir, and found a big stone on which to eat our second breakfast while Othon told us which were the passes for smugglers. Calvin, too, is supposed to have come over one of these cols, from the Valpelline, 'escaping from the persecutions of others, in the Val d'Aosta, to practise his own at Geneva.' But I learnt this later, from William Brockedon, and not from Othon. We went down and up to the Col du Sonadon, traversed across a sort of snow balcony towards the Testa Bianca, just inside Italy, and back again round the séracs to the middle of the Glacier du Mont Durand, a great level corridor overlooked by Mont Avril and Mont Gelé.

Once off this glacier, and down to the torrent of the Doire, we had to plod up again another 300 metres to the Chanrion hut. This ascent to a hut at the end of an expedition is a familiar sequence in the Alps, but no repetition ever makes it seem less unfair. I trailed up last. 'Come on, Dolly!' shouted Othon, five zigzags ahead. The Chanrion was a less austere (and less ship-shape) hut than the Valsorey perched on its stony shoulder. Here were cow pastures and a little lake, and a guardian willing to sell wine and milk, though, as at all Swiss Alpine Club huts, you had to provide your own food. We had all afternoon and evening to eat, sleep, and enjoy ourselves; as well as the usual volumes of the S.A.C. periodical, the hut had de Saussure's *Voyages dans les Alpes* on its shelves—the book that Ruskin had asked to be given on his fifteenth birthday. Two most agreeable and efficient young Swiss passed the time in laying out their stocks on the table and planning their menus for the next three days. They had already been snowbound three days at the Valsorey hut, so they must have started with a week's provisions. We had no such margin, and could only hope for fine enough weather to carry us over to Zermatt within the next two days. After supper we talked about quick climbing times. Othon had a story of taking a Dutchman up the Grandes Jorasses, leaving the hut at 2, doing the climb, back to the hut at 9.15, to clean, tidy and sweep, and down to Courmayeur at midday; only then did the Dutchman reveal that he had a finger frost-bitten; when he first noticed it he had not wanted to stop Othon for fear of spoiling his time-sheet.

There was rain the next morning, with mist higher up, and Othon thought there was no point in starting, because the Col de l'Évêque was hard to hit off in mist.   I read de Saussure, but the bench got very hard.   Eight elderly Swiss came up from the valley, rather wet.   There was more rain, with a few intervals of sun; then the sun seemed to be winning, and we woke Othon. He had a look, and was still doubtful.   Why not go up the Otemma glacier, we suggested; we could at worst come back to Chanrion.   But Othon wasn't easily deceived: 'Si l'on part, on arrive.'   At midday, though, he thought we might do it; and in one swoop, leading without hesitation over the misty tricky cols, he brought us to the rocks on the Arolla glacier under the Évêque, four hours and a half from the Chanrion.   We ate in the rain; the mist thickened; we came quickly down the glacier and off it at the Plan de Bertol, and again had a pull up at the end of the day. This time there was the compensation of the elegant little rock scramble in the half-dark up to the very door of the hut. It was the first solid bit of rock this year, and I did not spoil it by using the fixed rope.

Everything had worked out all right, but Othon described it as *marcher à l'allemande*—going off when you weren't sure you would arrive; all very well if you pulled it off, but leaving no margin for trouble.   Released now from the strain of finding his way through those misty corridors, he was in outrageously good form.   Jean Georges, the very pleasant guardian of the Bertol, had a nice streak of gullibility which encouraged Othon to tell story after story. Of course we had had a bit of difficulty crossing the stream to get to the Chanrion the day before, he told the company. 'Really?' asked Georges, hoping to pick up a bit of advice that he could pass on to other travellers.   'Yes, it was the pigs,' said Othon.   'The *pigs?*'   'Yes, they were on the wrong side.   I had to lasso one with the climbing rope, go over and get the others before our party could cross the torrent.'   Georges for the first time looked almost incredulous.   'But everybody knows you cross to the Chanrion on pigs,' said Othon.   'How else could you cross?' 'Sans blague?'   'Sans blague!'

There were three other climbers in the hut—a French couple, with a Dutch friend.   We suspected that Madame, very well made up and wearing natty skiing trousers, did not much like mountains. When we got up next morning she was in a tremendous temper. Her friend had suggested going on to the hut on the Wandfluh ridge of the Dent Blanche. She obviously pined for the valley, and reproached him bitterly: 'Tu sais que je ne suis venue à la montagne que deux fois!' From the platform in front of the hut we saw the sun rolling the mists off the Matterhorn and the Dent d'Hérens; and the light played tricks with our vision on the Ferpècle glacier, blurring the contours of the humps and hollows. Othon did some skilful steering in and out between the crevasses, and then we were on the Col d'Hérens, with the Matterhorn in front—a great triangular face of black rock, with another tiny triangle stuck on top, streaked and seamed with new snow, bounded by the airy white Zmutt ridge and the black jagged Italian ridge. This was the way that Michael had wanted to approach the Cervin, over the glaciers like a man and not up the railway like a tripper. We ate our last crust and sardine at the Schönbühl hut, marched down the tiresome moraine path, and came into Zermatt. The spell worked, the old excitements stirred. I pointed out the Rimpfischhorn with possessive delight, but I looked on the familiar landmarks with a new eye. After the doings of the last three weeks, I knew that I should no longer be content to sit in one centre and go up the climbs around in turn; I knew that the exhilarations of Alpine travel, even in mild districts like the Tarentaise, matched the exhilaration of climbing the classic Alpine peaks.

The uncertain weather had filled the street of Zermatt with patient, pipe-smoking guides and grey-flannelled, tweed-jacketed British. But there were signs of improvement in the weather, and over coffee in the bar opposite our Hôtel de la Poste, we discussed what to do next. I was all for the Matterhorn: I had not forgotten my earlier resolve to work up to it through all the other Zermatt peaks, but I felt it would be too fussy to bind Michael to that plan. And after all, it was six years since my first Alpine season; I could hardly accuse myself of greedily snatching the mountain. Both Othon and Michael agreed about climbing it, but put Monte Rosa first on the list—very reasonably, for it would give the Hörnli ridge two days to get rid of its snow. I felt I had had enough of snow mountains, and was sure the weather would not give us both peaks. My preference for rock started Othon off on what he liked best: tricky rock (with a wonderful account of a new climb he had done that summer on the Tour de Grand Saint-Pierre, in the Cogne district, where the handholds were all undercut), or finding his way through a complicated ice-fall, or system of crevasses. Then he talked about the best way of getting out of a crevasse—a problem that had given us a lot of thought in the Tarentaise. You might wait weeks for another party to come along and help you out on the Glacier des Sources de l'Arc or the Glacier du Mulinet, and it had seemed important for the two of us to manage rescue work alone. Our device had been a long loop of the climbing-rope, tucked into the end of the rope round our waists as we walked, ready to be pulled out and act as a sort of stirrup to stand in should we go down; but we still felt that the only really satisfactory solution on our guideless wanderings would be the Collapsible Man (non-talking), who would whisk out of the rucksack and be assembled as we reached the glacier, and be folded up again once we had safely attained the other side. Othon's system was to carry a short, spare line, and make loops with it on the climbing-rope, then step up: he had tried this in crevasses on the Dom and on the Tacul. We then asked him what was the hardest job he had ever had to do in the mountains. He smoked his pipe and thought, put his rope-soled feet on to a spare chair, and told us this story.

A German doctor arrived at Courmayeur, anxious to do the Requin. The only guide who was free was an old and lazy man, who said there was too much snow and suggested the Géant instead. When they got to the Torino hut, they heard that two Germans had just fallen from the Géant; so the doctor said that if, in the circumstances, the guide preferred not to go there, he would be happy to do the Requin instead; but, being a doctor, he would not be upset himself by the sight of the dead men. The guide (who was really unable to do the Requin) said that he did not mind either, and they would stick to the Géant. But next morning, when they got to the foot of the climb, he said they could not possibly go on, and cursed the German doctor for not showing respect to his countrymen. The doctor, who had foreseen this possibility the night before, was rightly furious; he rushed down to Courmayeur and sulked in a hotel for two days. Then (as Othon thought), wishing to score off the Courmayeur guides, he went to the guides' office and asked for a man to do the four Dames Anglaises without such artificial means as pitons, hammers, and karabiners. (The Dames Anglaises are the points on the great Péteret ridge of Mont Blanc, on the col between the Aiguille Noire and the Aiguille Blanche; the last was not climbed till 1912. They are ranked as *course extraordinaire, à débattre,* which means there is no fixed tariff, and you have to settle the fee yourself with the guide.) The office knew of no one capable of doing them who would be willing to take up a perfect stranger; Othon, dropping in later, was intrigued, and went round to the hotel to see what sort of a man this was. The doctor mentioned various things he had done in Bavaria and Tyrol—none of them meant anything to Othon—then said he had found the Grépon not at all difficult. Othon made an offer which he thought would be rejected—10,000 lire for the job, to cover all expenses. The doctor agreed, and Othon collected another guide, a couple of porters, and provisions, and took the party up to the Gamba hut. Before turning in he cut steps across the Fresnay Glacier to the Brèche des Dames Anglaises, and so got his caravan over next morning, to dump their loads, and back before the snow got bad. This saved an extra day's pay (each porter got 350 lire). Othon and the doctor bivouacked two days on the Brèche, and did the four Dames, without artificial aids. (Here Othon demonstrated the complicated manoeuvres, to the interest of the other drinkers in the bar.) As for the German, he was no better than a sack of potatoes, and simply had to be dragged up each one. They bivouacked for the third night, cold and hungry, for while they were climbing that day a stonefall had swept away some of their provisions, and the doctor's coat. At 9 o'clock Othon could stand it no longer, and led the German back in the moonlight to the Gamba, which they reached at 2 a.m. All this time the German had hardly spoken; but next morning, idling and sunbathing at the hut, he unburdened himself. He didn't know why he had done this; he must have been off his head, for he knew he was nothing of a climber, and the whole of this affair had not given him a moment's pleasure. As for the money, he was desperate; he was poor, and it would take him years to pay off the 10,000 lire. Othon also felt he must have been off his head when he took on the job—he told us now that he would never do it again with such a man, at any price. Soon after, the doctor went to Egypt to practise; in time he paid off the whole amount, and wrote to Othon for some years. Later Othon met the Chamonix guide who had taken him up the Grépon; he said he would rather have taken a mule.

But as for Othon's worst assignment, that was the shepherding of young Italian girls up to the Col du Géant, when he was twenty and in his first year as a guide. Often they screamed and cried. One took eight hours from the Cabane des Mulets (below the last zigzags) up to the hut, Othon putting her feet in the steps.

That night I dreamt that C. E. M. Joad (whom I have never met, nor particularly wish to) had fallen off Monte Rosa. Now, why?

Everything promised well when we got up to the Bétemps hut the next day in time for two delicious sunbaked hours on the scrap of grass outside. The hut filled up after us, mainly with a party of climbers who had been up Monte Rosa, but had come down too late to go on to Zermatt. Othon woke us at 2.40 next morning; I had vaguely heard noises of earlier departures. Bread, jam, sausages from a tin, and off we started at 3.15, with a starry sky, and a bright new moon which made the lantern almost unnecessary. We trudged up the glacier on good hard snow and I must have been in good training, for I have no memory of helping myself on with poetry. Two or three shooting stars flashed across the sky. Streaks of light showed over the Strahlhorn, behind our backs; and down the Gorner glacier the Matterhorn stood out very white with its new snow against the intense blue of the night sky. A pull up to the bergschrund, and suddenly, surprisingly, there was the rounded top of the Breithorn, with the sun slanting on it, below us. Puzzling, because it was only six o'clock. Above the bergschrund, Othon turned: 'Je suis orgueilleux de mes clients; vous avez très bien marché!' I laughed, because the night before

I had reminded Michael that a snow-plod tired me, and begged him not to let Othon go too fast. But this had been no effort!

Now the light was on all the hills, but our slope still lay in shadow: 'a long, cold, snow grind,' my father described his ascent of Monte Rosa fifty years before. We passed the last of the early starters from the hut, two very pleasant-looking elderly Swiss (this year's motto for ourselves, we had discovered, was 'last to start, first to the top'); poked our heads into the sun over the last rocks; enjoyed the elegant last step, a thirteen-foot chimney of excellent rock, and there we were on the top. There was Italy, a sunlit sea of cloud; here was Othon, most unusually shaking hands; beyond him the great Swiss peaks stood round. Here, on this highest point of Monte Rosa, I found again that pure shock of joy that is one of the reasons why we climb, but that does not come on every mountain top; when the splendour of the scene and the pleasure of the climb bring a sudden great sigh of elation, of fulfilment; when tears might come if it were not that they would complicate one's breathing. It is as impossible to recapture this fine shade of delight as it is to recapture those moments of illumination when we see the meaning and pattern of our lives; but we can remember that we have been blessed.

The only trouble about our three and three-quarters of an hour up was that it had suddenly made Othon wish to get down in fast time too. We bribed him with chocolate and raisins—Michael at this stage longed for a square meal—while we picked out the peaks that thrust up from the sea of clouds: Monte Viso, the Meije, the Écrins; then, in our own parish, the broad snowy Paradiso, defiant Grivola, gentle Ruitor; the Mont Blanc, the Combin, round to the Oberland and Engadine, as well as the Zermatt giants. The clouds parted and showed the Macugnaga valley almost directly below, yet very far away; it made one feel queer to think how steep and high the slope must be. This cleared up a problem that had exercised Michael on the way up. All the accounts he had read of Monte Rosa—by Kugy, Achille Ratti, not to speak of the illustrations to King's *Italian Valleys of the Alps*—had related to this terrific south side; he had an idea that Monte Rosa was like that all round, and had kept wondering where the horrors were to begin.

Once we were off the top, it was a pleasure to go fast; my new boots bit the snow magnificently, but then the snow itself was superb. Michael was too hungry to caper, but Othon and I were in high and noisy spirits, coming down the glacier with a sort of ski-ing motion, in a series of big swoops ('Were there many glacial passages?' asked a Scottish acquaintance politely, three months later), and we were back at the hut just six hours after leaving it. We lolled on the rocks; watched the crowds coming over the Gorner glacier to picnic at the hut ('une fourmillière,' said Othon, with distaste, and picked ourselves up at midday to go down the rest of the 3,000 metres at a more sober rate. We certainly came nowhere near the record of twelve and a half minutes established by my parents from the Riffelberg to the Riffel Alp forty-six years before. It is hard to understand now why, on such a fine day, we did not go on to some of the other points on the Monte Rosa ridge. Our hopes of the Matterhorn the next day perhaps accounted partly for this apparent lack of enterprise—also a lingering diffidence in the face of these highest Alps which had such long and famous climbing histories. We could cheerfully spend a whole day poking round the Ciamarella or the Pourri, but we felt ourselves lucky to get to the top of Monte Rosa at all.

As we started up to the Hörnli hut next day the sky was blue, but by the time we got to the Schwarzsee, there were too many clouds coming over from Italy. There would be sudden chills as they passed over the sun: everything looked a trifle bleak, and the heart was out of the day. Then the sun came out again, and we began to believe once more we should climb our peak. The final zigzags up to the Hörnli hut—I made them forty-four against the Kurz guide's forty-two—provided one of those rare and pleasant moments when climbing steadily on a good path becomes enjoyable in itself, and demands no effort of one's willing legs. At the Hörnli, most of the mattresses had sacks or bundles to reserve them; there were thirty people on the Matterhorn that day, the guardian told us, and many of them were still on. A worried-looking young man monopolised the telescope; we recognised him as one of the large party who had come down so late to the Bétemps the night we arrived. After their very long outing on Monte

Rosa they had spent the next day rather wearily trudging down the Gorner glacier and up the Théodule glacier to the Hörnli hut: this boy had been too tired to try the Matterhorn, but the rest had gone up, with their one guide; and now it was six o'clock, and there were still no signs of them. We suggested they might be spending the night at the Solvay, the tiny hut 4,000 metres up, intended only as an emergency refuge; but at seven he shouted that he could see them. We took our turn at the telescope; there they were, tiny little ants, but not so tiny that we couldn't see they were mostly sitting their way down. We also noticed a good deal of mist. At half-past eight we had another look; we could see a lantern or two bobbing up on the ridge; also summer lightning over the Breuiljoch. It would have been very impressive if one had been disinterested.

We turned in; the guardian, a slack man, had gone over to the Belvedere Hotel next door without making any effort to reserve mattresses for the late party (who had, of course, hoped to get down to Zermatt). About nine we heard them come in; their guide, a cheerful little man from Evolène, came upstairs. Othon commented on the time they had taken. 'Mais avec des types comme ça,' was the answer, reinforced with expressive gestures. There were seven in the party; the guide had taken two on his rope—one of them being a girl who had had her appendix out six weeks before—and the other five followed. This rope did not go further than the Roof; they had wanted the guide to take his rope to the top, come back, and in turn take them, but it would have meant an extra hour and a half at least. They had taken eight hours to get up Monte Rosa, so he had tried to dissuade them from the Matterhorn. But they were adamant: 'C'était sur le programme.'

That night I dreamt that I was trying to climb the Matterhorn, but was always being frustrated. Sometimes it was a person who pushed me back; sometimes a wall, or house, suddenly appeared in the way (the Matterhorn itself was a huge tower, like an iron pagoda). I got desperate. 'But I've got as far as this so many times. Please let me get on,' I cried, almost in tears. But they wouldn't let me pass, not even when I tried to sneak by on a motor-bike.

I woke to something as bad: Othon poking his head out at the weather and muttering 'Quelle charognerie!' 'Candelwett!' and other curses in other languages. It really seemed hopeless. 'If only we had done this first instead of Monte Rosa' —miserable, unfair thoughts chased round my head. An hour or two later there was a commotion. Othon, going down for a final look at the weather from outside, had found the late party lying on mattresses in the eating-place, many of them with no coverings, while there were places and covers available upstairs. What a guardian! Othon brought them up, took off extra covers from those already installed (including himself), and saw them comfortably wrapped up.

Nobody got up till late. The large party looked exhausted, but the burly leader signed the hut book with a flourish, while their guide looked at us and smiled. About nine we started down; the demon of competition possessed us, and we hurtled past two bare-kneed vegetarians and the large and straggly party, to reach Zermatt in an hour and a half. Othon, who started after us, did it in an hour and a quarter. Nobody said anything about coming down from the Torino last year, or the vices of quick descents. We had to work off our disappointment somehow.

On the train down to Visp we found the little guide from Evolène, now released. He asked a lot about Courmayeur; Othon suggested he should come over in September, and they would do some climbs. He often did this after the tourists had gone, and liked showing another guide round the district. The journey from Visp to Chamonix, in rain and mist, was cheered by Othon's clowning. He stood on the tiny open platform of the train, bawling 'En voiture!' at the stations to startled scurrying passengers. He followed the mild little ticket-collector, shouting 'Vos billets' in stentorian tones, to make both passengers and collector jump. 'Si les guides sont comme ça,' said the latter peacefully, 'je serai un sans-guide.'

At Chamonix, Othon rather hopelessly suggested that we should wait and do the Grépon. But obviously it would take at least a couple of days for the new snow to go; so far we had managed, in very mediocre weather, to keep moving, to travel to a new hut even when we could not climb a mountain, and we had no wish now to start hanging about a valley centre waiting for the weather. Nor could we afford it, for a guide as well as ourselves. So we waved him off the train, to go home over the Col du Géant, while we went on to Saint-Gervais.

It was an awkward parting, and our consciences were not entirely easy. We might be going to climb in the Mont Blanc range with another guide than Othon, and we didn't like to tell him. Earlier that summer we had seen, in the C.A.F. paper *La Montagne*, an announcement of a *course collective* organised by the Saint-Gervais section of the C.A.F. It struck us as a good opportunity to climb on a side of Mont Blanc we did not know, at moderate expense. You paid your share of the guides; but only for the actual mountains climbed, with no retaining fee for the blank days, and no guides' lodging. So next morning at Saint-Gervais we inscribed ourselves for the course, under Category A (*Bons alpinistes bien entrainés*), with the Aiguille Nord de Trélatête, the Aiguille des Glaciers, the traverse of the Bionnassay and Mont Blanc on our programme. We didn't want to be presumptuous with A2 (*Très bons alpinistes très bien entrainés*) on the north face of the Bionnassay, nor did we wish, out of excess of modesty, to confine ourselves with B and C to the Mont Tondu and Aiguille de Béranger.

The same reasons had inscribed another Briton in Category A —H. V. Hughes from Birmingham, to whom M. Chapelland, the courteous *guide-chef* in charge of the arrangements, had introduced us. He had been on last year's *course collective*, and enjoyed it very much, in spite of weather which only allowed him the Dômes de Miage and the Aiguille des Glaciers. He had begun this year in the Dauphiné, then walked over to join a Fell and Rock Club party at Arolla. M. Chapelland also told us that special terms for the members of the *course* had been arranged with the Hôtel Splendide-Royal. It pretty well lived up to its name, far above our usual level. There were one or two raised eyebrows when we appeared, with our only luggage a bundle of trousers and crampons that had come round in the bus from Courmayeur. Here and there, however, in the hotel dining-room, or in the streets of Saint-Gervais, we could spot fellow travellers of the *course*, conspicuously hairy and tweedy among the summer visitors.

We assembled in pelting rain next afternoon at the *bureau des guides*, twenty-two men and five women, and were put into a bus for Les Contamines. The Pavillon de Trélatête was to be our headquarters; we started up the narrow path in long Indian file. A fat girl with a nautical roll blocked half the party, till an outflanking move brought the British in front. Young Ernest Chapelland, one of the twin guide sons of the *guide-chef* (who, badly wounded in the war, was no longer active), set a terrific pace the minute the hotel was sighted. Michael was a close second, Mr. Hughes and I strung out third and fourth. The pavilion was charming—beds with sheets, delicious food—and the proprietor, Léon Orset, was one of our guides. At dinner, groups were formed, rather tentatively; one of our neighbours was a nervous little man called Flandin—no relation, he assured us, to the politician; all politicians were corrupt.

We were not called early for the Aiguille Nord de Trélatête, but spent the morning playing draughts and reading. It cleared a bit at midday, so after an early lunch we all set off for a walk up the Mont Tondu. The sun came out, and we saw Mont Blanc, also the Brocken—our own shadows on the clouds. It was all very impressive, but did not look like good weather. At dinner, the pleasant dark Parisian who had been appointed Commissaire of the party collected our share of the guides' fee for the Tondu: Groups A, B, and C sorted themselves out—there seemed to be no aces of A2 after all—and provisional plans were made for to-morrow.

But again, next day, we were not called early for the Aiguille des Glaciers. The morning passed in an orgy of Polish draughts. M. Flandin was taking everybody on, and winning with rather too much satisfaction. Michael, who had never played this variant before, went over and saw a few games played; then said he would like a turn. He scored a huge popular success by winning; Flandin was annoyed. By lunch-time, our idea of taking a little exercise on some near rocks gently faded out. In the rare intervals of clearness we could see new snow very low down on the green hills across the Bon Nant valley: it did not look as if anything high up would be possible for days. Everything was tried. Fatima of the nautical roll was very much to the fore in parlour tricks

and musical chairs. M. Flandin asked me for a book: I lent him
Flaubert's *Trois Contes*. He returned them in an hour, saying they
were not very nice. Hughes and I discussed an error in the
Northern Highlands volume of the Scottish Mountaineering Club's
guide. Signs of disintegration appeared. Various people gave up
the *course* as a bad job, and went back to the valley. The *Commissaire*
tried to hold us together by suggesting plans for next day—a
traverse of the Dômes de Miage to the Durier hut. The British,
by this time entirely sceptical, opened their own supplementary
provisions of sardines, anchovies, and tinned *hors d'œuvre*, to in-
troduce an exceptionally delicious dinner which worked up to a
climax of *mousse au chocolat*. But there were only half the party
to eat it.

We went to bed positive that we should have another long
night; and the knock came at 3.40! We dressed and packed our
sacks, but felt sure that someone had made a mistake. The other
remnants of the *course* straggled into the dining-room; the guides
sorted us out into three parties. Our lot was to traverse the
Dômes de Miage; a second was to climb the first Dôme, and
come back; a third go up the Aiguille de Béranger. The *Commissaire*
did complicated sums about our hotel hills. Provisions were promised, but did not appear. Outside, it started to snow. The British
got more and more sceptical: 'Of course they feel they've got to
give us the pretence of a climb. We'll be back for breakfast.'
Orset said nothing, but had obviously made up his mind to start,
so off we went at 5.20. There was no harmony in the party that
trudged up the Trélatête glacier, in new snow, and with more
snow falling, thin and wet; a thick mist crept over, and Michael
gave the joke a couple of hours to play itself out. It seemed a
bad ending to a year that had already given us disappointments.
However, these were the chances of a climbing holiday, and we
must try to he philosophical. Then suddenly I noticed that the
Aiguille de Béranger was clear, and very white, in an unearthly
cold sunlight—and, indeed, that it had stopped snowing. In five
minutes the miracle had happened. There was no mist ahead,
and no clouds straight above us, though all day they were massed
round the horizon. When we stopped to put on the rope under
the wall of the Béranger, the rocks were running with water from

the melting snows.   The new snow that we walked on that day was firm and good when over old snow, to which it adhered quite well, or when wind-crusted; but over ice, or rock slabs, it peeled off at once.

On one rope were Léon Orset, the *Commissaire*, an Alsatian called Muller, and a gruff solid porter.   Hughes, Michael, and I were on the other, with Ernest Chapelland.   Like many of the younger men on the Chamonix side, this young guide was something of a dandy; with his dark ski-ing trousers, nipped in with puttees to an elegant ankle, his white wind-jacket, gay muffler, and cocky beret, he looked very different from the homely peasant guides of Val d'Isère, or the large solid men of Courmayeur and Zermatt. One could easily picture him as a success in the dance hall, or a demon in a racing car.   We were on his rope continuously for two days, and could have had no better leader—quick, sure, and careful himself, understanding and patient with us.   Of course, on a casual short-term engagement such as this, his job was simply to get us safely up our peaks, and safely down again; he could not be expected to instruct and chide us, as Othon did, in order to make us better climbers.

Chapelland had heavy work kicking steps in new snow up to the Col de Béranger.   From that point, to our day's end at the Refuge Durier on the Col de Miage, nothing could have been more pleasant or exhilarating than our airy walk over the Dômes de Miage.   All the way we were on a ridge, and for most of it, on the frontier between France and Italy; on our left were the glaciers leading down to the Saint-Gervais valley, to our right the great south face of Mont Blanc; now and then, away behind us, we caught a glimpse of a very white Grivola and Tsanteleina.   Up and down we went over the three rounded domes, walking for the most part on good snow, in every sense on top of the world—until one of my thick woollen mittens, that I had stuffed into my breast pocket while blowing my nose, suddenly whirled away down to Italy.   Though not desperate, it was annoying, as Mont Blanc (which now began to look like our ultimate goal) was obviously the occasion for which I had been lugging the pair round all summer.

The laconic Orset had said something about sleeping at the
Refuge Durier; we knew nothing about it, and expected the usual
kind of hut. Suddenly here it was, right on our ridge, a one-room
box about nine feet cube. It was supposed to hold ten; with
eight it seemed far too full. We prayed that no other party had
had the sense to start this morning. (Orset, by the way, when
we asked him why he had started, said the wind had been cold,
so he had been sure it would clear.) We spent the afternoon
eating nut-milk chocolate and chattering about mountains; Hughes
entertained us with memories of enforced bivouacs—once, last year,
on the infernal moraine off the Zinalrothorn, and this year, on
the Râteau de la Meije—they got down to La Grave just as some-
body's sister was organising a search party. Then he remembered
another search party, in the Lakes, that had spent a week looking
for a missing climber. He was found three hundred miles away,
on a stolen bicycle, riding to Dover.

I woke in the night to hear the wind howling and the rain
pelting. The hut shook and rattled. 'No Mont Blanc,' I thought,
but without recrimination, for we were already one day to the
good after the morning's hopelessness. We all woke about seven,
and Orset said he had deliberately let us sleep, because it was
too cold to start before the sun was on our route. Hopes rose.
It was fine now, but the wind was blowing the snow round the
top of the Aiguille de Bionnassay in front of us, and, more vigorously
still, round the Aiguilles de Trélatête across the glacier. We had
lukewarm tea made on Chapelland's portable Meta stove; yesterday's
clothes were still wet from the snow, and though I had spare dry
stockings it was a cold agony putting on boots, and worse still
lacing on my crampons. (Orset put some old socks between his
boots and crampon tapes, thus distributing the pressure on boot
and foot.) We started second, waiting to clear up the hut, and
roped before we started. It was hideously cold; on Chapelland's
advice I curled and uncurled my toes at every step to prevent
their getting frost-bitten, and soon they felt quite snug. Instead
of my lost mitten I wore a spare sock, perfectly adequate, and no
bother even on rock. Crisp, firm snow took us to the rock ridge,
one of the unexpected delights of the day. From most points the
Bionnassay looks a predominantly snow and ice mountain, and

descriptions usually dwell on its long knife-edge eastern snow
arête.   But here on its southern side was about 300 metres of
admirable granite, solid as the Charmoz, with the sun well on it.
Half way up I took off my sock and remaining mitten, and felt
the rock dry and warm.   Michael took off his coat.   There were
no long or difficult pitches, but it was always interesting; I was
amused to find what little bother crampons were on this highly
unsuitable terrain.   Orset told us later that the ascent used always
to be made by a snow couloir on the French side of the face,
for the rocks had the reputation of being extremely difficult.   He
had been on one of the first parties to take them direct.

At the top of the rocks we moved off on to the Italian face
of the Bionnassay, and cut and kicked to the top.   It is a perfect
point, the intersection of two knife-edge ridges, and there was no
place to stand on it, so we moved straight off down the east ridge
towards the Col de Bionnassay.   Again we were lucky: Orset had
tales of cutting the whole way down in ice, a matter of three
hours or more.   We found good firm snow, and walked all the
way down the crest of a ridge which, though not itself very steep,
falls away on each side with tremendous drops.   It was even airier
than yesterday's Miage ridge, with an even grander view of Mont
Blanc's south face.   It would have been nice to pick out at leisure
the storied routes—the Brouillard ridge, that we shall always see
in terms of Geoffrey Young's great narrative, the Rochers de Mont
Blanc, and the early attempts to find a way up the Italian side.
But attention had to narrow down to the fifteen feet of curving
bounding ridge between myself and Hughes.   I was chiefly conscious
of the squeak of the ice-axe every time I pulled it out of the
snow, and the greeny-blue of the hole it left; and of Hughes's
imperturbable back and constant flow of chatter.   ('Did you see
a photograph of this ridge in the last *Mountaineering Journal*?').
He was first down on our rope, walking, in steps made by Orset
at the head of the first rope, at a pace so smart that *Doucements*
had to be frequently passed down the rope to him from the careful
Chapelland at the back.

Just over an hour brought us to the Col de Bionnassay, one
of the cols you can really straddle, with your right leg in Italy
and your left in France.   We had some bites of food, hut there

was really no room to sit; and after ten minutes our rope was off first, Chapelland leading us up to the Dôme du Goûter. Unlike the first part of this ridge, this bit was steep in itself as well as falling steeply away on each side, and when I looked at it I was heartily glad that we were going up and not down; but Chapelland kicked hard, the snow was still firm though it was one o'clock, and the climb up the staircase went remarkably well. In half an hour from the col we joined fresh tracks coming from the Italian route up the Aiguilles Grises. Beyond this point the angle of the ridge eased off, and the ridge itself broadened out; for the first time since we had left the rocks we were able to walk not exactly in each other's steps. To deviate a couple of inches from Chapelland's tracks was as good as relaxing in the sun on a hard-won peak. The Dôme du Goûter seemed absurdly broad; we stretched our legs happily, and were at the Vallot hut at half-past two. After the heavenly airy ridges it was a horrid place, dirty with snow and litter, and we spent a rather unhappy hour waiting for the other party to come up, waiting for the kettle to boil (it never did), drinking lukewarm tea, and getting very cold. We had a word with the two men whose tracks we had joined at the head of the Italian route. They asked about the way down to the Aiguille du Goûter and the Tête Rousse hut; one of them had slightly frost-bitten hands.

At last, leaving all the packs behind, we started off on the final stage up Mont Blanc. After the last two days' ridge-walking, this arête seemed a highway, and we walked up as easily as one would walk up Helvellyn from Grisedale Tarn. I tried to tell myself that this was the top of Mont Blanc, and feel the proper veneration and excitement; all I could think of was the hideously cold wind, which whipped the hard snow on to my face and the tips of my ears, barely covered by a too skimpy tammy. I wondered if any one had ever got a frostbitten nose. On the top, we looked round the horizon rather dully: the mountain ranges stretched away in every direction, but they did not look very interesting seen from above. Only here and there did a mountain—the Matterhorn was one—distinguish itself from the monotonous lines. We probably did not want to be impressed, for it was much too cold to linger, and after picking out the Grande Sassière and

another old friend or two we very willingly turned round and
went back to the Vallot hut, which we reached at half-past five,
a couple of hours after leaving it.   Once out of the worst fury
of the wind, interest in the mountain revived, and we picked out
the classic routes, *l'ancien passage*, the Grands Mulets.   We had
wanted to go down the latter way, but Orset decided that we
should make for the new hut on the Tête Rousse.   He said we
should sink deep in snow on the Grands Mulets route, and that
the hut was scandalously expensive; the clinching reason, we discovered later, was that his brother was guardian of the Tête Rousse.

We undid our crampons with frozen fingers outside the Vallot,
and looked rather wistfully at the observatory next door, which
seemed a snug and tidy place.   But there was no wind worth
speaking of on our way down over the Dôme du Goûter, and bit
by bit contentment took possession of mind and body.   The evening
was superb, the exertion was over, and we could realise what a
splendid climb it had been, this two-day journey on the airy
ridges, which swung us up and down, swept us over other peaks,
and always led us on to Mont Blanc, a noble way to reach that
noble mountain.   From the Aiguille du Goûter the ridges of the
Jura stood out black against a line of fire; the north face of the
Bionnassay, to our left, was indigo; the great chunks of ice and
sérac on the glacier at our feet were yellow and purple like a
Neapolitan ice.   Michael and I discovered afterwards that we had
both wanted to stretch out our hands and pick them up and see
if they were good to eat.

So far down our rope had led, and we had been slightly annoyed
at the repeated rests asked for by the *Commissaire* and Muller on
the other rope, though quite pleased to help with the tinned
peaches or pears produced on each occasion.   Now, on the crumbly
face of the Aiguille du Goûter, their rope led, and we were humbled,
coming far more slowly down the scree, shale, and small rock.
There was nothing difficult, but you had to be careful; Michael
and I were glad that Othon wasn't there to curse.   The lights of
Tête Rousse never seemed to get any nearer; it was quite dark
when we got on to the glacier, but Orset, whose party had unroped,
came back in a friendly spirit to guide us in.   When we blinked
our way into the Tête Rousse, at nine o'clock, there was the beer

we had been shouting for on the top of the Aiguille du Goûter, kindly ordered by the *Commissaire*.

The new hut, opened only a few days before, was crowded; in the forefront of the press stood Fatima! Our colleagues of categories B and C (whose existence we had entirely forgotten) had done their climbs the day before, and had now come up by the railway for an assault on Mont Blanc the next day. They were full of questions about the route over the Dôme du Goûter; we could only think of food and sleep. They were all abed by the time we had finished our excellent and protracted meal; the light was out in the *dortoir*, and we had to feel for the three empty bunks the guardian had promised. We discovered them, under a mild leak in the roof; someone had spread his belongings on one of the mattresses, but we moved them carefully away.

Far too soon the Mont Blanc party was astir. Fatima was evidently not to go, but she saw them off good-humouredly and noisily in bright pink pyjamas. The sleeper whose overflowing belongings had been displaced turned out to be the M. Flandin who had disapproved of Flaubert. Now he was fussy because he couldn't find his *chaussettes blanches*. I giggled, and thought of the White Rabbit. He made us turn over to show that we weren't lying on them, and still wasn't content, but muttered suspicions. We got very angry. Every one else left the *dortoir*, and we hoped at last for peace; but now Flandin pulled out a breviary and started saying his prayers. This was too much, and we put out the light.

We had the hut to ourselves for breakfast (save Fatima, busily writing postcards) and swung happily down the 2,000 odd metres to Saint-Gervais for drinks with the guides, settlement with old M. Chapelland at the *bureau des guides*, and a final lunch with Hughes. (I dislike calling people by their surnames, but he dislikes his Christian names even more.) At the hotel we ran into M. de Ségogne, who led the C.A.F. expedition to the Himalaya the next summer; he seemed very pleased to find some British in the *course collective* and was full of warm congratulations. Next morning, as I followed Michael to the bus stop, I saw him talking to a cleric in soutane and shovel-hat. I wondered mildly whom he had picked up. The cleric turned round, and there was Flandin!

Categories B and C had made a most successful ascent of Mont Blanc from Tête Rousse and down to Chamonix; M. l'abbé Flandin was delighted, and not a word was said on either side about the *chaussettes blanches* or the interrupted devotions.

The holiday was still not quite finished; earlier that year I had taken a step to ensure a longer spell in the Alps.   Late that afternoon we toiled up the Gran Credo, a spur of the Jura overlooking Bellegarde, first over hot pastures, then through steep brushwood; desperately I pulled myself up by hazel branches, but never in my life had I wanted to stop as much as I did now.   Kindly but very firmly Michael got me up above the tree-line, to camp at last by a well and a deserted chalet.   He put up the tent, collected the wood, made the fire, and produced a miraculous tiny bottle of Benedictine.   The next day we ambled along the ridge a mile or two, and camped by a shepherd's hut beside a small dewpond.   At night we looked down on the lights of Geneva, and then enjoyed our own illuminations as lightning played all round us.   We sloped off the ridge next morning by a gully on the north side and had an exquisite lunch of tinned lobster and wild raspberries by the mugful.   When we reached the road and were offered a lift into Bellegarde we didn't think twice about accepting.

As we walked up to the station to collect a bundle, a gendarme stopped us and asked to see our papers.   Always impressed by authority, I quickly scratched through the spare socks and tins in my rucksack to find my passport; but Michael, who rather likes a nice French row, was truculent.   'They can't have much to do in this town,' he said in French, rather loudly, and added some comments on a successful burglary which, according to a three-day-old paper, was baffling the Bellegarde police.   The gendarme was furious and hauled us along to the police station.   A sergeant was sitting at a desk in shirt-sleeves.   'I want to report this man,' said Michael.   The man who had stopped us was indignant; doubted the validity of our passports, and held forth on the penalties imposed for speaking contemptuously of the police.   'In England,' he said, 'you would be in a cell by now,' and it began to look as if he were determined that French justice should not lag behind. 'It is wise,' observed William Brockedon over a gendarme-and-passport incident at Briançon in 1824, 'for a stranger to bow with temper to these regulations in a foreign country; but no one feels the annoyance so much as an Englishman, and any unnecessary exercise of this power is sure to ruffle him.' Michael played the part of an Englishman to the full, and thoroughly enjoyed himself; I was unreasonably nervous because the name on my passport was no longer my legal surname; also, I was tired and grubby and longed for a bath and food. I begged Michael to be conciliatory. As a first step towards putting things on a better footing, he announced that he was a journalist. This seemed to produce some effect. The sergeant, who had been writing quietly at the end of the room, turned round with a smile and suggested that there was really very little cause for fuss. These people seemed to have their papers. Why had they been stopped in the first place? 'Mais voici,' said our captor, pointing to Michael's face, still protected by blobs of Crème Nivea, under his large black hat, 'quand on voit un type comme ça avec un chapeau comme ça . . .' There could be no more dignity or truculence. Michael asked our gendarme to recommend a hotel; he begged us to part from him *sans rancune*. *Sans rancune* it certainly was. The hotel he named was good and the water hot; and the *Chartreuse de Parme* (which had just seen me through the holiday) supplied the appropriate comment when we found some Asti on the wine-list: 'Un assez bon vin mousseux qu'on fabrique en Piémont dans la patrie d'Alfieri, et qui est fort estimé', surtout de la classe d'amateurs à laquelle appartiennent les geôliers.' We drank to the Bellegarde police.

CHAPTER VI

THE BEST YEAR OF ALL

Ô les fraises et les framboises,
Et le bon vin qu'nous avons bu!
Ô les belles villageoises
Nous ne les reverrons plus!

BY this time I had learned that the right place for the mountain classics is by one's own fire on autumn evenings, and not in one's Alpine luggage. Among the new discoveries, for me, were the Ladies, though for many years I thought they were but one. Mrs. Cole's *A Lady's Tour round Monte* Rosa, Mrs. Henry Freshfield's *Alpine Byways: by a Lady,* with their beautiful emblems, title-pages, and dedications, struck a humane and graceful note that later Alpine travellers seldom reached. In their agreeable, unpretentious narratives, and in the enchanting coloured lithographs, there was room for both the world of men and the world of rock and ice—in the foreground, the summer chalets raised on blocks of stone; behind them, the shining snows of the Macugnaga face of the Cima di Jazzi. Douglas Freshfield, too, delighted us; he is the humanist of the Alps. With his love of frescoes and campaniles, of descents from high snows to fertile chestnut valleys, Freshfield pointed the way to the richer pleasures of the Italian side; and George Yeld, with his delight in poetry and flowers, gave the Italian valleys of the Graians a morning freshness and a mystery which harmonized with our happy sight of the Val d'Orco and its milky torrent, when we sat on the Central Levanna and promised ourselves Ceresole. An early traveller to those parts, the Rev. S. W. King, produced a different effect. Towards the engraving of the Grivola, in his *Italian Valleys of the Alps* (1858), I felt much as I did towards Suilven; and I still do. There is a delicious shudder in turning over the page, a gasp of horror and astonishment when the monster mountain is confronted, and I echo Thomas Gray's opinion (of the Mont Cenis) that it 'carries the permission mountains have of being frightful rather too far.' Angry fretted rocks are topped by a cruel even slope of ice; the peak curls over like a breaking wave, as inevitably and horrifically as the Great Wave of Hokusai itself. It was with some alarm that I saw the Grivola imposing itself on our programme for 1936. But our winter reading had brought one small and comic aid to self-confidence: the discovery, in an old *Alpine Journal*, that the slope from the Col de Chalanson to the Glacier des Évettes, which we had gone up and down on our unorthodox way to the Ciamarella, had only been descended for the first time in 1921. Colonel Strutt, who had made the expedition with Pierre Blanc le Pape of Bonneval, spoke of it in gratifyingly respectful terms—'some 750 feet high, and exceedingly steep.' Perhaps, after all, I had no need to be ashamed of the qualms I had certainly felt.

Before our plans for the Italian valleys could be realized, there was another school party to be dealt with at Val d'Isère. There were some veterans of the year before, but most of the boys were in the Alps for the first time: two of them, having lived for a week on the succulent cooking at Pierre Rond's, said the Val d'Isère was nice, but they looked forward to seeing potatoes again at home. *Pommes sautées, pommes frites, pommes fricassées*, all the range at the Galise counted as nothing against plain mashed and boiled. The only casualty occurred the first day when, as usual, Michael dissipated train lassitude on the Aiguille Pers. A plump, urbane boy, who had been sent out by his mother for the good of his soul, announced on the Col de l'Iseran that he could go no further. There was a gentleman's agreement between him and Michael that as long as he had one top to report at home, he would be unmolested the rest of the time. So he was left to sleep in a grassy hollow in the sun. The rest of the party proceeded up the Aiguille Pers and came back to the col four hours later, to find no sign of the sleeper, nor any news of him at the chalet-hotel. They assumed that he must have come down to Val d'Isère; when they arrived and found he hadn't, there was real anxiety. Search parties were being mustered when a telephone call from the col informed us that he had just gone on sleeping in the same hollow, seven hours solid, and had never heard the returning climbers pass within ten yards.

The new road was now complete, up this side, and one busful

of tourists went up to the col every day. Val d'Isère was expanding, though as yet not very fast. There was one new hotel at the lower end of the village, one new shop where they sold films, toothpaste, postcards, Crème Nivea, and sun-goggles—one could not deny its usefulness—and a couple of private houses at the upper end, with some boards beyond them announcing plots of land for sale. M. Boch at the Parisien had a new café-lounge with comfortable plush seats; but he left two smart girls to deal with the cocktails ordered at the chromium bar, and himself continued to sit in the old snug two steps down from the road, in his shirt-sleeves, hat on head, doing his day's accounts at his high desk while the village people sat on wooden benches drinking red wine. Pierre Rond himself was on a prosperous road; a good winter season at the Galise had enabled him to buy the chalet-hotel on the Col de l'Iseran from the C.A.F. and the Touring Club de France, and he now ran it efficiently and smartly, with a couple of garçons in white linen coats to serve lunches to the tourists coming up in the bus. Only Madame over at the Hôtel des Glaciers seemed unaffected by the march of events; once across the humped bridge one found the same huddle of buildings, unenlarged, the old cartwheels against the wall, the flutter and cackle of hens, the occasional donkey or goat, the rickety tin tables, the faded awnings, the low, dark café where the génépy was as good as (and fifty centimes cheaper), and the coffee rather better than, what you got in the shiny new café-bar of the Parisien. Up at the Clitaz chalet, too, there was little change, and Michael did something to arrest the tide of progress when he hit his head against the oil lamp slung from the ceiling, new last summer. Two years later, when some friends of ours stayed there, it was still not working; but Madame bore no grudge. 'Monsieur Roberts l'a cassé. Oui, c'est lui-même qui l'a cassé. Mais il l'a payé! C'est un bon brave homme!' And in the hamlets up the side valley, Le Joseray, Le Goray, La Rosière, Le Manchet, nothing was different. The water was led down in open wooden pipes into the great troughs where the black-dressed women did their washing; the balconies were stacked with wood, and the barns loaded high with hay brought down from the stony hillsides. They were ruled here by mightier move-ments than the tastes of holiday-makers—by snow and avalanche and growing grass, by the need of winter firewood and fodder for the beasts.

I had my chance to potter round, and read *Le Petit Dauphinois*, and gossip in the gallery outside the post office, for I was acclimatizing slowly this season, in contrast to Michael. His record for the first six days was Aiguille Pers, Grande Motte (on a bad day, as far as the last rocks), Grande Motte to the top, Grande Sassière, Tsanteleina, Sana, all in doubtful weather, with rain or mist for part of the day. Another master, Bill Galbraith, had kept up to this rate of over 1,800 metres up and down each day; it was his first Alpine season and he grew blear-eyed for lack of sleep and desperate for lack of cigarettes, yet he never flagged. On the seventh day I joined them, and two ropes set off for the Méan-Martin. On a small plateau, very green, between the two tributaries of the Calebourdane, we saw five small mouse-coloured donkeys grazing; it seemed a happy omen, and indeed it was an absurd and delightful day. Mist came down as we reached the high, shaly plateau above the grass slopes, and gave a dramatic air to the landscape. Fingers of rock thirty feet high would loom up and then shrink to a mere six feet or eight; the caravan in front, hands in pockets and coat collars turned up, would plunge into a bottomless pit, and re-emerge across the unpassable gap within fifteen seconds. (After one of these reappearances, Bill Galbraith was detailed to linger thoughtfully on the edge of the chasm for the sake of a photograph in the next number of the school magazine. It turned out even more striking than we had hoped, and saddled him with a quite unjustified reputation for rashness.) We seemed to be following a rock-rib running more or less southward, and rising towards the watershed between the Arc and the Isère. If Michael had any doubts as to where we were, he kept them to himself, and led us on steadily. At last a thin glow of sunshine came through the mist. 'This is the top,' said Michael firmly, and sat down. It was *a* top all right, and somewhere on the watershed, and it was a good place for lunch (all the better for a new drink compounded of orange juice, brandy, and snow), but some of us whispered treasonable suggestions that it was not the Méan-Martin. However, there seemed nothing wrong with the ridge sweeping round to the north-east. We set off along it, towards the Col de l'Iseran, but after we had scrambled up and down a couple of surprisingly firm rock towers, the mist thickened again, and hail started hissing. We thought we had better call it a day, and follow a subsidiary rib down to a small glacier on the Calebourdane side of the ridge. When we were in the last couloir, with everything rotten, Michael from the back shouted us out of the way, as he had a twenty-ton rock balanced on his toe. All scrabbled quickly out except Max Black, an amiable philosopher, in the middle of the last rope. There was a wet ledge six feet above the bed of the couloir to which he could not pull himself; Michael tried to play him on the rope from above— 'You only need to *roll* on to it, man' —we pitched and jerked from below, and the philosopher was safely on the shelf as the rock bounced and banged past. There were no other incidents, but we felt we had a claim to christen the gully; and the 'Couloir des Pantalons Déchirés' was added to our list of routes that were new only because we could not imagine any one having wanted to come this way before. Over coffee in the snug at the Parisien we pedantically nailed down our bogus Méan-Martin top as the Pointe Occidentale du Pélaou Blanc.

We took the school party to Bourg Saint-Maurice and sent them off with a cheer—eleven boys and four masters who at any rate now knew that mountaineering was not just a rich man's game. It had taken Michael years to find this out: he had once, after walking down from the Col du Bonhomme, stood and studied the guides' tariff at Les Contamines and wondered if he would ever possess the £10 that seemed necessary if he was some day to climb Mont Blanc. No one had told him that it was possible for two active young men to do good climbs in the secondary ranges for the price of a rope, boots, and ice-axes, and he knew no one who climbed or wanted to climb. Some of these boys now rattling third class back to England might never come to the Alps again, but new possibilities had opened for them. Two summers later postcards would come, from members of this party, from the Lofoten Islands, and from the Black Sea. But every year there would be two or three who would find themselves entirely happy and at home on this kind of mountain holiday, and they would later be heard of collecting gear for a camp in the Dauphiné or

Tyrol, borrowing volumes of Gaillard, or asking us to sign their applications for membership of the C.A.F.

We went back to the Hôtel des Voyageurs at Bourg Saint-Maurice and discovered that though chromium-plating had invaded the café, the food was still delicious, and Madame Marin-Laflèche still as ready to laugh at all we said and to take charge of queer bundles of crampons and spare shirts. In the morning we took the bus up to Peisey, in the valley on the other side of Mont Pourri, and at the Bellevue began a beautiful *déjeuner* with a dish of colossal tomatoes, scooped out and filled with peas, beans, chopped tomato and carrot, in a sauce of cream and chopped egg. Reproduced six weeks later in England, it tasted quite different; perhaps, for the lack of great fluted pumpkin-like tomatoes.

A day's idling and eating was paid for next morning when, starting for Champagny by the Sommet de Bellecôte, we landed ourselves on a hillside of small rhododendrons and junipers. We were well soaked and scratched before we reached the high pastures above the Chalets de l'Arc. In dry weather, once you have plodded up to the ridge, you can probably romp along to the summit on a regular path. I have a postcard showing about six light-hearted parties on it, and such numbers are usually a sign of a *montagne à vaches*. But the bad weather of the last fortnight had given the ridge a delicate cornice of very clean new snow which had been whipped by the wind into toppling walls and curling waves. We made our way along cautiously, now on one side of the ridge, now on the other. A white mist muffled everything, but it parted occasionally, to show the summit looking very pretty against a blue sky, and, once, the dome of Mont Blanc, floating on mist, and unattached to anything substantial below. The vision appeared again later, after we had taken off the rope and were glissading down the tiny Glacier de Bellecôte: to slide smoothly down the mountain, poised and controlled by the axe behind, and see before one's eyes that insubstantial faery dome, seemed the very refinement of mountain delight.

We came back to earth with a bump an hour later, when the path down from the high chalets took a great sweep to the right before the final step down to the valley. Lateness and tiredness made us think we knew better, and we pushed down a gorge to take us more directly to Champagny-le-Bois. By the time we realized we were wrong we were too tired to go up again, and the day ended with a maddening hour and a half of tentative descent on grass terraces that ended in rocky drops, all too like my descent from Suilven four years before, with the additional torment of seeing our village directly below, and almost smelling the dinner that we didn't reach till 8.15.

The *salle* at the Hôtel Ruffier was a little musty and best-parlour -like, with immortelles and stuffed birds; not many visitors came there, and as we sat on a bench in front next morning everybody stopped for a word. There were a lot of little girls, dressed exactly like their mothers with boots, black frocks, and straw bonnets, off to help with the hay. Any ascent on an off-day is an effort, and we only dragged ourselves up 300 metres above the valley to read *La Comtesse de Cagliostro*, take photographs, and follow the shadow round a great cleft block. Next morning we had reached the same level before daylight, without effort, for the day was on a different scale. We were on our way to the Grand Bec de Pralognan: Ball says it 'may be attained without any difficulty' from the Champagny valley, but he probably did not meet the sheep. On the highest pastures, just under the Becca Motta glacier, they pressed round; I realized uncomfortably that the hillside fell away in rocky ridges only a few yards to the left. Michael, who did not seem so attractive to them, heartlessly ran on to take a photograph of the lot of us; I reckoned that the sensible thing to do, if they rushed me, was to lie down flat—those matchstick legs could surely never push me far. Eventually they lost interest, and the affair became a family joke, though it wasn't till I re-read *The Alps from End to End*, years later, that I realized they had been hoping for salt: Conway there describes a similar scene on a hillside in Glarus, when a flock 1,700 strong knocked Carrel off his feet and then rushed over him as he lay on the ground.

On the Sommet de Bellecôte I had been cheerful and sanguine while Michael groaned over tiredness and boots that needed an extra sock. Now, on the snow ridge leading up to the Grand Bec, I was the gloomy member—gloomy at being on snow when I thought we might have been on rock, at going into mist, at walking up a steep slope that would be horribly soft in the afternoon.

Michael sensibly ignored all this, and hit off the top, in mist, at midday; the photographs he then unkindly took are as useful as a hair shirt in taking down pride. And, to mock my grumpiness, the descent, by the same way that we had come up, was child's play, and even I ran down the snow slope that had loomed so steeply in my apprehensions. No doubt I would have thought nothing of it on a clear day, but the mist had conjured up vague horrors.

The mist really lifted as we got off the glacier; we ran down through the woods and reached Champagny with our tongues hanging out. But even drinks were forsworn for the moment, in a new obsession to get down to Bozel in time for the bus to Moutiers. We picked up our second sack at Ruffier's, and some vaguely hopeful remark about a possible lift in an army car, and whizzed down the ten kilometres to the junction with the road up to Pralognan. 'Ah, c'est de vrais touristes,' said an old peasant as we bounded past. But at Villard we found that all was lost: the Champagny clocks had been slow, and we had missed the bus by about ten minutes. Angrily, we stumped on to Bozel, where I sank into a chair outside a cafe and swore I would never move again. Michael went off on a mysterious errand, and came back with news of a taxi. The beer and lemonade was nectar now.

At Moutiers, where the taxi dropped us, we had an entirely admirable dinner, with melting *vol-au-vent*, at the station hotel; then sleepily visited several cafes in the effort to keep awake till the bus came in to meet the eleven o'clock train. There were only a couple of passengers who wanted to go on to Bourg Saint-Maurice; the four of us rattled and banged in the bus which leapt terrifyingly from side to side of the road and hooted non-stop through the sleeping villages. We had a rendezvous at Bourg with Hughes, our companion of the *course collective* the year before. When we reached the hotel, M. Marin-Laflèche in pyjamas assured us that he was here, and we sank into bed at midnight, after twenty and a half hours out.

Hughes it was indeed next morning, with an ingenious pair of trousers of his own design and making. At first sight they looked like breeches; but what were the buttons for, half-way up the thigh? He expounded their threefold use. Breeches, as we had seen; but by letting them out and down, there was a pair of airy bell-bottomed slacks, suitable for town life; now, by folding them back and buttoning them up, here was a pair of shorts for hot walks up to huts! Elaboration of further uses, from bivouac tents to sponge bags, became an easy joke. He had come from a Fell and Rock meet at the Montanvert; the mizzling weather that had let us reach our tops in the Tarentaise had put their important climbs out of the question. He wanted to be on the move again, and we decided to cross the Little St. Bernard and explore the Italian valleys running up to the frontier chain. We hoped for a few peaks, but at any rate we would keep moving.

By the time we had stocked up with provisions, and started asking about buses, the last one had gone. After complicated bargainings, we found ourselves sharing a taxi with about ten other people; they looked as if they thought we should be paying for an extra place for our crampons. This expensive taste for mountain taxis was closely related to another of our mountain habits. The only book officially allowed in our packs, beyond the necessary Gaillard and the filleted edition of Ball, was the *Annuaire de Poche* of the C.A.F. This fascinating and practical handbook told us what hotels and mountain railways gave reductions to C.A.F. members (there was even a jeweller in Lyons who gave you five per cent); had lists of huts, guides, and porters; and printed sound good sense on mountain accidents and other emergencies. But the pages we always turned to, over coffee at Val d'Isère or in the snug 'Chez Louis' at Bourg, were those giving the guides' and porters' fees for all the mountains in the French Alps. 'Mont Pourri par la Brèche Puiseux,' we would say, '205 francs; I think we might have a Cointreau each.' For however much we joked about it, we got into the way of half-believing that we had saved the fee of the guide whom we had never dreamt of taking and could never have afforded. I have never been able to remember for two seconds the categories applied to British mountains, and have often shocked adepts by genuinely believing that a 'difficult' was harder than a 'severe,' or a fourth-class climb in Skye easier than a second; but I can rattle off: 'Ciamarella, fr. 110; Grand Bec de Pralognan, fr. 150; Grande Casse, par le Glacier des Grands Couloirs, fr. 160'—even the *indemnité de retour* from Valgrisanche

to Sainte-Foy. Michael's seven days with the boys at Val d'Isère
had given him a comfortable nest-egg in this hypothetical currency;
we felt half justified in our taxi up to the pass.

At the Little St. Bernard we changed into the Italian bus, so
full of smoke and people that when we got out halfway down the
Italian side at La Thuille, we had to have cold drinks to clear
our heads. The *citrons pressés* were also a way of putting off the
slog up to the Margherita hut for the Ruitor. It was already five;
no one felt like climbing. Our start was unpropitious. In the
woods at the entrance to the Ruitor glen was a large camp of
Fascist militia. We were stopped by two cocky young men and
commanded to show our *documenti*. These had already been scrutinized
(very civilly) by the frontier guards on the pass: the militiamen
had no shadow of right to call for them, and Michael's John Bull
was rising. I was the appeaser—I didn't want to retrace any steps
that evening—and our passports were produced with a bad grace.
Unfortunately this was the summer after sanctions, and mine belonged to the era of Sir Samuel Hoare; this, the only word
the militiamen could recognize, set them mocking loudly. Rather
luckily, we could only grasp their intention, and not the wordy
detail of their gibes.

La Thuille is 1,441 metres, the Rifugio S. Margherita is 2,494;
as far as I was concerned, every metre up was gained with toil
and sweat. 'Few walks in the Alps so beautiful,' wrote William
Mathews in 1864, and lyrically described the cascade, the clefts,
the gigantic boulders clothed with larch and the cembra pine.
With my pilgrim's enormous burden on my back I noticed hardly
anything; I saw vaguely how lovely it must be, but I was chiefly
thinking whether I could decently ask for a rest half-way up the
zigzags on the rock face, or whether Hughes would think with
disgust that this was the sort of thing that happened with a
woman in the party. Higher, my thoughts centred passionately
on a drink of water, yet when a clear burn crossed the path I
refused to stop, because I could just keep going, and felt it would
be fatal to break rhythm. Abstinence induced reflection: one of the
appeals of climbing, I decided, is that it makes you long with your
whole being for some object that you can attain—to stop moving,
to reach a summit, to see the other side of the ridge, to drink water.

A cool breeze came off the snows; suddenly I knew the meaning of the phrase 'air like wine.' Hughes told me at the hut that he had offered to carry my crampons; bound up in my own sensations, I had never heard him. The last step was downhill, to the little lake, the chapel, and the chalets; at the hut the water was like wine, and the wine like heaven. I kept hitting my head against the lamp out of sleepiness, and when we had eaten, stumbled to my mattress and relaxed with complete and delicious exhaustion.

The guardian saw us off next morning with some advice about the best way down to Valgrisanche. We walked over the stones and boulders in the half-light, and on to the level glacier that makes the Ruitor, seen from Mont Blanc way, look so gentle and humane a peak. Later, we decided that we had put on the rope somewhere between the only two crevasses on this even table-cloth. On the Col Ruitor we ran into two or three parties who had come up from the Valgrisanche side; there were several soldiers among them, and after the militiamen in the wood we expected some mockery of the British, and were touchily ready to reply. Not in the least; a couple who reached the top as we did chatted pleasantly to us, part in French, part in English, as we pieced together the view. From our breakfast place on the rocks by the col we watched the parties going down the Glacier de Morion, easy enough, but with a steep little slope to start off. First went a rather unhandy ropeful of civilians, with little shrieks and squeals, slippings and slidings. They were followed by a soldier who had brought his goat up from the military post below the glacier. We had already admired the animal, capering confidently on the easy summit rocks. Now, on snow, it exactly recapitulated the nervous tourists, slithering, dithering, moving sideways instead of down. The soldier, walking down with the easy assurance of the practised ice-man, got impatient with his temperamental companion, and tweaked the rope. My sympathies were all with the anxious goat.

We capered down ourselves, glissading down the glacier and crossing the military path to find a heavenly idling place on the alp above Le Fornet, with a burn running across a green and level lawn, then falling in a small cascade. We sat there in the sun, looking down to a blue-green pool among the dark trees in

the valley. Full in face of us, on the other side, was the Bec de
l'Invergnan.   Michael and Hughes turned a vague idea into a
definite plan, discussed routes and approaches, while I washed
myself and all our stockings in the limpid water of the burn.

We reached the valley three kilometres below Fornet and trudged
up dustily.   There was no sign of a pub or shop; we thought we
would try our luck at a hamlet up the road.   Midway between
the two, Michael decided to turn back to Fornet for bread, while
Hughes prospected the hamlet.   I sat where I was by the side of
the track, and slept.   Hughes came back empty-handed; we walked
towards Michael, who had good news, as well as two or three
pieces of bread.   While he had been collecting the bread (which
is scarce in these parts and can be obtained only by pathos,
cajolery, or guile), an old man had seen him and offered to give
us a meal in his house.   We stepped in from the midday heat
to a bare, clean, whitewashed room, with a scrubbed wooden table
and benches.   The old man called his wife, an old lady with a
sweet patient face, and they set bread and wine, cheese and butter
before us, and asked us how many eggs we would like in the
omelette—Nine!   While she prepared it, and we ate it, he talked
to us in French (the only paper we saw there was a church
magazine published in Bordeaux).   He had been a guide, and still
had his badge; by and by he produced his guide's book and we
saw his name: Giuseppe Domenico di Pietro.   He had never gone
far beyond his valley; as with the peasant guides of the Tarentaise
his guiding was an occasional diversion from his real work, and
the Ruitor, and the passes to Val d'Isère, were his main expeditions.
There were a few English names in his book, which went back
to the nineties.   We asked him if we could write our thanks in
it for his beautiful hospitality.   When we inquired how much we
owed, he answered simply: 'Comme vous voulez—moi, je ne suis
pas aubergiste.'

Stumbling out into the sunlight at four o'clock, I felt my legs
like water and my pack like lead.   The old guide had told us
we could probably sleep at the Alpe Nuova, and had shown us
the beginning of the path; but in the woods it seemed to go the
wrong way.   Michael struck straight up through the undergrowth;
I groaned my way from bush to bush.   At last we rejoined a sort

of path, in an open space, sat down for a blessed rest, and were eaten to bits by midges. Out of some ruined chalets appeared a cheerful boy with a load on his back. When we said 'Alpe Nuova' he nodded, and led us up the path at a great rate, Singing and whistling. Michael just kept up with him; Hughes and I plodded gently behind. At last we came out on to bare open pastures in a high valley, heard cows, turned a corner, saw the chalet, staggered up, dropped our loads, and changed our dripping shirts.

A cheerful old cheesemaker ran the chalet, with several boys; he said we could sleep in the straw and make our supper on his fire. I stood minding our soup and coffee, crying with the smoke and acrid smell of cooking cheeses. He asked where we had come from, and if we had passed through Paris. He had been a cabby there in his youth; he had enjoyed driving the fine couples through the Bois. Now he talked of 'ce nouveau système'—it took me a minute to realize he meant Fascism—rather detachedly, as if it were something that had but faintly altered his life. He came up to the chalet for four or five months; making *fontine* was hard work, and not much profit at the end of it. Still, he could stand it. He stirred and poked his huge vats; everything to do with the cheese, muslins, presses, vats, and ladles was scoured and fresh.

We ate our supper outside, by the lade diverted to the chalet from the stream. Then we walked up a wooden plank like hens, to the hayloft above the cattle; various boys seemed to creep in later. All night the cattle stirred underneath, and their melancholy bells were hardly silent. Several times, it seemed, there was milking or some other activity afoot—Michael believed the cows were calving all night long—and the boys and the man sang together, a rough haunting song like the one we had once heard peasants singing in Bonneval to bring in the New Year. The boys' voices rose high, but cracked and rough—a melancholy music. Some such den may have been in the mind of the Hon. Frederica Plunket when, writing in the 'seventies, she delicately alluded to the great drawback of many of the most interesting ascents— 'the necessity of sleeping in a cave or small hut, containing but one room. Of course in this matter every lady must be the best judge for herself. . . . Of these places I only speak by hearsay.'

Less scrupulous than Miss Plunket, I slept surprisingly well, in spite of the real hazards of rats and insects; but it was days before I got the last of the straw out of my hair.

The night's unrests were forgotten in the breakfast that followed: Michael had cooked thick rashers of bacon on the choky fire, and at 6 a.m. we ate them rather shiveringly by the stream. At 6.30 we started up the path to the Col de la Fenêtre; a nice walk up gently sloping pastures to a big split rock where we dumped two of the sacks. We cut across to the Glacier de Rabuigne, and in crampons stepped up on good hard snow to a high col under point 3183 on the main Bec de l'lnvergnan ridge. Here we left our crampons, put on the rope, and started our exploration of this long northern ridge of the Bec. We forgot who was meant to be leading: Michael would take us along a ledge on the east side, come to a stop, we would all turn, and Hughes would find a passage ten metres further up. Whatever happened I was stuck in the middle. I grumbled a little, on principle, but could hardly have enjoyed myself more. The rock was certainly not sound, yet the ridge was delightful: a new valley on our left, to which we were bound; to our right the stony Valgrisanche which the old guide and the old cheesemaker had placed securely on the map of our affections; in front, a peak of obvious dignity and importance, which had yet been little noticed by British climbers. Even George Yeld had nothing to say about it. But two compatriots were remembered and honoured when we sat on the top, after a very pleasant last pitch of almost perpendicular rock up which Hughes led in best Wasdale style. These were the Misses Pigeon, who in 1875 had crossed the Col de la Grande Rousse—not so much a col as a nick a little beyond the summit, with rock falling away towards the Val de Rhêmes, snow towards the Valgrisanche, with equal steepness.

Our ridge had been, in comparison, easy going; but we sat on top very well pleased, looking over the next valley, to the next crossing, and to our goal beyond that, the Gran Paradiso. Halfway down the ridge we stopped where we had eaten on the way up; then, there had been mackerel in white wine; now, in the empty tins, was fishy, winy water from the snow we had left to melt. By a happy variation on the last step of the ridge, Michael found a nice difficult chimney in solid pink rock. He had lost patience with looking for corridors and ledges—after all, we had come all this way to climb. A stretch, pull, double, undouble, balance, pull, and up he was on the very top of Point 3183; Hughes and I, with several inches less reach, did it less elegantly. Coming down the steep top bit of glacier, up which it bad been so easy to walk in the morning, I felt like the goat, and eventually slipped; I was pulled up by my own ice-axe, and by Hughes above and Michael below. It was silly and humiliating, and Michael galumphed gaily down behind me, to show me how absurd it was to make heavy weather of it. My nerve and common sense returned, and the two of us pranced down, waving our spiky boots and cutting enormous capers like dancing elephants or bears. Down at the split rock Hughes got tea going over Meta, and we laid out a delicious meal on the grass—the chief treat was some apricots that we had left to soak while we climbed. Hughes groaned at the idea of plodding up to the Col de la Fenêtre, but I felt I could do anything, sack or no sack. We were up in half an hour of easy zigzags; it really was a window, without a top, and as we put our heads between the two perpendicular blocks that formed its sides, we saw right down into our new valley.

On this eastern side of the col the good path disappeared under a hard bed of dirty snow. Michael started to glissade, I followed him, but the snow was too hard and ridgy to give us much fun. Hughes appraised it from the top, then hitched off his sack, put on his crampons—'Well, I may be silly, but I like it better'—and stumped solidly down. When the path reappeared it took us over some grassy alps, by a chalet or two, then plunged down steep zigzags, which by this time we could barely see, to the Val de Rhêmes. We stumbled up the white road in the dark, past a row of cypress trees, to Rhêmes-Notre-Dame. Out of nowhere appeared a *carabiniere*, to ask if we had come over the Col de Rhêmes (the pass that leads over from Val d'Isère, under the Tsanteleina). We satisfied him that we had not used this forbidden entrance to Italy, and he politely told us that the inns were further down the valley. So back we trudged past the cypresses, to the handful of houses at Chanavey. There seemed to be two inns; we chose the Albergo Grande Rousse because we could see people still eating in the lighted rooms. Although it was nine o'clock, we were soon ourselves having a meal of soup, omelette, veal, peaches, grapes, and wine. Then Madame, an enormous key in hand, asked us to follow her; she went out of the inn, and up a cobbled alley, and stopped at a massive wooden door. She flung it open with a welcoming gesture, and revealed an enormous room furnished, as it seemed to my tired eyes, with beds of every size. I fell into the nearest, and in two minutes was asleep.

Ten-thirty is not a good time of day to start for the Col de Sort. It is a mistake to cross the Col de Sort at all, as we realized later that day, sweltering up the messy waste of boulders on its western side. The sensible thing would have been to take the Mont Tout Blanc in our stride over to the Valsavaranche. But on the Bec de l'lnvergnan the day before we had light-heartedly pointed our fingers at the col, waved in the direction of the unseen valley beyond, and said (with the airiness of height and a successful climb): 'Yes, we'll nip over the col, down to Valsavaranche, and up to the Victor Emmanuel hut for the Paradiso the day after.' Over our *caffè espresso* in the hotel it had still seemed a good idea; we were too sleepy to remember the horrors of climbing 1,000 metres at the end of the day. Now, after our lazy late breakfast in the trellised veranda it did not look so attractive, and we dawdled to postpone the moment of effort. We stopped to admire the Grand Combin shining high at the foot of the valley, and took a long time buying food at Rhêmes-Notre-Dame. My pack, which I had hardly noticed up to the col the night before, once more became a pilgrim's burden of sins. An hour and a half's dragging up through the woods seemed to call for an hour and a half's rest over lunch on the high pastures. It was almost as pretty as our resting-place below the Ruitor, but we could not relax to enjoy it. The beastly col was still 700 metres above. When we did start again, everything seemed hot, tiring, and disagreeable. We lost the path, or rather the path lost itself in stonefalls. Instead of the hoped-for mechanical slog, there were irritating decisions to make—to go straight up the scree, or to make a detour by the boulders; to explore the hint of a track, or to take a direct route from point to point. Three pleasureless hours, with the sun beating down, dust flying up from the scree, and with no difficulty to make it interesting; but at last we stood on the col.

We looked across the Valsavaranche to the lion couchant of the Grivola, and the snows of the Paradiso; we could almost see where the Victor Emmanuel hut must be, and kept up a flicker of pretence that we meant to get there that night (it was now five). 'If we contoured round, and struck the valley higher up, we should save ourselves eight kilometres of road'—other ridiculous fantasies were proposed. Then we got side-tracked on to the money question. This year the lira had two values: there was the ordinary rate of exchange, about seventy to the pound, and the tourist rate, about ninety. Each traveller could buy so many lire at the cheaper rate; but this exchange could only be made at certain banks in Italy. Since we had crossed the frontier at the Little St. Bernard we had been nowhere near a bank, and had paid our expenses in the Valgrisanche and Val de Rhêmes out of the small sum of lire we had bought in England at the ordinary, dearer rate. Now the supply was nearly exhausted. Absurd suggestions were made— 'There's sure to be a bank at Valsavaranche—it's a place you hear a lot about'; 'There's a bank at Lochinver, and I don't see why there shouldn't be a bank at Pont'—all the arguments that the weary bring forward to stave off the effort of changing plans and making new decisions. Then a snag was remembered: was tomorrow Sunday? We couldn't think. Hughes started counting from the day he left England for the Montanvert; we had an idea we had spent our lazy day at Peisey on a Saturday. Our reckonings never agreed, and we couldn't stay all night on the col. Ball had buoyed us up with his reference to the 'king's hunting-path' down from the east side of the col; it started off royally enough, but there had been great stonefalls since the first Victor Emmanuel had hunted bouquetin on the Col de Sort, and we had to struggle down over disorderly boulders. Later we learnt that when cattle had been driven from one valley to another it had been worth while keeping up the paths; but now they were taken round by lorry. Down on the prosperous-looking alps, musical with cowbells, the path improved, but it made a long detour before falling to the valley. We remembered the gorges of Champagny, but took the risk and made straight down the hillside for Eau Rousse;

everything went easily and we were having dinner in the inn before it was dark.

Next day *was* a Sunday, but it didn't matter if the banks were open or not, because of course there were no banks in Eau Rousse or at Pont. So there were long sums over the bill, as some of it had to be paid in francs. There were a lot of officers in the hotel, a lot of soldiers all the way up the charming wooded road to Pont, and a great camp at the head of the valley, with little groups of signallers, sappers, and gunners working away in the noon-day heat. The zigzags up the further hillside went easily and pleasantly, some of our heavier sins seemed to have been shed on the fiendish Col de Sort.

The new Victor Emmanuel hut startled us: a gigantic aluminium dog-kennel stridently out of keeping with the setting of pasture, rock, and snow. There was something queerly horrid about it: like the Calton Hill monument in Edinburgh, but far less pleasantly, it spoke of the vanity of ambitious projects not backed by material resources. For the section of the C.A.I. that had started it had lacked the money to finish; and, much relieved, we turned into the old shabby stone refuge and quickly bagged perches on the straw mattresses. It took some time to find a place outside to laze in that wasn't also a dump of tins and rubbish, but the afternoon passed pleasantly with *La Cagliostro* se *Venge*, and lazy scrutiny of the Paradiso, the Ciarforon, and the Becca di Monciair. The hut was full, and we had some time to wait for supper; luckily we had finished just before the army arrived, dozens of them, to be fed in batches. We lay in our straw and listened to their talks and jokes and discussed tomorrow's plans. Hughes and I had some doubts about traversing the Paradiso with heavy sacks; we knew little about the Cogne side. Then it turned out that a monkey-faced little Italian in a neat corduroy suit, who had chatted with us outside the hut, had often climbed the Paradiso from Cogne. We thought that made it all right for us.

Michael had not before led up a 4,000-metre peak, but he had no luck on the Gran Paradiso. Infuriating sums with our francs and expensive lire kept us in the hut while the soldiers got well away. Hughes and I left Michael to negotiate, and counted the men as they stepped on to the glacier. There were just fifty, fine, fair-haired upstanding northern Italians, obviously a hand-picked group (I mentally contrasted them with the cheerful rabble streaming down from the Great St. Bernard the year before); we guessed university students.   Their ice-axes and boots looked first-class, and they carried crampons, neatly tied on to their long cloaks rolled round their sacks.

We were able to take our own line at first, up a different tongue of the glacier.   An hour from the hut the sky, which had never looked very settled, began to cloud over, and we heard queer noises—our crampons humming on our backs.   Looking back, we could see a black storm coming up over the Grande Casse, nearer and nearer till it burst on us in a torrent of hail; in five minutes everything above and behind was clear again, and the storm was beating itself out beyond the Paradiso.   There seemed no reason against going on, and we soon joined the army's tracks.   The Paradiso from the Victor Emmanuel hut must at any time be one of the very easiest of the high Alps; to-day, with this highway beaten out in the snow, it was rather less trouble than the ordinary path up Goatfell.   It seemed unlikely that any masked crevasses could lie in wait for us after the passage of fifty pairs of army boots, and it was mainly for form's sake that we put on the rope. The obvious bridge over the bergschrund was well kicked about but still held us; and the only real difficulty of the climb was finding a place to stand on the top.   The soldiers were all chattering in groups, and the groups did not always correspond with the ropes—there was a fine possibility of entanglement.   Their rope management generally seemed a weak point; most of the parties had arrived with loops of slack between each man and his neighbour, sodden with dragging through the snow.

Hughes and I looked with some alarm down the far side; it seemed to fall extremely steeply to the Tribulation glacier.   Our way down, however, began by retracing our steps across the bergschrund, then up across another smaller bergschrund to a nick in the rocky ridge, at right angles to the summit ridge; the guide attached to the little corduroy Italian looked across to see we struck the right one.   Hughes, now in front, looked through this little window, shouted cheerfully, and led us down a nice little fifteen-foot pitch of rock to a flat platform, just above a scree

gully leading down to the Col de l'Abeille. We lunched on the
platform, in very good spirits, and in twenty minutes rattled down
the gully to stand on the col, and respectfully remember the
insensible bee found there by Coolidge, and later restored to life
at the Victor Emmanuel hut.   At the foot of the steep slope
leading down to the Tribulation glacier we met a party of Italians
plodding up to the Paradiso; I was overcome with superior pity
for a party with so far to go, so late in the day. The snow was
still in good condition and the crevasses were bridged, but the
tossed and tortured Tribulation glacier exacts respect, and we came
down very carefully; On the moraine, and the steep grassy ridge
below, we took different lines; and when Michael and I at last
struck the Valnontey path we found Hughes with a fire of pine
branches in full swing.   It was a delicious tea, and we could
enjoy it with easy, satisfied minds—the mountain crossed, the high
snows left behind, nothing now between us and our dinner at
Cogne but a walk down the glen of pines and larches.

But a censorious spirit invaded my benevolent mood after an
hour and a half's smart walking had brought us to the edge of
the village. Perhaps it was annoyance at the sight of the great
box-like hotels starting up from these lovely lawns, but I suddenly
became critical of Hughes's costume. His shirt had no collar; his
braces flaunted shamelessly above his famous all-purpose trousers,
and at this moment I was less conscious of their ingenuity than
of their peculiarity. Alpine snapshots recall only too vividly what
I probably looked like myself, with scarlet face and linen hat
pinched from a schoolboy at Val d'Isère. Michael, as usual, looked
a trifle villainous, but I decided that Hughes was low, and lagged
behind to dissociate myself from the pair of them. However, the
Hôtel de la Grivola took us all in (though their 'three rooms'
turned out to be two windowless cupboards and a bathroom). For
all its name it catered, quite clearly, for those Italians who come
to Cogne to breathe after the heat of the plains, and stroll agreeably
a mile or two up the Valnontey; certainly they all looked very
tidy. We kept our end up by asking twice for everything on the
table-d'hôte, then found our level at the café opposite. Heavy
showers drove us indoors from our table under the trees, and
when a party came in at ten from the Paradiso they were soaked

to the skin.

We still had not found a bank, but next morning we managed to do some shopping in francs, and had fresh bread to take up to the Vittorio Sella hut under the Col Lauzon. A royal hunting-path, unspoilt by stonefalls, marched us up the steep side of the Valnontey, where the Lauzon cascades through the trees, to a grassy corrie in the upper glen where we ate. After an hour's peace by the stream which tumbled round the grassy hillocks like any Border burn, we slung on our packs with the usual reluctance of climbers facing a couple of hours uphill after lunch. Forty minutes later we topped a little rise, and there was the hut. Everything about it was as unexpectedly delightful as our quick arrival to it. It had been built as a hunting-lodge for Victor Emmanuel, and it belonged to the landscape as naturally as the unpretentious kind of Highland inn or shooting-lodge, like the inn at Cluanie Bridge. There were two long narrow one-storey buildings, whitewashed, with roofs of grey-green lichened stone, built across the line of the valley, with the ends that pointed uphill tapering into a wedge-shaped projection, solid all through, to take the force of the spring avalanches. The guardian's quarters and the big living-room were in one; the other, once the stables, contained the dormitory, and a few narrow slips of bedrooms converted from stalls.

Now we were in a countryside which I knew through W. P.'s eyes. When he died, I had been given his *Climbers' Guide to the Mountains of Cogne;* at first I could not puzzle where the district was, for the map in the pocket did not seem at any point to touch any of the Alpine districts that I had heard of. Now his *Guide* had helped to steer us over the Paradiso, and turning it over at the beautiful hut this night, I saw in his hand at the back: 'King's Lodge, Val Lauzon, *altitudine sul mare metri 2588.*' The blank pages had sketches of the Ciarforon, Roccia Viva, and Becca di Monciair, that suddenly looked as familiar as the sketches of Goatfell and the Bay with which he usually ended his letters; and there was a note on the path to the Comboe chalets, dated August 1916, when the Alps were accessible only in memories and hopes. In his pencilled comments, so clear in the tiny margins of the *Guide,* Alps and Highlands met: as in the letters he wrote from the Alps. The

Piantonetto hut was 'a little stone house, well buift, lined with wood—a but and a ben—on the top of it a high rock looking down a beautiful valley—with Ceum na Caillich on one side of it,' and Arran was again in his mind when he described the Roccia Viva as 'not more than the height of Goat Fell above this.' At Macugnaga, he spoke of 'breakfast on the rocks, just where the Garbh Allt was beginning to run out of the snow,' linking Alpine torrents with half a hundred stormy Highland waters. The Scotch tourist whom he claimed to have heard referring to 'the Taynuilt top of Monte Rosa' was a joke, but a joke after his own heart (though 'I do not wish to hear him speak of the Nordend or Höchste Spitze of Cruachan'); it was no joke, but delightful truth, when he once walked up the Great St. Bernard with an Italian *commendatore* who carried a stick bought in Fort William.

W. P. saw the likeness between alp and corrie, burn and torrent; he also saw the likeness between the lives of people who take their cattle in summer to high pastures, and live in shielings, sæters, or chalets; who pick blaeberries, and call the mountains that block their valleys Sgoran Dubh, or Aiguille Noire; Jungfrau, or Cioch na h-Oighe, the Maiden's Breast. When, at Macugnaga, the peasants sang mass 'moderately out of tune,' it made him think that the Ballads must have been sung in much the same way. The last letter he had written me was from Zermatt in 1922 (characteristically dated 'Glasgow Fair Saturday'). He spoke of a walk he had been by himself the day before: 'Up through woods to a high valley, what they call an Alp in this country, where the people go up with their cows and pigs for the summer. It is a beautiful place—more like Scotland or Cumberland than most of these Swiss valleys are—no steep sides but gentle slopes and a flat floor—the river winding like Water of Rosa. They are building a chapel there, and it looks as if they meant to keep up the settlement. Two years ago in September I met them all coming down—cows and furniture—the cows went down by the good looped road—zigzags—*les lacets du chemin*. Most of the men with furniture went down on sledges—a long straight toboggan shoot through the woods—it must be rough work bumping over stones.'

At this royal hunting-lodge, too, the mountains and humanity had come to terms. We were not grimly clinging to a crag, like the Bertol Cabane, nor precariously perched on an icy col, like the biscuit-box of the Refuge Durier. We were on a path that had been stamped out by men and mules, for necessary traffic between two valleys, long before it had been enlarged and smoothed for Victor Emmanuel's pleasure. Cow-bells jingled from every grassy hollow; the guardian of the hut, a nice black giant with deceptively fierce whiskers, had more solid attachments to his mountain than the needs of holiday climbers. Boys came round the corner of the building, singing and clattering milk-pails. We found clean sheets on our beds. For dinner we were offered roast chicken and zambaglione. If there were metaphysical monsters waiting for us on the Grivola tomorrow, the milder spirits of vale and fountain were attending us to-night.

Our good genius still seemed to hover next morning. The grassy Alps, grey-green before the dawn, made the start less shivery than a first step on to rock or snow. And there was the royal path, an offshoot from the main track over the Col Lauzon, to carry us up in a sleepy daze, with no need to consider one's foot-steps or one's route. The *Climbers' Guide* mentioned no routes up the Grivola from this valley, for at the date of its publication the hut was still a hunting-lodge only. But we knew the general direction, and if the satisfactory path now took us a little far to the east, as it seemed, no doubt it was to strike out a better line up the reddish shaly rubble above the pastures. The path climbed confidently, and so did we. Soon we saw a well-marked col above us, and as we reached it the mists thinned, and there was a rough, red rock-face above us, ribbed by the fan-shaped shallow gullies that we had studied in the large photographs of the Grivola at the hut. With the sun on it, it was a striking and heartening sight. 'That peak's as good as ours,' shouted Hughes with un-characteristic rashness. Michael cut some steps across the hard, steep snow, and we scrambled up some rocks to the foot of one of the gullies. This Trajo glacier looked smaller than we had expected, but then glaciers recede, and it was forty-three years since the *Climbers' Guide* had described it as two kilometres wide. And, unmistakably, to the right of the peak, was that north-east arête against which the *Guide* so sternly warned us, pointing out that it appeared tempting, easy, and direct, but in fact offered 'so

many and such great difficulties, that both the strong parties which
have taken it, were forced to rejoin the ordinary route.' It certainly
looked tempting, easy, and direct, but we braced ourselves against
the monster's stratagems and set to work up one of the many
couloirs of the face 'which can be and have been climbed.'

With that assurance—which transforms an impregnable Matterhorn into a tourist mountain, an impossible Grépon into 'an easy
day for a lady'—we started up in good heart. Somehow the gully
looked less human the longer we climbed. The shallow V-shaped
trough was tilted outwards, at the angle of a partly opened book
held sideways to the light; obviously anything on the lower wall
would roll off, and (our plunging eyes confirmed) bump on to
the lower wall of the next gully, and the next, and the next. We
cramped ourselves on to the angle, and the upper wall, and gained
height mainly by rather painful finger-pressure. Nobody said much
about the stones, because we all hoped they were an accident and
would presently stop. We could not always see them, but their
pings and whizzes never stopped. Big pieces of rock came away
in our hands: why had no one told us that this face of the
Grivola was rotten? The north-east ridge looked now not only
tempting, easy, and direct, but safe. On the worst pitch of the
gully hold after hold shook and trembled as Michael tested them;
somehow he got himself up, though neither of us below could
secure him properly. But the effort decided him to retreat: this
could hardly be the easy popular way up the Grivola. It was
very bad watching him come down that horrible scoop again, and
I suddenly got cramp in one leg, and became even less use in
case he should slip. As for Hughes, his answer to Michael's shouted
question was prompt and desperate: 'I couldn't hold a fly.' As soon
as we could move easily, we fled from the valley of stones to the
south-east ridge, about which the *Guide* seemed to have nothing
to say. But now we were using our own judgement, and not trying
to work out what someone else's judgement had once established.
This rocky ridge looked good, no matter what was its Alpine pedigree,
and we were not disappointed. Good, clean rock, with now and
again a moderately stiff pitch; now Hughes, now Michael was at the
top end of the rope as it swarmed up pillars, crawled through
tunnels, popped up first one side of the ridge, then the other. It

was Hughes in the lead on the last little joke of a spiral staircase leading under and through the summit rocks. He poked his head through a hole on the western side and, echoing the tourist in one of Samivel's drawings, who puts his head over the top to see cows grazing, 'We are deceived in our peak!' he cried. Across at least two kilometres of unretreating Trajo glacier glowered the unmistakable genuine Grivola, a larger, greyer copy of the peak we had come up. The monster had scored.

Sitting on our top, we worked out our mistake. The Italian military 1:100,000 map which we had been working on marked no peak here at all, so we had not realized there was a possibility of error; too late, we drew out the map from the pocket of the *Climbers' Guide* and found the Punta Rossa clearly indicated. Our only possible gesture was to run down the 'deceptively easy' north-east ridge in twenty minutes. On the practically invisible mock-Trajo glacier an elegantly skirted lady from Cogne was taking a stroll with two cavaliers in dark suits. We skedaddled down to the hut in another half-hour, and decided that the day had been well worth an *omelette au rhum* for pudding.

The real Grivola next day was, except for one incident, almost an anti-climax. We quickly turned off the easy hunting-path, set there to deceive us, and a steep snow couloir took us up to the Colle Nero and the glacier. The gullies spread fan-wise on this face of the real Grivola were set at a much more convenient angle than those on the Punta Rossa; we did not feel as if we might be tilted off. Some stones fell—Hughes got a small one on his head—but by keeping to the top of the rib between two gullies we were pretty clear of them. We had to be careful all the time over loose holds, but there was really no difficult passage, and on the top we decided that our yesterday's south-east ridge on the Punta Rossa had been a much more entertaining climb. But the view was superb; gazing entranced at the Paradiso, I dropped a large roll, which bounced from rock to rock. Our own descent was easy and exhausting, stepping down interminably from shelf to shelf; Hughes, still sensitive about his head, came last. We put on crampons at the foot of the face, for the sake of the couloir down from the Colle Nero. The snow was soft; we glissaded a little, still roped, Michael in perfect control, I not so sure. Near the foot of the couloir we stopped to take off rope and crampons. We were all bending over, rather tangled with ropes, tapes, and rucksacks, when Michael shouted 'Jump left!' and jumped. Hughes and I jumped too, in the same direction, and an enormous boulder came crashing down the couloir over the place we had been standing. Nobody said anything. At the hut, an hour later, we began to realize that it had been a nasty business.

Our last dinner at this heavenly hut began, surprizingly, with a marmalade omelette. Michael had tried to order a plain one, but they had misunderstood his sketchy Italian, grasping only his insistence that this kind of omelette came before the meat. A red object, seen dimly in the dusk in our chicken casserole, turned out to be not a tomato, but a cockscomb; but we could find nothing wrong with that dish, nor with the zambaglione. Happy as kings, we talked to a sad Frenchman who was dragging his eight-year-old boy and his ten-year-old girl on a walking tour which they obviously hated. We warned them earnestly off the Col de Sort.

Warmed by the climb, the food, and the scene, Michael revealed his true ambition. 'I should like,' he said, dealing out the second bottle of red wine, 'to give my name to a village square somewhere in France. The Place Michel-Robert needn't be very large, and the villagers needn't remember why they named it after me. It'll do if one of these days they answer, when asked who Michel Robert was: "Un zèbre quelconque." But there must be plane-trees, and a café, and the sound of someone playing bowls.' Hughes asked him what he proposed to do to 'deserve this honour, but Michael seemed indifferent. 'Oh, anything you like—editing a *de luxe* edition of Arsène Lupin, or taking the President of the Republic up the Sassière, or marrying the fireman's daughter.' Unsympathetically, I pointed out that this avenue was closed, and that a more direct way to put his name on to the topography of France would be to come to a bad end on the mountains and get his friends to name a hut after him. Hughes, with memories of the Dauphiné, did not agree that this was a desirable immortality. 'No name could sound as musical as Adèle Planchard,' he said firmly, 'and no hut could be as foul.'

Money troubles loomed up again the next morning, but the guardian was touchingly trusting about taking our French money at the rate we named. Our Italian must have been improving, for we understood most of his chatter. People still came up to the hut to hunt, he said; though licences were now needed to kill bouquetin. The first beast cost about 5,000 lire, the second and subsequent ones were increasingly dearer. Later in the season he was expecting the King of Egypt. We left him, and his squat wife, making cheerful Fascist salutes at the door, and in a couple of hours were back at Cogne. We rescued a curious bundle of torn trousers and spare rope from the smart luggage at the Albergo Grivola, and took the bus to Aosta. Soon we left the pines and larches, and were down among the vines; there were rosy apples on trees by the roadside; a slender Roman bridge nobly and impressively spanned the valley. At Aosta I had to leg it from the station to the bank—the bus had agreed to let us pay at this end while Michael and Hughes stayed behind as hostages. Thank heavens it didn't seem to be Sunday, the bank was open, and our tourist lire at last collected; but that afternoon it took half a dozen water ices in the colonnade to get our mutual indebtedness with Hughes cleared up before he started for Chamonix over the Great St. Bernard.

The year before we had only passed through Aosta on our way from Courmayeur to Bourg Saint-Pierre. Now we had a day and a half to take in the singular charm of this Roman town. Courmayeur's spell derives from the mountains; the immense white precipices of Monte Bianco dominate the imagination and leave no room for any other contemplation. But 'Much more of humanity in it than any other I have seen in the Alps,' wrote W. P. of the view from the Grand Combin, and Aosta spread like a domino below. Standing in the square at Aosta we could see the snows of the Combin shining far above, but had eyes too for the works of man—the fan-shaped pattern of the paving stones in the big square, the dignity of the colonnade, and, down the road, the great Triumphal Arch. Here, in Augusta Praetoria, were all the reasons that make the western Alps the greatest mountains in the world. Beside Augustus's arch, or at the foot of the great pass, one felt the Alps, not as on the fringes of European civilization, but at the heart. Over the St. Bernard went one of the greatest roads in the world, the pilgrim's road to Rome, linking the maize fields of Piedmont with the fells of Norway, Renaissance with Gothic,

Giotto with Dürer, Dante with Ockham. There were homely links, too, for the British. Canute had complained to Rome of the violence done by brigands to Englishmen crossing the St. Bernard on pilgrimage: they had to cross the pass in companies of four or five hundred. 'The notorious and haughty St. Anselm' had been Bishop of Aosta before he was Archbishop of Canterbury.[1] Aosta, asserting its history and humanity against the full height of the Grand Combin, satisfied deeper needs than the wish to score another four-thousander.

Our first meeting with Othon this year lacked the usual exuberance. He had come down from Courmayeur by train to meet us; it was 16th August, the day after the Guides' Feast, and he thought eight in the morning a shocking time for a rendezvous. On the train down to Châtillon he scolded us for not having explained our plans for the next ten days. (Our unspoken defence was that there wasn't much use making them without him.) 'Je suis homme de famille,' he said severely, making us feel giddy and irresponsible; 'il faut renseigner ma femme où je suis.' Indeed we knew how good and dutiful a family man he was, telephoning or telegraphing Mme Bron whenever we got to a post office. Horace, a delicate child, gave him anxiety; after ringing up Courmayeur, Othon would join us, cheerful because Horace had taken a good dinner, out of humour because 'il ne mange pas—il suce du lait.' There were many jokes about le petit Bron leading a hypothetical petit Robert up the Péteret Ridge some day; but Othon's serious plans for Horace were different. He was not to be a guide.

This morning, however, we guessed that Othon's real trouble was the too successful junketing at the Guides' Feast the day before, with, perhaps, a slight additional grudge that we were not having one of our Alpine taxi rides. A lorry at Châtillon, painted Roberto Michele, eased the situation by making us all laugh at the same moment. Othon's temper was restored by Breuil, but he was clearly not very well.

[1] A connection which cannot have pleased the Rev. Dr. George B. Cheever, who crossed the pass several hundred years later: 'The city of Aoste, lying under an Italian sky, and out of the way of communication with the Gospel, has always remained in allegiance to the Pope and Tradition.'— Wanderings of a Pilgrim in the Shadow of Mont Blanc (1845).

From the bus up the Valtournanche, we had one or two superb views of the Matterhorn, but the sky soon clouded. Over lunch at Breuil we discussed the situation. In Othon's view, the south ridge of the Matterhorn would not go for a few days. There was already a lot of snow on it, and the weather was uncertain. Our one principle was never to hang about waiting for a peak; so we decided to go up to the Théodule hut, see what the weather did, and be well placed to come down in a day or two to Zermatt, or to Breuil again.

The first section of the new téléphérique up to the Théodule pass had only been opened the day before, and Othon was eager to try it. I regard these cabins slung in the air over precipices with alarm and distaste; I felt we deserved it when this one hung still in space for about fifteen minutes owing to some breakdown. We calculated the distance from the ground, and eyed our rope; it would reach, we decided, to within fifteen feet of the ground. Then, thank heavens, we were off again with a wheeze and a grind, and landed at the Plan Maison. We walked up to the Théodule hut in soaking rain. Othon went to bed with nothing to eat; we dined with a charming couple from Paris, who were enthusiastic about the comfort and cheapness of this Italian Alpine Club hut compared with the privately run Gandegg on the Swiss side of the pass—' ah, quels voleurs!'

Surprisingly, next morning was fine; but Othon was still unwell. We refused to let him get up, and promised to behave soberly on the Breithorn without him. Othon used to regard our guideless doings in the Graians with indulgent amusement: 'Encore des montagnes à vaches!' he would exclaim after hearing our news. But on real Alps his own reputation was involved, and he wanted us to do him, and the mountains, credit. He could, of course, have earned a living in a good many other ways (and did); and he did not think guiding was really worth while unless it was something more than dragging one new client after another up a familiar mountain. Part of the pleasure in climbing, for him, was in watching his pupils improve from year to year, though he always discriminated between those who wanted to break records or bag peaks and those who had 'la passion pour la montagne.' Once, talking to Michael, be said that he liked his clients to be about the same age as himself, able to go fast, and with the same idea of a joke.

Two hours and a quarter took us to the top of the Breithorn, which was as crowded as Lochnagar on a fine summer Saturday. The snow was perfect, and I had no qualms whatever about rattling down the only steep slope of the climb, near the top; but the two fat men, helplessly sliding down, tugged back now and then by their solid philosophical smoking guides, probably remember the summit, and the view, more keenly than we do. Othon was at the hut door to meet us, complimentary because the rope (his own) wasn't wet. He said he felt much better after his good sleep in the empty hut, and after lunch he was ready to start for the hut on the Hörnli ridge of the Matterhorn. It was a most beautiful traverse under the great mountain; sometimes we were shut into a world of snow walls and crevasses, with eyes only for the next step down; but for long stretches we walked conscious of the tremendous rocks above us on our left, and down on the right the green twists of the Vispthal. On the last passage, an ice slope in the angle of the Furgg glacier and the Hörnli ridge, Othon turned round and asked if we wanted the rope. We said no, with perfect confidence; Othon cut a few steps, with apparently casual flicks of his axe, and without the least difficulty we were across. Just before reaching the hut, Othon turned round again: we had improved a great deal since last year. 'One more year, and you can go by yourselves, always, anywhere.' We knew this was a way of saying that he felt better now, but of course we were pleased all the same. Traffic was slack on the Matterhorn that day, and we discovered the hut telescope had been turned on us. 'What imprudence!' exclaimed an elderly French trio on the tiny terrace, and went on to give grisly details of every accident, known or conjectured, that had happened in the district that summer. They looked at Othon with disapproval: with his bare head, bare chest, and bare legs, he must have looked to them suspiciously lacking in the solid respectability of a Zermatt guide.

Upstairs in the dormitory we found two Italians who had started to cross the Matterhorn from Breuil the day before we came up the Valtournanche. After spending the first night at the Savoia hut, they had been caught by a storm high up on the Swiss arête, by the shoulder, and spent their second night up there. Conditions had been appalling all up the Italian side.

No Matterhorn ogre disturbed my dreams in the crowded hut this year, and the next morning was clear and starry. Othon refused to start early. It was absurd to set off for the Matterhorn at midnight, as some people did; at two or three we should only have to stand in queues; far better let the others get well ahead, then we could go straight up. However, when we came out of the hut, roped, at 4.15, the tail of the string of lanterns which danced up the Hörnli ridge like will-o'-the-wisps was not far away, and we caught it up at the first pitch. Othon was extremely impatient. He made one attempt to take a higher line than the crowd, and so cut in ahead, but the Zermatt men were naturally so concerned at the possibility of our knocking down stones that they shouted to him to rejoin the tail of the caterpillar. So we stayed in our places till the Solvay hut. The climbing was very like the Grivola—the real Grivola—a progress from ledge to ledge, with here and there a chimney. On the whole, the rate of the caterpillar (which we reckoned to be about forty people, in fourteen parties) seemed quite creditable. Obviously, about six of the clients were in no sense mountaineers, but enterprising holiday makers who wanted to climb one mountain, and that the Matterhorn. With one guide to pull, and one to push, they got on quite briskly if not beautifully. A small man in black velvet corduroys and black beret turned out to be one of the alarmist French trio of the day before: his two female companions were not present. I kept on thinking how funny it was that this circus show should be the Matterhorn; yet oddly I did not resent it as I should have expected, in the instinctive mood of the child who finds a Sunday school treat picnicking in the particular valley he has at last managed to explore. The Matterhorn was large enough to carry with dignity even such a curious company as to-day's (of which we were certainly part), and the moments of waiting while Velvet Breeches was patiently tugged and hoisted up a pitch passed pleasantly in remembering the first ascent, and speculating where Whymper's party had spent the night.

At the Solvay hut the caterpillar paused to breathe and breakfast; with a rueful look at each other, for we were hungry too, Michael

and I followed Othon straight up. He could take his own pace
now, and we passed two or three parties by the fixed ropes on
the shoulder. One of them was led by an old guide who had
told Othon the night before he wasn't going to be first up in
case there were any steps to be cut. As soon as he saw us now,
he begged us to go on ahead. I had often heard good climbers
dismiss the Hörnli ridge as too easy to be interesting, and it had
long been an ambition of mine to climb the mountain first by
the Zmutt or Italian ridge. But with a thin coating of snow over
everything, I did not feel at all inclined to make light of the
ordinary route. The shoulder certainly was not outrageously steep,
but there was nothing much to stop you if you did start slithering.
And no one who has read and re-read Whymper can climb the
top stretch unmoved. Above the last rocks, the scree was frozen
under a layer of snow—in dry years there is almost a track here,
we were told—and the summit ridge was deep in snow, curling
over in a great cornice to the south-east. Across the Zmutt valley
the Dent Blanche was seamed and streaked with new white. I
tried to realize where we were, not very successfully; our climb
had been too natural, and the Matterhorn is a legend.

At the fixed rope on the rock on the way down we met a
tangle of parties and a cat's cradle of ropes. There was a short
argument with some Germans as to whether they were coming up
or we were going down. Further down we ran into our elderly
gentleman in black velvet. 'Est-ce que c'est loin au sommet?' he
asked anxiously. 'Je pense que je n'ai plus de courage'. We
assured him that half an hour would see him up, and that it was
well worth the effort. Obviously this was the big adventure of
his life, and it would be a pity if he didn't complete it.

At last, after six hours' movement, we stopped to eat just under
the Solvay hut; but not for long, because we were anxious now
to get down quickly and avoid stones from the parties above.
The last lap to the Hörnli was a rather monotonous jogging, with
nothing exciting or difficult, and yet no moment when we could
relax. We managed not to let down any stones, and no one was
near enough to let them down on us. Hot and untidy, with the
rope still on, we clattered on to the platform by the hut: some
parties who had walked up from Zermatt cheered us as the first

rope down. We were extremely embarrassed. 'What club is this badge?' said one lady, pointing to a trumpery little brooch of a boot and ice-axe that Othon has picked up somewhere and stuck in my wind-jacket. I was too thirsty to stop and spin a story about the exclusive Club Alpin sans Blague of which Othon, Michael, and I had constituted ourselves foundation members. Further down, at the Schwarzsee, we were met by the two elderly Frenchwomen who, with our black-velvet friend of the Matterhorn, had watched our arrival the day before with such disapproval. One of them, dressed in flowing black, accosted me with tragic voice: 'Vous venez du Cervin? Est-ce que mon mari est sauf? Y aura-t-il un accident?' I did my best to reassure her; told her that though he might not be down for hours, he was with the best and surest guides, who could not fail to bring him back safe and triumphant. But I left them still tragically gazing upwards.

Michael and Othon waited for me at the entrance to the village. We walked through Zermatt as I had always wished to do, past the Monte Rosa and the guides on the wall, with the knowledge that we had climbed the Matterhorn. Next morning, loafing round the shops, I stopped to look at a photograph taken outside the Monte Rosa in 1864. On the edge of the group was Miss Walker, who I knew had been the first woman up the Matterhorn, in 1871. I thought of her, and of the French girl my father had met when he went up the Hörnli ridge—'in boy's clothes with father (or keeper) and six guides.' By modern standards, Miss Walker's clothes were impossible, and the French girl's six guides absurd; but if I, who had fallen heir so easily to the territory they had won for women climbers, could claim a tenth of their independence, initiative, and courage, then I could be well pleased with myself.

Up at the Trift Hotel that evening we met a young Zermatt guide with a dashing white wind-jacket who said airily 'Oh, if you're a good party, you'll get up the Rothorn in seven hours'; also Pierre Blanc le Pape of Bonneval, who was climbing with two English girls. While we gossiped with him about the Levannas, the Col de Chalanson, and the new hotel at Bonneval, Othon took a look at the beginning of to-morrow's route, and read about it in Kurz. He had never been over the Zinalrothorn before, but next morning he led us unhesitatingly up the maddening moraine in the dark.   Going up the curtain of rock, where I had been turned back so sadly seven years before, I felt free and happy; this climb had been worth waiting for.   Everything went so easily on the upper snow field and the narrow snow ridge that I could hardly believe we were already under the top rocks.   Othon moved fast, for the weather was obviously spoiling and he wanted to have at least a glimpse of the unknown way down the other side.

Five hours from the Trift we were on top, eating genuine plum cake that Michael had run to earth in a *pâtisserie* the day before. Ten minutes only, and then we were off into a fierce wind.   Sometimes it was really snowing, sometimes the wind blew snow crystals about so that it seemed as if it were snowing.   My eyes were stinging and crying, Michael's glasses blurred over as fast as he wiped them.   Othon, for once wearing his cocky green Tyrolese hat, was in his element, cheerful and gay—though he was exceptionally careful on all snow passages, playing us down one at a time and whenever possible securing his own rope on a rock. Indeed, we all enjoyed it, for not even the wind and snow could spoil the beautiful rock that day: Leslie Stephen's party straddling the ridge on the first ascent had always been one of my favourite Alpine pictures and it gave us an extra tang of enjoyment to find ourselves recapitulating their spread-eagle attitudes.   The one place I found tricky was the traverse round the Sphinx, which Michael led in one easy movement.

By now we could not see ten metres ahead, but with compass and altimeter (this year's new toy), Othon hit off exactly the shoulder where the route to the Mountet hut and Zinal leaves the ridge.   After the exhilaration of Sphinx and Razor, I found it hard to keep up a rhythmical pace on the snow slope.   'Ça, c'est le meilleur système de tomber dans une crevasse,' said Othon severely as I did a slither and check.   We reached the Mountet hut just eight hours after leaving the Trift, and found three French guideless parties who had started for the Rothorn that morning and turned back.   We felt superior, and pleased; then noticed that the practice climbs they were imposing on each other on the slab behind the hut were far harder than any pitch on the ridge.   The kind, elderly guardian brewed us gallons of Maggi to fortify us for

the dreadful Mountet glacier.   We walked endlessly down dirty
ice and dirty moraine, I banged my watch on a boulder, and
swore never to go up from Zinal to the Mountet but always to
reach the hut by some back door.   Down on the meadows at last,
Othon quickened the pace, to keep us in training, he said; but
the glacier had destroyed my morale. We walked through Zinal
and on to Ayer, expecting to find a bus there at four.   We arrived
with half an hour to spare, and then found the bus went at six.   I
refused to walk a step further for the sake of training, so we sat at
the café, drank wine, wrote postcards, ate hard peaches and pears,
and talked to two little girls who were washing their linen in the
village trough beside the café, dressed in the costume of the Val
d'Anniviers—black boots, black-and-grey striped frocks that went half-
way down their legs, and fascinating black hats of pleated ribbon.

Suddenly, familiar figures came round the corner—the Swiss
brothers whom we had met a year ago at the Chanrion hut, so
business-like with their menus and equipment. They had traversed
the Rothorn the day before with Camille Bournassien, the little
Evoléne man who had herded that unwieldy party up the Matterhorn,
and unburdened himself about them to Othon on the train to
Visp.   Gathering up these last year's threads was oddly satisfying,
though there was one loose end I never tidied up—a tin labelled
Pussy on the dump beside the Hörnli hut; I had half expected
to see it again this year, but no, the problem still teases me.   By
now the weather had quite mended, and we could look back at
our Rothorn rising very white behind the black stump of Lo
Besso.   The post bus came at length, bright yellow, trailing a
little yellow carrier behind for the mail, and driven by so solid,
blue-eyed, and dependable a Swiss that we passed the steepest
hairpins with hardly a tremor, and the three-note posthorn echoed
musically from side to side of the rocky gorge.

After a night at Sion the slow progress by railway down the
Rhône reduced me to my usual regrettable valley temper.   Also,
I had discovered that the knock on the Mountet glacier had quite
disorganized my watch.   I refused to stroll round Martigny with
the others, and muttered protests against the expense of a lunch
in this charming town of apricots and roses.   I was unfairly
rewarded by finding, in a hotel copy of *La Suisse*, a reproduction

of a drawing by the Dutch artist Jan Hackaert, of whom I had never heard before. He had visited the Grisons in 1656, and looked at mountains with an eye like Francis Towne's for their structure and solidity. Where J. R. Cozens and Turner let their mountains trail off unsubstantially into mist, clouds, and romantic atmosphere, Hackaert and Towne revealed the permanent architecture of the mountain beneath the temporal changes of light and weather. 'It seldom happens that mountains in a very clear air look exceeding high, but these, though we could see the whole of them to their very summits, appeared to me more majestic in their own nakedness than our imagination could have conceived them to be, had they been half-hidden by clouds, yet showing some of their highest pinnacles.' Dorothy Wordsworth's observations on the hills of Glencoe apply also to the mountains of Towne and Hackaert.

We talked late that night at Chamonix, in the café within sound of the Arve. Othon had had a good year. He had been at Sestrières as usual from December to February, as instructor and organizer of the ski school; though this winter he had had a pupil who set a pace almost too high for him. She was a physical training instructress from Berlin, a beautiful skier; but her idea of fun was to go up after a snowfall, pick a steep slope, and ski down on top of the avalanche she had started. Even Othon thought this excessive. In spring he had done his favourite ski-tours on the great snowfields at the base of Monte Rosa, sleeping at the Bétemps or Britannia hut. One couple he had taken up from Breuil had been noble, but undisciplined: they had objected to putting on the rope on the run down from the Théodule pass to the Gorner glacier. 'Il n'y a plus de duc, plus de prince'—Othon had been firm—'à la montagne, il n'y a que le roi; et le roi, c'est moi!' There had been no more nonsense.

Towards the middle of June, he had realized a plan that he had discussed with us the year before: 'L'École du Ski et de l'Alpinisme,' on the Col du Géant. In these early weeks of the season, before the hut was crowded, he could keep ten or twelve people up at the Torino, where they were ideally placed for learning the elements of glacier skiing, rope management, walking on crampons; and on the Tour Ronde and Géant they could learn to climb rock. It was largely a family affair: Othon's brother Léon was now guardian of the Torino, and his brother-in-law Octave Ollier, Jock Butler's guide in 1934, was one of Othon's chief helpers. This first year the school had gone well.

Then we talked of next year. It must be the south side of Mont Blanc, cried Othon, perhaps not the Péteret yet, but certainly the Brenva ridge. Then, the year after, the Péteret; that was a climb! He described the ascent to us, stage by stage. 'Now if we three were caught in a storm, high up above the Fresnay glacier, this is what I'd do.' We gripped the café table while Othon lashed us to our axes, moved us one at a time across the dangerous snow slope, ingeniously contrived belays; not till he got us safely down to the glacier did we dare relax.

Chamonix was a good place to get away from next day after a hairdresser, finding me helpless in his drying-machine, had wreathed my face in curls. Othon and Michael spared me nothing. The curls bobbed unnaturally round my brown and shining face, and in spite of showers, lasted long enough to make the trip up to the Montanvert a misery. It was a Saturday, and late in the evening the place filled up with week-end climbers from Geneva, cheerful, wet, and noisy. There were several parties on the Nantillons glacier next morning. We left them to breakfast on the Rognon while we cut straight up the rocks at the side, in excellent condition this year. So was the Charmoz-Grépon couloir, which we had viewed with guilty memories of slithering down it two years before. To-day it was dry and easy, though I managed to let down one stone, for which I was well told off by Othon. We sat in the sun for a few minutes at the nick between the Charmoz and the Grépon, while Othon changed into rubbers, whistled, sang, and shouted jokes at the parties coming up the couloir. Then we went out on the Mer de Glace side, back on to the other, and there, within a few feet, was the Mummery crack. Othon saw the rope well belayed, then danced across the rock to the platform part way up. Infected by his high spirits of ten minutes ago, I let out a cheer. He turned on me in a flash; *this* wasn't the moment for noise. He always moved so lightly and easily that one sometimes forgot the tension that underlay this perfect co-ordination of will and muscle. He was up the crack in a minute; it was as easy as that. The occasion was impressive to a frequent reader of Mummery; it was too fine a day to feel overburdened by it, but I kept on remembering that there was no place to stop till you got to the top. Instructed by Othon above, I swung across to the platform like the weight in a pendulum, with the party's sack bobbing and bouncing on the rope above me. I looked straight up the crack and saw Othon's brown face leaning over pinky rock, heard his 'Montez donc,' and there I was, finding the crack far easier than I had expected. The holds were very good, and there seemed to be several places where one could rest a second if one should want. But I knew very well that we had an exceptionally good day—and that I was held from above. Othon welcomed me with a grin, swore he hadn't pulled, and took Michael's rope from me; so I squeezed the last bit of pleasure out of the occasion by watching Michael and reclimbing the pitch in sympathy.

The rest of the climb was dry, warm, and gay. Wriggling through the Trou de Canon (so reminiscent of our antics on the Punta Rossa) seemed an odd way to climb a great Aiguille; on the Grand Gendarme I behaved disgracefully. I had not roped down for two years and could not, on the brink, really believe that it was all right just to sit back over space and start. I found the Râteau de Chèvre considerably stiffer than the Mummery—arm-pulls have never been my strong point—but it was a superb climax. We lay on the top for an hour, licking up water from an ice-covered puddle, and listening, on this airy perch, to the cheerful noises of humanity. Othon shouted instructions to a couple of Genevese who wanted to know the best way of coming down the Grand Gendarme. From the Chamonix side floated up the music of a brass band; from the Mer de Glace a fanfare of trumpets blown by the Chasseurs Alpins who were helping to inaugurate the enlarged Requin hut. We could see the crowd winding like a caterpillar up the Mer de Glace.

The two Genevese joined us, and we arranged to share *rappel* ropes with them on the way down, so that each party would only have to pull its rope down every alternate pitch. Now that I had got the feel of the motion again, I found the *rappels* delightful; these, and the music from below, and the pleasant group on the Rognon for lunch, made the day something of a party. The

Genevese topped it off by standing us beer and lemonade ('la champagne des pauvres') at the Montanvert, while we watched the procession straggle back from the junketings at the Requin hut.

Plenty of the celebrants, though, had stayed on to inaugurate the hut's new regime with a climb, and we had a most social walk up the Mer de Glace next afternoon.   Nearly every guide we met had something to say to Othon, and we ran into both the Chapelland twins who had been with the *course collective* the year before at the Trélatête.   Up at the hut we found Georges Cachat, last seen in a snowstorm on the Col du Géant.   The two young Americans he was climbing with came over and talked to us about to-morrow's climb.   They had come from Zermatt, where they had climbed the Dom and Monte Rosa guideless; they had only enough money for one climb with a guide, and were banking on fine weather for the Requin—our peak too.   All the world had come up to sample the extended hut.   The new *salle* was big, as hut *salles* go, but it was packed.   Matters were made no easier by the guardian and his family resolutely tackling their own supper, and ignoring any one else's demands.

As with the Grépon, the Requin next day was so entirely delightful and smooth that the memory is left with little to grasp.   The long, vertical crack at the Colonnes struck me as harder than anything on the Grépon; the *rappel* down the Grande Cheminée was so charming that I wished it twice as long.   From the top we looked at the great east face of the Grépon; it seemed astonishing that any one had climbed it.   This face was a sore point with Othon.   One of his earlier clients this summer had been the daughter of an Italian admiral: a girl of about nineteen, active and keen, but new to the mountains.   He took her up to the Torino hut, with the Tour Ronde and Géant in view, and a possible finish with a Chamonix Aiguille   But at the hut she got into conversation with Gervasutti and Lucien Devies, the Italian-French couple whose climbs 'of the sixth degree of difficulty' we used to read about with admiration and alarm in *La Montagne*.   'My dear,' they had said in effect to her, when she spoke of her hopes of Chamonix, 'it's a fearful bore going up the Grépon the ordinary route; the only possible way to do it is by the Mer de Glace face.'   She was a strong-minded young woman, and it had taken

Othon the best part of an evening to make her understand he meant No.   The clinching argument had been his remark: 'Of course if you insist on it, I shall have to be entirely free, and you will have to carry my rucksack, my boots, all our food, and extra clothes for the bivouac which we shall certainly have to make.'   The only point on which he met her wishes was to go down to Montanvert at once and climb from there.   Two days later, after a traverse of the Petits Charmoz, which she had found agreeable but strenuous, she handsomely admitted he had been right.   But he still growled at the irresponsible ace-climbers who had filled her head with wrong ideas.

Cachat and the Americans were within hail most of the way over the Requin and the shouted greetings from Épaule to summit, the shared rope down the Grande Cheminée, gave a delightful friendly note to the day's climb.   Othon looked approvingly at Robert Bates's casual grey-flannelled legs swarming neatly down the *rappel*, and thought he must have climbed a good deal before. We said we understood he had done something in Alaska.

We came down the glacier as gaily as we had come down from Monte Rosa the year before, laughing and talking (but the rope was always taut).   I collapsed entirely once, from nothing but mirth.   We had the rest of the morning for idling in front of the hut, and gazing at the astonishing and beautiful peaks all round, ourselves profoundly satisfied.   We had spent friendly days in our familiar territory in the Tarentaise.   With Hughes, we had explored new country, and found what lay on the far side of the hill. And with Othon we had climbed four classic peaks, long read about and hoped for, in the gayest and happiest companionship. We had always been able to start for the climb we had planned the evening before, and (except for Michael's first day on the Grande Motte) we had never, once started, been turned back by bad weather.   The only major plan that had not come off had been the traverse of the Matterhorn from Breuil.   There had been no riding out of storms in high huts, no hanging about in valleys for the tops to clear.   And all this in a season generally considered bad!   We felt astonishingly lucky.   Michael was going on across the Col du Géant for a few more days in the Tarentaise, and I was due for home, but I had hardly a regret as I said good-bye to Othon in front of the hut. Never had we had a more perfect summer's climbing.

Nor was the gaiety over. I left Michael and Othon to go up the glacier while I went down with Georges Cachat and the Americans. Cachat embarked on a sort of follow-my-leader at express speed; we skipped, jumped, and bounced our way down the Mer de Glace in just over an hour. I reckoned that if I waited for the train at Montanvert I would have no time for a bath in Chamonix. I left the others and rushed fiercely down in another hour, my whole being longing for fruit or water, beer or lemonade or milk. I bought grapes, and ate them in my bath. David Robertson and Robert Bates, just down by train from the Montanvert, came to say good-bye, and we promised to do another climb together some day. The train drew out; I ate half a kilo of peaches and half a kilo of grapes as I looked good-bye at Mont Blanc.

Yet, for each of us, there was a coda to the summer's climbing. Michael went to Courmayeur with Othon. At the Col du Géant Othon had repeated, but this time sadly, what he had said under the Hörnli: 'Next year you can go by yourselves.' Then Michael made for Tignes; he liked ending a season where he had begun, and measuring the change—the apples by the road at Séez now red, that had been small and green when we went up in the bus with the boys; the hayfields by the cascade, then wavy and bright with flowers, now shaved and yellow. He had a last climb, over the Pourri, acting as second porter to the curé of La Gurra who was guiding a party of two men and two girls. He arrived home with a great line of blisters on his left hand made by the sudden pull of the rope when one of the party fell off on the way down to the Brèche Puiseux. But it had been a good day, and as they sat on the top the curé had talked of peaks and passes, snow bridges and chamois poaching. 'Ce sont des gens honnêtes,' he said of his parishioners, 'but they have more respect for the laws of God and the decisions of the commune than they have for the laws of the Republic—or of the Kingdom of Italy. It happens'— here he had looked at the first porter, judiciously fitting a piece of cheese to a hunk of bread, 'that now and again one of them will knock at my door late at night. "I was coming over the Col de la Galise," he'll say, "and I left a big parcel under a rock just this side of the frontier. I wonder if you could lend a hand . . ."'

For me there was a week in Argyllshire, where Elizabeth Monroe let me lead her up the Church Door Buttress of Bidean nam Bian, in the wet. The climb went all right (except for a stone I let down on her wrist before we ever began), but in the mist I brought her down into the wrong glen. Three days later we did the Crowberry Ridge of Buachaille Etive (the original route, it seemed to be), in weather so nice that when we came to the Crowberry Tower we danced up and down it three different ways. It was a good ending to this wonderful summer.

CHAPTER VII

TWO WINTER JOURNEYS

With Death and Morning on the silver horns.

I

OUR ramblings in 1935 had made me feel as free on the hills of Savoy as in the Highlands, but I still thought of a skiing holiday as a matter of booked rooms in a big centre, with an expensive new uniform as the necessary passport. Indeed, like many other people, I thought of Alpine skiing as something different and remote from the world of the ordinary modest hill-walker, who could not afford to spend a lot of money on his holiday. True, I possessed skis, skins, boots, and ski-gloves already, owing to careful birthday and Christmas present policy; but I fancied they wouldn't operate without an intervening ski-suit of extreme expense and stylishness, in an atmosphere of funiculars and fancy dress balls. When, in the autumn of 1935, the Southern Railway Continental time-table appeared about the house, I raised this question of clothes. 'Haven't you got climbing breeches?' asked Michael, genuinely puzzled, 'and a wind-jacket?' It was as simple as that.

In Edinburgh, just before Christmas, we picked up a Paris newspaper which said there was good snow in the Jura: we thought of La Cure, and the runs on the Dôle. But at the Gare de Lyon, just after Christmas, the *bulletin d'enneigement* was discouraging; there seemed to be a thaw everywhere, and the only chance was to go high. Why not Tignes? Michael had been there twice at Easter; he thought that up at the lake, at least, we should find some snow. I went off to the time-table boards: 'The train's at 10.35, so we'll have heaps of time for dinner.' Back at the station again, well fed, the truth crept slowly over me: 20.35 was not, as after a tossy passage of the Channel I had thought, 10.35; and the Bourg Saint-Maurice train had duly left an hour ago, at 8.35. Michael took it magnificently. But as we had only nine days, it seemed a pity to waste one of them waiting to get to Bourg. Where else could we go that night? There was an 11.20 to

Modane, so we planned to try the valley of the Arc instead, and perhaps reach our original objective in the Val d'Isère by the back door over the Col de l'Iseran.

It was the winter of the Italo-Abyssinian war, and Sanctions, and there were miles of empty trucks on sidings between Saint-Michel and Modane. The station itself was queerly lifeless, with only a few passenger trains going through to Italy by the Mont Cenis, and no goods at all. We stepped out into unpromising slush and rain, but our spirits rose when we saw several other skiers in the electrobus for Lanslebourg. Small boys, Chasseurs Alpins, natives, and a gruff tax-collector kept us warm. We made slow progress up the valley, with old women popping their heads in at the stops, to ask the tax-collector why they had been assessed seven francs instead of six. At Lanslebourg there was snow, but wet and heavy-looking; the skiers disappeared into the Hôtel de l'Europe. We stood looking at the Valloire, where we had stayed a few months before. It was closed, but the proprietor came out and, recognizing us, invited us in. He gave us hot water to wash in, and a very good lunch in his own parlour. Lanslebourg at once seemed to me a good place to stay in; historically its record was auspicious, for one eighteenth-century Englishman who had crossed the Mont Cenis in winter had enjoyed the descent *en traineau* so much that he stayed a week in the village 'for the purpose of risking his neck three times a day.' But Michael, thinking of the possible crossing to the Val d'Isère, felt we should get up to the head of the Arc valley while we could. So, with some rather regretful looks on my part at the slopes of Mont Cenis on the right, we started to ski up to Bessans. We had a sledge-trail to follow, but everything was slushy and slippery. It took us an hour to trail up the two and a half kilometres to Lanslevillard. We thought we would be quicker walking; Michael carried his skis, I trailed mine behind on a piece of string. Some distance beyond Lanslevillard we put them on again for a short descent. Michael made a nice little run of it, but with my sack dragging on my back and my skis either shooting away uncontrollably on the slushy sledge-ruts, or refusing to move at all on the dead and sodden snow at the side, I felt cross and tired. These wet bumps and half-hearted slithers in a fading light seemed to be quite

different from the light-hearted little runs I had made with Hans
Graf at the Jungfraujoch, or from the odd hours I had spent on
Aberdeenshire slopes.   These had all been fun, even when the
days had not been sunny, because you could stop when you were
tired or wanted a cup of tea; now, skis seemed an unhandy wearisome
way of making an interminable journey.   Clearly we had to reach
Bessans to-night—and now it was nearly dark, and clearly we had
to use our skis, or at any rate not lose them.   On the level I
took them off and, towing them again, followed Michael along
the track, thinking with feeling of Good King Wenceslas. There
was no sign of Bessans.   Michael himself was so tired that he
sat down for a minute on his skis.   This made me feel better
about my own tiredness, but rather spoiled his role as Wenceslas.
The river Arc looked extremely black and cold.   I thought of
Horace Walpole's poor spaniel Tory, eaten in these parts by a wolf.
At last I spied a light, and in no time at all we had staggered
across the bridge to the Hôtel du Mont-Iseran, and discovered it
was only a quarter-past five!   There were one or two lights in
the hotel, and two women directed us in.   We plunged downstairs
from the road, into the family's winter quarters, half-underground,
separated only by a low screen from the cattle.   The horse, cows,
and calves stamped, champed and munched, and gave out warm,
comforting exhalations.   I suddenly realized that perhaps Mary
and Joseph had not been put into the worst place at the inn that
winter night in Bethlehem.   The cattle gave off an even heat,
and through the door behind us Madame was busy on her stove.
We had not long to wait for a *potage*, *bifteck*, and coffee; then, with
regretful backward looks we followed M. Clappier up cold dark stone
stairs to a bedroom with clean sheets and hot-water bottle, a tiny
focus of warmth in a freezing room. We slept for thirteen hours.
      Gratefully, we scrambled down to the living-room-cum-byre, for
café au lait.   Outside it was misty, and the snow was falling
lightly; the going was very heavy as we went up in the Bonneval
direction.   We only stuck it for a couple of hundred metres, then
practised running on a gentle slope where I fell monotonously,
and wetly, at the end of every run.   When we came in to lunch,
we found they had lit a stove in a little room on the ground
floor, papered with *Le Petit Dauphinois*.   It was quite snug, but

the stove was not as even and reliable as the cows' breath. About a dozen skiers came up from Lanslebourg, having taken five hours; two men came down from Bonneval, having taken three. Every one agreed that they were lucky not to have been caught in one of the avalanches that sweep the road after each snowfall. The Bonneval couple had tried the Col de l'Iseran early that morning, but found it too dangerous. The dark wooden crucifix just outside the hotel carried great oozy lumps of snow on each arm; from time to time a lump would slide off in a wet flurry. We went back to our practice slopes, then walked a little further up the valley on our skis; two peasants jogged along the sledge track on a mule, on their way to Bessans from the hamlet a little higher up. It cleared slightly and Michael took a photograph. Weeks later when it was developed, we discovered that a little black triangle sticking up below the sledge track was the gable end of a chalet, otherwise submerged.

Next day was sunny, bright, and cold. We went out early, for M. Clappier was entertaining four or five men, as large and dignified as himself, on the benches beside the byre. Now and then they would get up, look over the screen, prod a beast with appraising comment, and come back for another glass of red wine. We went up the slopes over the bridge, where we had seen the hay-hoist working in the summer, and practised diligently. It was easier running than yesterday, the snow less heavy; still, I fell monotonously on each run. At midday the village boys rushed out, with skis made out of roughly shaped boards; one had a box-lid on each foot. Down the steepest slope they flashed, the one I had not yet dared to take direct, waving their sticks and standing very upright. To preserve my dignity I went much further uphill, and had a longer run down. By now the sun had gone behind a cloud, and it was difficult to make out the bumps and variations of slope on the trackless snow. I didn't fall till I was nearly at the foot. The boys rushed down to the village, so I went back to the nursery slopes, did several runs without falling, then began to be surprised when I did fall rather than when I didn't. All the same we went in very wet to shove-ha'penny and the study of Arnold Lunn, whose *Skiing in a Fortnight* was our only literature. Just before dinner we went out for a few minutes' walk as far as the post office. The sound of dripping water and slithering snow had ceased, the snow now creaked underfoot, and our breath turned to thick cloud in the frosty air. Under the shadow of the houses, three old women in their black Savoyard dresses (tightly stretched over several layers of clothes) and their *frontière* head-dresses, were talking quietly. A boy came down the street dragging a load on a sledge. That was Bessans in winter: a world scarcely stirring in its hibernation, content to wait till the snow melted from the pastures, and the old routine of a year's work crowded into six months would begin again.

Another day of practice raised our spirits. The long run down was enlivened by the hotel dog, a sporting mongrel who rushed after us, sometimes riding down on the back of the skis, sometimes swimming through the frothy untrodden snow. The weather still held, and the place now looked tidier: the loose blobs of snow had fallen off the telegraph wires, the crucifix was bare, and the night frost had kept the snow crust firm and trim on the house-roofs, with no messy trickles and drips. The hills themselves looked more orderly, the rocks and trees plainly black, no longer greyly smeared with thin snow. For the first time since our arrival, the courier went down with letters to Lanslebourg. The boys were out again; the one with the box-lids had bad luck, for one came off as he was beginning a run, and shot down ahead of him. He skied down perfectly on one leg, then that lid shot away too, and he skidded the rest of the way on foot.

The better weather revived our hopes of crossing the Col de l'Iseran; next morning we were back to a misty drizzle of snow, with the frosty tang gone from the air. We laid out a course with twigs, turning in and out between them; I practised snow-plough and turns. By midday the snow had almost stopped falling; we thought we might go as far as Bonneval that night. After lunch M. Clappier, a courteous old man with pale blue eyes, brought us a wonderfully modest bill and a bottle of *liqueur de marque*. He filled our glasses and excused himself politely for not taking a full glass himself because, it being New Year's Day, he had already drunk many toasts. He did not try to dissuade us from going to Bonneval, though he warned us against trying the col beyond; but he asked us to telephone our safe arrival. Otherwise, he said firmly, he would send out a search party.

This courteous concern sent us off in rather an Excelsior spirit; but it turned out to be a far quicker and easier walk than our sad plod up from Lanslebourg. All the way up the valley there was some sort of track, made by sledges or skiers, and not obliterated by the latest fall. Our skis slid forward easily; in spite of the constant thin snowfall and the poor visibility, I enjoyed the walk. We met two people—the postman, on skis, and a girl in a white sweater, with a rucksack on her back, walking. She was the schoolmistress, and in winter she divided her time between Bessans and Bonneval, sometimes spending weeks in one place while the road was impassable, and giving the children in the other village a holiday.

A little above Bessans, where the hills crowd in on the valley, there is the two-kilometre stretch where the big avalanches fall; we saw no sign that any had come down recently. In about two hours we were in Bonneval. As we expected, the C.A.F. chalet-hotel was shut, but at the post office, where we telephoned to M. Clappier, the old lady in charge sent a child with us to a brand-new little concrete box at the far end of the village. Immediately a talkative proprietor appeared. For the first minute we could hardly understand his accent; then we learnt that this was the Hôtel des Glaciers des Évettes, and we were among its first guests. Inside, everything was new, clean, and hygienic; pitch-pine doors that didn't quite shut, freshly distempered walls, electric heaters. We ate our dinner by one of them. It was not so cosy as the byre at Bessans, and we fidgeted with our chairs, and with our heater, to get the best results; but the food was carefully chosen and well cooked. While we ate our host talked, and his unusual accent was explained. He was an Italian, an engineer from Turin; he had been in the Socialist movement when Socialism was as exciting as polar exploration, and he told us how he had paid for Mussolini's drinks when they were both in Switzerland in the good old days, he on a job, and Mussolini as a political exile. M. Cusino did not tell us when he had finally left Italy, but we gathered that he felt safer over the border. Now, installed in this new hotel of his own building, he had great plans for the development of

Bonneval. Skis would be borrowed from Modane, so that the village children could learn properly, and later play their part as guides and instructors. There ought to be a road for sledges up to the Évettes hut, and the hut itself should be enlarged and provisioned, so that skiers might penetrate to the glaciers—and that would prolong the season until spring. Avalanches? Yes, he admitted, the local people talked a lot about them; but he had not seen any yet, and surely a great wall could be built above the threatened stretch of road, to break their force. It took new men to bring big ideas into country places like this, he said; and later, when the peasants came in to drink wine and sing in celebration of New Year's Day, it was as one man of the world to his sophisticated equals that he apologized for their rough noises. All the same, he was glad that they were celebrating here, for it gave his hotel a status and reality in the winter-bound village; this was the second time, for they had all been up on the 11th of November.

They certainly were rough tunes, but queerly moving. Slow, minor, now one man's voice joining in, or another's breaking off, as the glasses were put down or taken up. We preferred them to the wireless that was switched on at intervals, when all were hoarse, or drinking. The tinkle of tunes from *Congress Dances*, charming in a warm plush cinema, stood up as poorly to this rough male music as would an organdie frock to the wind on the col above. All the local guides were there, the Blancs. We remembered that Pierre Blanc le Pape had been to the Himalaya, and seen more of the world than we had, and probably more than M. Cusino; there did not seem to be much need to apologize for rustic limitations.

There was the same soft mizzly snow next morning, and after three-quarters of an hour's plod up to the first bend of the road to the col, we had to turn back, because in the bad light we could not see the snow-drifts. Also, there were avalanche tracks further on. M. Cusino was at the door when we came in, and before we could explain our prudence he dramatically told us of all the people who had been engulfed. A little later he appeared in the parlour with a villainous-looking man who he said could go with us as porter to-morrow. We made it clear that we would use our own judgement about taking him.

M. Cusino, it appeared, was not a skier. The afternoon passed
with a little practice in sticky snow, word games with paper
and pencil, and sighs for an Arsène Lupin and a new James
Thurber ruthlessly jettisoned at the Gare de Lyon. It would
have been a good afternoon to spend with Arsène in the Fontaine
de Jouvence, the miraculous lake that drained in a night to
reveal a world of grottoes, springs, and Roman labyrinths that
might have been conceived by Hieronymus Bosch. Michael looked
at the plain hygienic walls, with never a *Petit Dauphinois* to
cover a crack, and thought regretfully of the shabby inn at Les
Chapieux and its series of 'Road to Ruin' prints. The story
of the young Savoyarde who, betrayed by the lieutenant, follows
the regiment to Paris and marries the colonel, would have been
good for an hour's distraction. But with dinner we had a
double spate of conversation. We learnt that M. Cusino had
been in the troubles in Turin in 1923 when the workers seized
the factories; had been barricaded behind mattresses while Fascists
besieged the buildings; had done something about pregnant
women in the workshops; thought Laval mad and Herriot no
longer a pure-minded democrat; considered the British *forts pour
la politique*. His wife, simultaneously, told us that she had been
a dressmaker in Modane, but got sick of it when every one
took to artificial silk, ungrateful stuff to work with; and that
she was making a skiing jacket of marmot skins for a typist in
the bank at Modane, who was *folle pour la montagne*.

Another muggy, misty day kept the col out of reach, and gave
us a horrible trudge up to L'Écot for exercise. Crossing the
narrow bridge by the C.A.F. chalet-hotel—a single plank with a
handrail, and the snow piled up to a height of a metre—gave
something of the impression of walking on a tightrope, except
that the tightrope was made of cotton wool. Michael crossed on
top of this crazy structure, which reminded me of the nightmare
landscape of *Dr. Caligari*, and then had difficulty in getting up
the bank on the far side, which was a mass of loose wet snow
covering the osier bushes. I thought he would slip into the
stream and called him back; also, I was frightened of crossing
the bridge myself. Michael, exasperated at catching the points of
his skis in branches and getting masses of wet snow down his

neck, answered sharply.   He got up, and in a fit of bad temper
I followed him.   We trudged up the valley wondering whether we
had come here to enjoy ourselves.

We gave up when we were in sight of the hamlet, though it
was difficult to distinguish the houses humped with snow from
the rocks on the hillside.   At 2,000 metres, L'Écot is the highest
village in France that is inhabited all the year round; but we saw
nobody about, and no tracks down to Bonneval.   There were signs
of avalanches on the opposite bank; we kept carefully down by
the river.   It was a bleak day, but not fruitless.   I discovered, at
any rate on the way back, that travelling on skis over level ground
need not be a matter of walking with heavy weights tied to your
feet, but that you could develop a kind of slow trotting movement,
helping each step with a push of the sticks, and sliding two yards
for every one you walked.   Back in the village we searched for
tobacco, and discovered some at last in an underground cave. No
one was about, except the snapping hungry village dogs.   Inside
the houses, beside the cattle, the women were working and the
men were playing cards, discussing the points of their cows, and
smoking away the long village winter.   The day before we had
seen them rake out basketfuls of dung to make tidy heaps on the
snow in the fields, ready for the spring; but that, and the bringing
in of straw, was not more than a quarter of a day's work.   Last
year, we were told, the road up the valley was open for carts till
February; this winter it had been blocked by the beginning of
December.   Cusino was puzzled by Bonneval's winter idleness. 'At
Val d'Isère,' he said, 'the women make lace and the men carve.
Here they do nothing.'

After a huge lunch—stuffed eggs, roast veal, sauerkraut, cheese,
and fruit—Madame produced her treat for us: a copy of *Weldon's
Ladies' Journal*!   We had long since exhausted the narrative interest
in *Skiing in a Fortnight*, and its practical instructions were ironically
useless on those mushy slopes.   While Michael unselfishly did
puzzles with numbers and philosophically twiddled his thumbs, I
rushed through   *Weldon's* greedily—patterns for open-work blouses,
a toddler's play-suit, a recipe for a beautiful complexion which
would be a passport to successful matrimony, gripping stories of
typists marrying rich and good young men.   Madame popped her

head in: would I like another? She was a subscriber, for she thought the patterns more practical than those produced by French papers, which seemed to aim at clothing the impossibly bony figure of a fashionable chromium-plated model. So she brought a second, and another, and another, and as the latest were on top of the pile, and she worked downwards, it meant that I read the Warwick Deeping serial backwards. It seemed a good way to read a Warwick Deeping serial.

And with dinner M. Cusino produced *his* treat. We had that morning thoughtfully selected a partridge from the game that hung outside the landing window, noticed the absence from the collection of salted jackass, on which George Yeld once feasted in this village, and wondered if we should stay long enough to work up to the handsome blue mountain hare. Our bird was delicious, and now M. Cusino appeared with great bowls of *crème fraîche*, personally collected by himself that morning. Always go to a house with several cows if you want *crème fraîche*, he advised; if you go to a single-cow place, they will make up the amount with some of yesterday's cream.

Fortified, we hoped for the col to-morrow; but we woke to mist and more snow. At ten o'clock it seemed to clear, so we paid our bill, packed our sacks, and warned M. Cusino we might yet be back for lunch. We zigzagged up near the line of pylons, well away from the big loop of the road where the avalanches come down. We joined the road again high up, where it goes into the mountains after climbing their outer flank. Now, through the gorge leading into the upper valley, came a great rush of icy wind from the north, stinging our cheeks and whipping the snow into our eyes. We came on patches of hard wind-slab snow, and slid cautiously across; then the whirling snow-cloud whipped up by the wind got thicker and thicker, and we could only see a few yards ahead. At noon we sheltered in the stable of one of the empty chalets and decided to give the weather twenty minutes to change. We got colder; it stayed the same, so we turned back gingerly over the wind-slab. Back on the slopes above the main valley the major troubles of wind and blindness were over—though most of our upward tracks had been blown away—but not the humiliating irritations. I had not before run down with such a considerable sack-load; now I found that this new handicap destroyed the balance I had so newly gained. The weight dragged me back, and I sat down while my feet went sliding on; or it pushed me over, and I dived into the snow ahead of my skis. Everything else I had learnt was lost to me; I leant forwards from the waist, held my knees stiff, let my hands drag behind. I fell, I couldn't get up, my bindings came off, my heavy gloves slid down the slope. After ages of this disgrace and misery I came down to the road and the field. Michael, who had arrived long before, came out to take my sack on the last lap. The Cusinos had kept a sharp lookout, and when they saw us reappearing had set to work on *ravioli* and veal cutlets skewered with bacon and a sage-leaf. It turned out that we had not quite exhausted yesterday's *crème fraîche*, and a couple more *Weldon's Journals* let me pursue Warwick Deeping almost to the beginning of his story.

From a spyhole in the auspiciously frosted window Michael saw clear sky next morning, and got me up early; this was the last day we could hope to cross the col before we had to go home. M. Cusino was much more cheerful when he saw us off at half-past eight; instead of search parties and memorial crosses, he talked now of the quick time we would make. He gave us a key for the cellar of the chalet-hotel on the col, used in extremity as a winter refuge. Madame pressed francs on us, asking if we would kindly renew her *Weldon's* subscription when we got home. The snow was appreciably harder than yesterday, and the tricky bit of wind-slab round the turn into the gorge made us walk very delicately. We had climbed into the sunlight, and saw clearly into the upper valley, with its summer settlement of chalets now showing as humps of snow. A sea of hard snow, pressed into wavy ridges by the wind, took us down to the bridge by the chapel. I turned as I crossed, and looked back astonished at the clear, and beautiful, and known mountains beyond the valley from which we had climbed at last. All the week we had moved in a muffled and constricted world, occasionally seeing the whole way up the slopes immediately containing the valley, our horizon more often limited to the sad leafless willows leaning over the chilly river, itself the one black line in the indeterminate grey of mist and snow. Unconsciously I had come to assume that this was the Alps in winter, and had become as resignedly accustomed to it as, in summer, to the deadening effect of looking at landscapes through dark goggles. Each time one pushes down the glasses, one is astonished and delighted by the sharpness and brilliance that have come flooding back into the world; and now, looking back at the tip of the Albaron against a deep and radiant sky, I shouted with surprise and happiness. The winter was this, as well as warm drinks beside the cows, and tiring trudges up the misty roads: it meant huddling in the villages, but also walking on the tops. With a sudden stab of remorse, I saw that M. Cusino's hopes of skiing on the Évettes glacier were not entirely fantastical.

Where the road stuck a great elbow out above the upper valley, we saw there had been avalanches; so we took a line not far above the gorge, and across the hillside which had once hurled boulders and spattered us with earth. We climbed up quite easily, though carefully; on the backward turn of each zigzag we could see the Charbonnel. We struck the line of the road again after it had passed the tunnels; the snow had drifted steeply all over it. When we came to a hard crusted stretch where the slope fell steeply to the upper gorge, Michael said that it was usual to do this bit on foot. The walking was easy, for though the slope seemed hard to skis, boots broke quickly through the crust to make deep steps; but it was tricky work dragging the skis on a string, for of course they swung down the slope, getting scratched on the rock, and putting a great strain on the green picture-cord on which I was towing them. This cord passed through a ring, made of a pipe-cleaner, attached to the little hole in the tip of the skis. Once, when I had shortened the lead and had them close at heel, the cleaner snapped. I managed somehow to grab the ski before it rushed down to the gorge. We mightn't have had Othon's Grands Charmoz luck in recovering it, either. As it was, this mildly *mauvais pas* cost us about an hour; if we had risked it on skis we should probably have been across in ten minutes, but I might have had a nasty slip, or the crust might have avalanched. We didn't feel we had chosen wrong, but we were glad that we could push on steadily the rest of the way. We crossed the river by the road bridge above the Pont de Neige, and Michael filled the water-bottle. Then we climbed easily on crunchy, honeycomb-patterned snow into the sun again, and to the sudden delightful sight of ski-tracks on the Aiguille Pers. The familiar little peak sat at the head of the view as we climbed. I looked at the stream coming from the *pays désert*, and forgot that the col is sharply to the left, well out of line with the direction from which we had come. So I was startled to look round and see the snow saddle broadening out, and the chalet-hotel, with smoke from a chimney, and skis stacked outside! I could have shouted hurrah; the days of misty little runs in the valley had made me disbelieve we could really cross the pass.

It was 2.30, and we had taken six hours over the thousand-metre rise from Bonneval. There would be barely two hours' more daylight, so after twenty minutes for Kendal Mint-cake we started down, my skins wound neatly round me as a sort of cummerbund or jerkin. My sack was still heavy, but I now had confidence—I had got up, so I could get down. Also, yesterday's fiasco had forced me to find the attitudes and motions in which I would not be the plaything of my load. The first stage was delightful, easy gradients down the upper valley, with always a mound on the other side of a trough to check the running if it seemed too fast. We got very quickly to the half-way house and the open slope above the Isère. One of the skiers from the col caught me up and joined Michael ahead; I tried to follow his line, but when I realized that at every turn I fell, I threw dignity to the winds and did standing kick-turns. Somehow I managed to keep ahead of the rest of the party; pride was gratified, and I told myself that but for my sack I would have done real turns. The hamlet of Le Fornet jumped a move closer every time I looked up; the last gentle field down was so nice an ending to the run that I boldly took its mild slopes direct, and landed in a heap behind a garden fence beside a startled pig. This made about eleven falls in the hour from the top of the col; by my standard, I was not too displeased.

In perfect happiness and satisfaction we jogged down beside the line of willow wands which marked the track to Val d'Isère. On the corner of the hillside where the road came down from Le Joseray were hundreds of skiers; at least so it looked to eyes fresh from the solitudes of the valley of the Arc. Michael went on ahead to announce our arrival at the Galise; he came back on foot to meet me at the entrance to the village. I proudly kept on my skis, a most hazardous undertaking as the path consisted of frozen ruts a foot deep, and seemed four times as steep as ever it had been in summer. There, at the door of the Galise, was Pierre Rond, rotund with extra jerseys and unsurprised as ever. 'Thought we might be seeing you about now,' he said, and helpfully kicked my heavy toes to get the boots out of the skis. Last summer's waiter shook us by the hand and brought us tea, biscuits, bread, and jam. Everywhere were gay and noisy young men and women. Arriving with a dash from the practice slopes, stopping themselves with a deft half-turn just at the front door; turning on the gramophone; tinkering with the wireless; singing American dance tunes; shouting across the *salle* and laughing. A white-faced little boy of six came in with his mother and sat at the next table for his evening bowl of soup: 'Maman, j'ai fait trente kilomètres.' He really meant metres, *maman* explained.

Upstairs we discovered Mme Rond, who was now doing the housework, and had no time for novelettes. I helped her with our beds, and heard about Val d'Isère's first big winter season. Sixty people they had had in the Galise over Christmas and New Year, she exclaimed; many of them had to sleep out. We had more local gossip from M. Boch at the Parisien over the Cinzanos which he insisted on standing us. He had had a hundred and fifty over the Fêtes, and was anxious that the road to Tignes should run under tunnels right through the gorge, so that it could be kept open for cars all winter. Now avalanches blocked it, and all supplies, and half the visitors, had to be sledge-hauled from Tignes. The Hôtel des Glaciers had even had to bring up half its extra beds by sledge! Like Pierre Rond, M. Boch was surprised and congratulatory at our crossing of the col; no one had been over for six weeks, it appeared. He wanted to know what it was like in Bonneval and Bessans, and if they were having many visitors. He found our answers reassuring.

The Galise did us well at dinner, which began with delicious cold cauliflower in a piquant sauce; hut noisy card parties drove us over the humpbacked bridge to coffee at the Glaciers. The hotel was nearly empty again, and Mme Bonnevie was tired; too much noise and scurry with these winter crowds, she said; she preferred an easier tempo. I spent a restless night, dreaming of our day, then waking and thinking about it, while the man overhead chucked boots round his room.   After breakfast we went round to telegraph our safe arrival to M. Cusino, and post back his key. We were startled at the warmth of our welcome from the postmistress, sister to Max Costa the guide.   Last summer we had walked in awe of her.   She had been sharp when we came in for single stamps without the right change, and the telegram from Laura Riding had taken a lot of living down.   But now she shook hands warmly, said she had heard of our crossing of the col, and asked for details to write to her brother, who was as usual spending the winter months as electrician at the Odéon in Paris.   There was not a trace of sourness except when she described the morning when a hundred skiers came in for stamps; at this point in came a pretty, very lipsticked girl.   Mile Costa refused to take a ten-franc note, with a scowl; then smiled as she gave us change when I remembered I wanted another postcard.   Climbers, it now appeared, were decent sober folk compared with the giddy winter sports crowd who demanded postcards, stamps, and stationery in fantastic quantities at absurd hours, and thought nothing of sending three telegrams in one morning.   We felt that perhaps this approval had more to do with the hours necessarily kept by climbers than with their innate virtues, but we said nothing to check the unusual flow of praise.

The young men had already gone out when we came into the Galise, but the girls were breakfasting in their dressing-gowns and playing the gramophone—they couldn't face the practice slopes till the sun came on them, they said, and put on another record. We said good-bye to the Ronds, thinking it wise to retire with dignity to Tignes and not spoil our reputation as intrepid skiers by giving ourselves away on the nursery slopes.

The sun was up as we walked down to the gorge, and behind the Pourri the sky was the wonderful deep blue of a Poussin landscape.   The winter track followed the line of the old road, which is deserted and overgrown in summer, but comes into its own again in winter because it avoids the line of the avalanches, which then completely block the new motor road.   In the gorge it was still dark and the surface was icy; but we came into sunlight where the valley opens out, and ran happily down through the fields into Tignes. The slopes behind the village were alive with skiers, and after we had dumped our sacks at the Grande Sassière, we passed a large group of Chasseurs Alpins, leaning on their ski-sticks and listening to a lecture from a young lieutenant. We pottered happily about the slopes on the little col towards Les Brevières. Here, too, the path was marked by willow wands, and three peasants trudged doggedly up on foot in the deep soft snow. Michael set me a course, and said any fall over six must be paid for in Cinzano at the Sassière; I had only four, and felt cocky. Cockier still, after lunch, when I picked out little mounds and hummocks to run down direct, whiz round, and jump from, till a too ambitious turn landed me as hopelessly twisted and tied as any tyro in one of Samivel's skiing pictures. I couldn't get my legs apart; I couldn't see where I could begin to untwist and heave up. Luckily Michael was near, but I couldn't tell him which boot belonged to which leg. I seemed to be sitting on one binding and the other was frozen stiff, so that a tug might have dislocated my knee; he had to unlace my boots before I could be sorted out. Humiliation, warning, and a torn trouser-seat!

The drive down to Bourg in the dark on slippery roads with snow falling was less hazardous than we feared. At the Hôtel des Voyageurs Mme Marin-Laflèche gave us caviare, but was all reproaches that we hadn't telephoned our coming, for then there would have been partridge too. Next morning the Gare Saint-Lazare was crowded with other returning British skiers, mainly from Austria; most of the girls wore dark skiing trousers, fur jackets, and smart hats. They laughed and shouted jokes about someone's spill on the slalom course, and the second-class test. I no longer envied them their central heating and practice slopes presumably free from avalanches; they had enjoyed themselves hugely, but after the journey of two days ago I would not have exchanged any holiday for ours.

II

The first joke was against us, when we met William Empson at Victoria next December. We had impressed on him that there must he no suit-cases or overcoats to clog our plans; but in spite of this we had allowed ourselves a small cheap attaché case that could be jettisoned without remorse. Bill eyed it, and our bulging sacks, and asked, with no irony whatever: 'What *have* you got in them?' His own sack flapped almost empty on his back, and his only spare clothes were his Japanese ski-skins and a pair of rabbit-fur ear-muffs which he had bought from a newspaper boy in Tokyo.

No mistakes were made about the train this year, and we arrived in Bourg Saint-Maurice near midnight, after stopping at Chambéry to buy skis for William, show him the four magnificent stone elephants, back to back, and dine at a favourite restaurant of Michael's. From the street of Bourg next morning we could see the snowy tops quite plainly; the Pourri was sparkling white from top to bottom as we went up by bus to Tignes. While Michael and I picked out all our landmarks, Bill drew Buddhas in the neat squared note-book he had just bought. The long puppy ears, the almond eyes, the faintly asymmetrical face—one could get the general impression even on a jolting bus. At the Grande Sassière at Tignes, Mme Bertoli was a little surprised to see us, nearly a week before Christmas. The hotel was in undress, with the red check curtains not yet up in the café; floors were being scrubbed and rooms aired, in preparation for the guests expected in a few days. But an elegant and excellent lunch was produced in half an hour, and Mme Bertoli cheerfully agreed to keep our small case while we went up to the hotel by the lake. With her jaunty scarves and her gay make-up she introduced a note of slightly foreign chic into the village scene, but she was always kind and helpful, and once, when the hotel was burstingly full, and Michael arrived late, she took the trouble to rig him up some sort of mattress in the *garage des skis*.

I stress these small points because 'the inn at Tignes' once had a bad name in Alpine literature. There is Charles Weld, who

arrives in 1849 after a twenty-mile walk from Lanslebourg over
the Col de l'Iseran Next morning he comes down to breakfast.
"'Ah, sir!" said the host, rubbing his hands, "I shall be able to
give you a capital *déjeuner à la fourchette*. See, sir," he added,
holding before me an animal freshly decapitated and skinned,
which my defective comparative-anatomy education led me to con-
ceive was a hare, "here is a magnificent fellow; see how fat he
is," and he poked his dirty fingers into layers of dingy yellow fat
on the animal's sides. "Ha!" I said, "a very fat hare, I see." "A
hare, sir!" replied M. Bock, starting aside at my profound ignorance.
"No, sir, a cat!—a tom-cat—and as fine a one as ever was seen.'"

Ten years later there is William Mathews, who was led 'into a
den behind called by a playful metaphor the *salle à manger*,' and
fed on soup composed of bad grease and vermicelli, and salted
mutton which he likened to slices of mahogany, cut with a blunt
knife. There is Thomas Blanford who, after good days on the
Dent Parrachée and Grande Motte in 1864, comes down hungry
to Tignes, is kept waiting two hours for dinner, gets 'gruel flavoured
with tallow,' sleeps in a 'den,' and of course is presented with an
extortionate bill.   Thirty years later comes Conway, using even
stronger language: 'I doubt whether all the Alps hold a fouler
inn. No cheesemaker's chalet that ever I entered compared for
filth with this loathsome den,' and he walks an extra seven kilometres
up to Val d'Isère to avoid sleeping there.   Finally, in 1908, the
Rev. W. E. Durham, arriving after a long day on the Pourri, sums
it up with: 'Worse than what we endured would be unendurable.'
The name which thus stinks in the noses of Alpine readers, the
Grand Hôtel des Touristes chez Revial Florentin, is there no more,
and M. Florian (the splendid mayor of Tignes) at the Grande
Motte, and Mme Bertoli at the Grande Sassière, deserve to have
its ghost exorcised.

After lunch we climbed on skis to the Lac de Tignes, now a
beautiful white round, with the homely Motte presiding over it
like the White Queen.   At the chalet-hotel they were in the full
tide of preparations for Christmas visitors, but gave us rooms. The
central heating was magnificent and, at night, too hot.   Next day
on the Col de la Tourne we sat content, and looked at the Sassière,
Tsanteleina, Dôme de la Sache, and Grande Motte, all our summer

mountains, their shapes familiar, their surface newly bright. It was clear that William was much the best skier of the three of us; it leaked out later that he had once passed a Ski Club of Great Britain test (second class), an ordeal regarded with respect as well as amusement by freelances like ourselves. He came down a wide gully of hard snow in a series of linked turns while Michael and I proceeded more cautiously with long zigzags out on the softer snow on the sides. In four or five days of perfect weather, and mostly on good powder snow, we made the most agreeable expeditions, to the Aiguille Percée (with the Géant and the Grandes Jorasses appearing as we reached the ridge), the Col de Fresse, the gap between the Tuf de la Tovière and the Tufs du Paquier. The sun was hot, and we climbed in shirt-sleeves; on one occasion Bill stripped to the waist, then fell into a snow-drift. I learnt to manage the changes from soft snow to hard a bit more handily, to bite into the firm snow with the side of my skis as I climbed across a slippery slope, to check myself on a straight run down by a quick half-turn. But in the hard shadowed gully of the Santel early one afternoon, when we were going over to Val d'Isère by the Col de Fresse and the Col des Grands Prés, I felt I might never have learnt anything at all. The only way I could lose height quickly, I discovered, was to half-fall, half-toboggan down on the back of the skis. The run down the hillside above Le Joseray, and warm soup at the Hôtel de la Galise, restored some self-confidence. Pierre Rond was full of plans for the summer: he thought he would let the Galise and devote all his attention to the hotel on the col—he fancied there would be more buses coming up this season. At the Parisien, M. Boch gave us coffee and told us that he was expecting nearly two hundred people for Christmas and New Year; but on 2nd January, he promised, he could offer us 'des conditions très intéressantes.' We skied down the road to Tignes for shopping and tea at the Sassière. Bill came in with a huge cake of pink soap. 'What on earth do you want that for?' asked Michael, startled. 'We've got plenty.' (He had a piece about the size of a bus-ticket.) Later I had to explain that, looking at postcards in another corner of the shop, I had heard Bill's request but had not felt able to intervene. With firmness and dignity, he had demanded 'savon pour les dents.'

The shopkeeper was puzzled, produced an ordinary cake of soap. 'Non, savon POUR LES DENTS,' with increased emphasis. So he fetched the vast pink cube. Tooth-paste was procured before we started up to the lake, but Bill still maintained that the soap would come in handy.

I wanted more practice in turns, and on hard snow, so next day I let Bill and Michael go off to the glacier at the foot of the Motte, while I went up and down the slope to the second cross on the way to the Col de la Tourne. At dinner time the porters came staggering up with luggage—one man, incredibly, had a cabin trunk strapped on his back; another carried a four-year-old sleepy child, papoose-like in her bundles. The owners of the burdens struggled up behind, mostly on skis, one or two middle-aged women on snow *raquettes*. The hotel was filling up. The *garçon* now appeared in a white coat, and contrived a natty little bar with a few planks, high stools, and red oilcloth, at the corner of the *salle*. At the end of a nice afternoon's practice I was persuaded by a young Frenchman to take the last steep slope to the footbridge direct. Slightly against my better judgement I did so, and collapsed, exactly in the middle of the single plank, by a mercy, and not in the black water below.

Bill and Michael had found their glacier very windy, and had run down to the Col de Fresse, and over it to reach the Val d'Isère at La Daille. Running down in semi-darkness, Michael had seen a wall loom up in front, had swerved sharply, caught his skis in the top of a bush, and turned a double somersault. No bones were broken, but something was wrong with his knee-cap, and wisely deciding to get home before the joint had time to stiffen, he had dragged himself down to Tignes, and up to the lake, but it was clearly most painful. Next day the knee was stiff and swollen, and we left him in bed, in charge of Madame, an *ancienne infirmière* whose plump, cheerful, and competent appearance banished any mistaken associations of the ancient and infirm. Bill and I repeated the run he had done yesterday with Michael, up to the Motte glacier, in a cold wind, and in shadow; then back to the Col de Fresse, and in sunlight to the valley—a heavenly run on powder snow. We lingered over coffee at the Sassière, and it was quite dark when we started our climb back to the lake. Coming out on the slopes above the trees, white in the moon, I heard the church bells below ringing for Christmas Eve, and saw gay red lights at the Hôtel de la Grande Motte. Over the brow of the slope dashed four helter-skelter figures—porters, snowploughing so extremely on the icy path that their skis seemed to make one continuous straight line. By this time the walk up at night had become transformed from a tiresome necessity to a magical moment of pleasure. We were now well enough trained not to feel the effort of climbing, and experience had shown the best ways of dealing with the awkward hard slope up from the stream in the woods (side-stepping), and with the wind-blown stretch above the chalet at the upper bridge. We could move upwards with no conscious effort (and yet in little more than half the time of the first afternoon's wearisome ascent), and the attention was set free to notice the shadows of the trees, the pattern of crystals on the moonlit slope, the lights of chalets under the Sassière when a zigzag brought the other side of the valley into view; to hear the steady upward swish of the skis, the creak of hard-pressed snow, the scrunch under the ski-sticks, the occasional slide or plop of snow from the branches, melted in that day's sun, and underneath all the roar of the unfrozen torrent.

We found Michael still stiff, but cheerful and ready for the great Christmas dinner. His day in bed had been a good preparation, for the feast began at 8.45 and went on till 11. There was a delicious cold clear pink soup; lobster and mushrooms on little dishes; a macédoine of vegetables with artichokes, carrots, and peas; turkey, with chestnuts and olives cooked in its juice; cheese; and a great ice-pudding borne in by a beaming chef, along with *Palmières*, puzzling on the menu, but simple when we saw the wafers stamped with 'H. & P.' There were forty-five people now in the hotel, and the noise was tremendous. With coffee in the *salle* came a Christmas tree, crackers, streamers, and paper hats; and just before midnight lights were seen on the practice slopes across the bridge. About twelve of the best skiers had gone up with torches and fireworks; with stars and roses exploding above, and brandishing their torches high, they came whizzing down the slope to the bridge, and when they arrived we saw they were wearing enormous comic masks, an old woman, a cheeky sailor, a grinning black. We wished each other a merry Christmas all round.

Still more people arrived, and the practice slopes were beaten hard. Just before Christmas the instructor had appeared, a handsome, fair-haired Austrian with melancholy eyes, and an astonishing range of mountain clothes: white jerkin and green plus-fours, with thick white Arlberg stockings; neat blue trousers clipped in at the ankle, topped by an embroidered sweater; or Mephistophelian in skin-tight black from head to heel. He had a French assistant, from Chamonix. The local guides were either away in winter, like Max Costa, or, like Gunié, self-taught skiers, they occasionally conducted parties on the runs over the cols, without much ambition to do the necessary training for the French Ski Federation's instructor's certificate. We ran into Gunié one day in Tignes, looking exactly the same as he did in summer, in his old tweed suit and battered hat. He looked a little sheepish at being caught shovelling snow on the road, but gave us his usual friendly grin, revealing his three remaining yellow teeth. He explained that he was taking it easy now, but looked forward to the spring snow, and some days on the Motte. From the top to the Col de la Leisse, three-quarters of an hour; from there to La Daille by the Col de Fresse, another three-quarters. There was a good run for you!

Meanwhile, le Professeur Marchhart conducted his classes with obvious efficiency on the practice slopes. I knew I ought to join one, but in this heavenly weather it was hard to keep off the hills, and two days after Christmas Michael decided that although he could not walk he could ski (you don't have to straighten your leg so much in skiing). A four-day tour round the Col de la Vanoise and the Col de la Grande Casse—that was what was wanted, he said. Bill and I thought this a drastic cure, but Michael put himself right by leading us all the way up to the Col de la Leisse on the morning of 28th December. We had another perfect day. Behind us were our summer mountains, the Tsanteleina beautiful as ever with a shining crown, but throwing long and pointed shadows towards the candid Sassière. And when I looked back just below the col, there was the *gros Mont Blanc*, its rocky ridges giving now, by their blackness, some idea of their immensity. Over the col it was an easy run down the Vallon de la Leisse, and we thought with some satisfaction of the slow and stifling plod it must be, either way, in summer; the four skiers whom we met, who had started from Termignon early that morning, looked hot and weary enough. About seven kilometres down the valley we stopped to eat. 'What's puzzling me,' said Bill, 'is what you do if you have to spend the night out. Richards says that you can dig a hole with your skis and——' 'We're not going to spend a night out,' said Michael. 'Or there's the igloo technique,' Bill went on. 'There's a man eating my dinner,' said Michael, 'come on.' 'Yes, yes, of course,' Bill answered, fixing his bindings; 'you're the officer type. Now, when the war comes, I shall rush for the ranks'.

Just below our halting-place the valley begins to bend to the left; if we followed it down to Entre deux Eaux we should have to climb up again on the steep slopes straight ahead. It would mean 300 metres extra climbing, and a considerable danger of avalanche. So we decided to contour across, keeping up on the right-hand side of our valley, on the lower slopes of the Grande Casse, and so reach the Col de la Vanoise direct from where we stood. All the same, we had to cross three avalanche tracks, where the spilt snow had frozen into hollow skulls, broken auk's eggs, and monstrous white roses. It was finicky work, treading over them on skis. Further on, where the slope went straight down to the gorge, we had to kick sideways into the hard steep snow at every step. Michael found that nerving himself to do it was rather more exhausting than the pain on the bad knee itself: 'It's like deliberately hitting your thumb with a hammer every three seconds. It isn't the pain that tires you; it's just the repeated effort to force yourself to do it once more.' Up in the long and shadowed corridor of the Col de la Vanoise the wind had laid bare great patches of grass, and it was hideously cold; mercifully the Félix-Faure refuge was open.

This hut, from which we had fled so eagerly two summers before, had not seemed to promise a cosy ending to a day of winter travel, however geographically convenient. But the minute we stepped in we saw it had been transformed. In summer it had been dirty, dark, and cold; now, in the fading light of a December afternoon, it was airy, clean, and warm. The stove was giving a steady heat that was apparent two benches away; upstairs, there were piles of blankets neatly folded on each mattress in the dormitory. The reason for the improvement was obvious—a new guardian, a man from Chamonix, who understood that the hut existed to serve the needs of mountain travellers. At once he had our wet clothes on a line, and was courteously offering us the choice of thirty pairs of clogs in exchange for our boots. There had been a heavy fall of snow in October, he said, but little since then. The hut had only been opened before Christmas, and he had not so far had many people staying. Later in the spring he hoped to organize a Pralognan to Chamonix tour, with himself as leader, and the Félix-Faure as the first stage on the way.

So snug it was that we decided to spend a second night there, and enjoy a day unburdened by sacks up on the Glacier de la Réchasse. It was a steep climb up, but the glacier itself was smooth as a table-cloth, and gently sloping. We pottered across to the Signal du Dard, and the saddle below. ('Ce col offre cette particularité singulière de ne pas toujours exister,' instructed Michael, quoting Gaillard.) We kept on stopping to look at Mont Blanc, the Paradiso, Monte Viso, and, across the trough of the Col de la Vanoise, the Grande Casse, bearing on its dark and rocky shoulders the great Glacier des Grands Couloirs.

For all the sun, the cold wind drove us down soon after lunch. With angry shame I did endless kick-turns on the 300-metre drop from the glacier to the hut. There was a slalom practice in progress on the slopes behind, with the guardian's boy streaking and doubling between the markers and making the other two skiers, themselves skilled by our standards, look like beginners. The sunset poured pink down the Glacier des Grands Couloirs; the twisting, turning skiers stood out sharp against a greeny sky.

'Do you know any propositions of the form A is B,' said Bill suddenly after dinner, putting down his beer glass. 'God is love, beauty is truth, might is right,' answered Michael promptly. 'Yes—I want to know what the verb "to be" means there. The *Oxford Dictionary* is interesting, but it misses the point. Love is God, truth is beauty, right is might, are quite different propositions. I want to analyse the A is B form. I think there's a book in it.' 'What about A is A?' asked Michael. 'Business is business, boys will be boys. The odd thing is that they aren't tautologies.' 'Yes, that's a new class,' said Bill, getting out his Bourg Saint-Maurice note-book with the Buddhas in it. I listened placidly—'time is money' seemed to be giving them a new kind of difficulty—but the voices grew fainter and fainter. I yawned my way to bed; but woke up to help Bill complete Yeats's *Byzantium*. How the transition had been made, I do not know.

The other skiers, bound for the Dôme de Chasseforêt, were out of the dormitory early; we left at 8.30, burdens on our backs, for the Col de la Grande Casse and a back door down to Champagny. We were soon up the glacier and put on the rope, but the crevasses were hidden, and after a time Bill asked: 'What have we got this rope on for?' 'There are a lot of big holes below us, and we might go through,' answered Michael, who thought it was always wise to stick to Basic English when explaining mountaineering technique to Bill. It was an impressive walk up the smooth glacier, with the black cliffs of the Grande Casse on our right and the yellow rock of the Lepéna on our left. Gradually the two walls drew closer together until only a few yards separated them. A narrow snowy col hung between them. It is just over 3,000 metres above sea-level, so we had come up more than 500 from the Félix-Faure, and with very little trouble. Not knowing what kind of snow we would find on the other side of the col, we kept on our skins, and the rope, and skied down cautiously on the glacier, avoiding an ice-fall, and twisting neatly round some large open crevasses. We were delighted to find that we could turn without being tripped up or pulled over by the rope. We could now see well into the Champagny valley, and the village of Le Bois stood out plain. How to reach the valley was not so clear, for all the helpful directions of the guardian of the Félix-Faure. On the ski-map the red line swung down confidently; it did not show us how to avoid the little outcrops of cliffs that we guessed, from the general line, must interrupt the snow. The sky was cloudy, and we lunched coldly and briefly at 12.30—the wine was frozen in the bottle and even the bread tasted cold in our mouths. Then we started running down, unroped, in cautious zigzags on the hard snow. At one point we had to cross the top of a steep slope that ended abruptly in a drop. Very suddenly, as I seemed to he moving nicely, I slipped sideways; my skis had not bitten into the snow at all, and I found myself diving head first down the slope. I did not think at all about being dashed on the rocks below, but I did wonder very much if one ski would catch; it seemed likely then that I might break a leg. I turned two somersaults, slowed down a little, saw I was coming to a point at which the slope eased off for a moment, and managed to stop myself. I was quite unhurt. In a second I had my skis off, and was scrambling up to retrieve my cap, my hair-ribbon, and one ski-stick that had come off my wrist on the way. Only later did I realize that there was something funny in hopping so confidently half way up a slope down which I had so lately hurtled. Michael and Bill had hurried down to join me. They too seemed to find the slope much easier once the air had become charged with real excitement. But it was a nasty slope, and looking back up it I asked Bill why he had come down. 'Oh, I wanted to be in at the death, you know,' he explained.

Anyway I had lost height quickly, and that was all to the good. We now had to go down a series of steep narrow couloirs. Bill kept on doing patient zigzags from side to side; Michael and I went down most of the way on foot, towing our skis. There was a final slope to be crossed before a big and shallow gully, which would clearly take us without difficulty to the valley bottom. The snow looked steep, soft, and slidy, exactly the sort of slope that did not show me at my best in summer, and now I had no nails in my boots. 'What are you waiting for?' shouted Michael, half way across, as I stood and boggled at it. Then half in exasperation, half with the feeling that because I had fallen I needn't be afraid of falling, I decided to walk like a man and not dither like a tourist or a goat. Of course it worked. I strode across as if it had been the heather slopes of Benachie—indeed it was in no way more difficult—and found that one effort of the will could banish the old bogy of the snow slope; but the fall helped too.

Down at the Chalets de la Plagne, after a warming last lap down on skis again, the work seemed as good as over. We had come down our 1,000 metres from the col, and had nothing to do but follow the valley down to Champagny. I, at any rate, forgot that there was another 500 metres' height yet to be lost. To begin with, the running was fairly easy, but over the two or three hard patches where the slope fell straight to the gorge on our left, I edged my skis in fervently. Michael was getting tired of the long struggle with his crippled knee, and he couldn't stamp hard enough with his right leg to get a grip of the slope. This meant a lot of taking skis off and putting them on again, and now, between four and five, the light began to go. Luckily, while we could just see, we hit some tracks of ski and foot; at the valley step, where the summer path zigzags steeply, even Bill went down on foot, and we reached the empty hamlet of Laisonnay in fairly good order. But it was quite dark now, and we had carelessly not noticed that the map told us to cross the river here. Knowing there was a footpath in summer on the right bank, we stubbornly stuck to it.

Soon we were in difficulties; huge ribs of hillside blocked the way, only to turn into gentle banks. Abysses yawned black; careful prodding with a ski-stick revealed nothing more than a ditch, four feet deep. However innocent, these obstructions took their toll of time and resolution; we progressed painfully and slowly. Worst of all, when the moon came out from the clouds, there was a double line of fence, that could only mark the level road-on the other side of the black stream. But it was too late to go back. We were forced to keep close by the river, then got involved in the frozen debris of an avalanche. Bill and I struggled across; Michael, utterly tired, paused half way to rest. We took off our skis, and went back to help him with his. After lying listless a moment or two, he struggled across the lumps and holes while we followed, each towing a ski on a string and, once more across, again put on our own. The best chance for Michael's knee seemed to be to let him hobble along on foot; he certainly went ahead now with new energy. Bill managed his extra burden well; I stuck for ages at the foot of what seemed an enormous slope. Every time I stepped sideways up it, the ski brought down the soft snow and ended on the level it had begun. I dropped a ski-stick; back to the beginning. Michael's towed ski danced and jibbed. At last I was up; it must have been at least six feet! Nervously I started running down the other side; how absurd it seemed to have all this fuss and bother when we had really reached the valley. We had won, and these extra obstacles were nothing but spite. I shouted; no answer; but the ground seemed to level out, and the gleam that I had reckoned was a star appeared clearly as a light in a house, close at hand! This was the hamlet of Friburge, the last above Le Bois, and here was Bill waiting on the bridge. Michael must be on ahead. The road was now beaten hard and icy, so we took off our skis for the last time. I carried mine, Bill both his own and Michael's, the weight making him lurch across the track. More lights shone gaily down the valley, then round a corner we saw a new cluster, nearer: Champagny at last, and I cheered in my heart, though I was too tired to make a sound. Less heavily burdened, I went on ahead, and roused all the sleeping dogs of the village. 'Bon soir, monsieur,' said the dogs' owners, when they came out to stop the row.

At the inn I found that Michael, who had had qualms of conscience about leaving us to carry his skis all the way along the level road, had used his time and talents to good advantage. He had announced, brazenly and incorrectly, that it was my birthday, and that if Madame could by any chance make a special effort at this unreasonable hour . . . Then, not at all sure that the Hôtel Ruffier, even on its mettle, could do very much at eight o'clock on a night in midwinter—they had been startled enough at the arrival of any traveller, especially one from the head of the valley—he had knocked up the village shop. It had been shut, and the shopkeeper in bed; but he had come down in his shirt and trousers when he heard the knocking, let Michael take his choice of raisins, figs, chocolates, sardines, and biscuits, and made not the least difficulty when Michael remembered that I had all the money. No doubt we should be here till morning, he had said, and gone back to bed. We were surprised it was still as early as eight, for we seemed to have been struggling in the dark for half the night, but three hours and a half after sunset was a reasonable bed time for Champagny.

I had looked forward to Ruffier's hotel, as to the Félix-Faure refuge, with no particular pleasure. There were chilly memories of that best parlour in which we had eaten our dinner last summer after the struggle down the wrong way from the gorges. But once again we were pleasantly surprised, and realized that winter travel had its own advantages. We were shown into the comfortable café, next the kitchen, and well warmed by its stove; *la p'tite mam'selle*, one of the little girls we had seen off to help with the hay five months ago, gravely stood and watched us change our wet clothes. A very creditable meal, with fried veal cutlets as the mainstay, arrived from the kitchen: we supplemented it with Michael's dainties from the shop. After doing justice to *vin ordinaire*, we decided that our day had earned us a bottle of Seyssel. Bill, entering into the birthday spirit, made one of his rare excursions into the French language. 'Café complet,' he demanded, and *café complet* duly arrived. (Encouraged by his success at Champagny, he worked up to a magnificent last holiday order in Paris on our way home. After studying the long menu in the restaurant off the Boulevard Saint-Germain, 'Garçon,' he declaimed with a great commanding gesture, 'un canard complet!')

The good things came to an end. Showing me into a freezing hell of a bedroom, Madame explained that she had given us no water as it would be ice in two minutes, but there were two *bouillottes*. I found that they, and my own body, warmed the patch on which they lay, but if I rolled one inch either way it was to find sheets stiff as a board.

After we had paid our bill at the shop next morning, and waxed our skis, we fell into chat with an old woman in the black dress of the Tarentaise, voluminous over extra clothes, sitting on a cart outside the inn. She asked us where we came from, and was astonished that people should come to Champagny from as far away as England. How much had the skis cost? I answered hastily with the price of Bill's, bought at Chambéry, by far the cheapest of the three pairs; suddenly I felt ashamed that mine had cost what would have kept the old lady in black dresses and tisanes for the rest of her days. But she made no complaint at this inequitable division of material goods. Clearly, she thought it odd that any one should come to Champagny in winter—should actually *pay* to come to Champagny in winter—to slide about on boards. But with a great gesture of tolerance and understanding, she summed it all up: 'Enfin, c'est toujours une distraction!'

For us the distractions began all too soon. While the old lady jogged merrily on her seat of sacks down the road to La Chiserette, we were painfully climbing up the zigzag path to the high pastures—the path we should have taken down last summer. The snow suddenly gave out, and there was nothing for it but to shoulder our skis up those bare wind-swept patches of path. At one point I could hardly have staggered further if Michael had not come back to take my skis. On the pastures things went better, though once we found ourselves having to kick into the slopes on our right, the hard way for Michael's knee. It was hot work up to the Col de la Chiauppe, but the minute we sat down to eat the wind developed a sting. Here we were on the ridge of the Sommet de Bellecôte, away to our right; and below us was the Peisey valley, our object for to-night. We began our run down on a mixture of hard and powder snow, according to the slope. Where the valley falls abruptly I took off my skis and plunged gaily down; Michael walked too, more slowly; Bill indefatigably zigzagged. As I waited for them, I found myself looking at a dome high in the air; suddenly I grasped that it was Mont Blanc. I should have enjoyed the next stretch down very much, from the Chalets de l'Arc, if the light had not been fading, muffling the contours, and making the skis surprise me by their sudden plunges up and down on snow that looked dead level. At the empty chalets of Les Bauches the ski-tracks began, any number of them: Peisey must be having a winter season. The path through the woods was beaten to an icy chute; I took off my skis without shame, so did the others; towed on a short string, they clattered and slithered, but came down docilely enough. Now, through the trees, the lights glimmered away in the Isère valley, below Bourg Saint-Maurice; then we saw them in Peisey, a little below us; then in Nancroit, just across the stream. At the Hôtel Tarentaise they thought for a moment they were full, but after dinner rooms were found. It was 31st December, and the other visitors may have seen the new year in duly, but we never knew; by nine o'clock we were dead asleep.

The hotel had a handy, warm ski-garage, with an iron, so we got well waxed before starting on our last stage over the Col du Palet and back to the Lac de Tignes. We had a pleasant walk up the valley past the empty summer hamlets of Les Lauches, Les Bettières, and La Gura. After this there was a steep climb to the upper valley; a hard slope, with here and there a muddle of frozen avalanche debris. In summer, one would be up the path in ten minutes; to-day we took an hour. Altogether we took five hours to the Lac de Plagne. Mont Blanc de Peisey seemed to dog us on our right, and it took a great effort to push it well behind. We ate quickly, above the frozen lake, for we wanted to be well over the col before the light went. The last stretch was easy going. I was fascinated by this humpy, downy country at the back of everything. It was difficult to see where the actual col was, with a small mound or ridge always starting up when we thought we could see a way clear; but there were now plentiful ski-tracks. I got up first, on tiptoe for the run down. When Bill arrived, I asked him what line to take, as he had once been up this way by himself from the Lac de Tignes. 'Oh, it's all the same, don't you know,' he said, with an airy wave of his ski-stick over the bowl-shaped depression on the Tignes side. Only after we had come down a bit of horridly hard snow did he remember, to our considerable and expressed annoyance, that of course there was delightful powder over to the right. After this the only worry was the light; otherwise the slopes down to the lake gave a perfect ending to our winter journey.

Long ago I had learnt from W. P. that the pleasure of a whole mountain day is always greater than any of the separate incidents of rock or snow, however exhilarating. Now in the same way I knew that this extreme pleasure of rushing downhill (even the extremer, and rarer, pleasure of rushing downhill in perfect control) was only an incident, and not the whole for which we had travelled all the way from England to Champagny. That whole was still the same as in the summer mountains; it was still the sequence of motions and rhythms, moods and sensations, in their constant variety and interplay; it was still strength and skill, intelligence and feeling, all stretched and all satisfied on a long day of mountain travel.

Back in the hotel by the lake two young men came up to ask us about the route to the Motte glacier. They treated us with respect because we went high on the mountains; I looked on them with admiration because they swung down the beaten path to the valley in a brilliant whisk of stem-christies, and took the narrow bridge direct. I knew which of the two branches I preferred; but there seemed no reason why one shouldn't do both. Next year, I resolved, I would begin with proper lessons.

CHAPTER VIII

AN END AND A BEGINNING

That more esteemeth mountains as they are
Than if they gold or silver were.

I

IN 1937 the Alps existed for me only on the postcards which arrived
from Michael in the Tarentaise and Dauphiné. He took the school
party this year to Bonneval, and along with the ropes and ice-axes
went a sheaf of fashion papers for Mme Cusino. (The French-speaking
climbers were kept busy translating knitting instructions.) They did
the Méan-Martin, Western Levanna, and the by now traditional Aiguille
Pers; then Max Costa came over from Val d'Isère and with him they
did the Ciamarella (but not by the Col de Chalanson), the Albaron,
and the Charbonnel, though robbed of the last hundred metres by
a new fall of snow. Then with the boys happily dispatched from
Modane, Michael and Denis Hardie climbed in one day from the stuffy
valley over the Dôme de Polset and the Aiguille de Polset to the Péclet-Polset
hut; then traversed the Pointe de l'Échelle ('a real Punta Rossa route
on to the summit'), and had a night in the hay at the Plan Sec chalets—'the
usual chalet night—mooings, champings, and bleatings, and the cat kit-
tened just beside Denis.' The Dent Parrachée next day (165 francs),
and the descent from 3,700 metres to 1,100, earned them a taxi ride
for the last six kilometres of road to Modane. Then Denis went home,
and Michael found himself extending his experience as an uncertificated
local guide. At Entre deux Eaux there was a girl anxious to do the
Roc Noir, and up at the Félix-Faure three English schoolmasters who
wanted to plod up the Dôme de Chasseforêt. Then came a good day
on the Aiguille de Lepéna with the young Pralognan guide Robert
Amiez, and when they got back to the hut in walked, with shouts
of recognition, the girl who had fallen off the Pourri at the end of
last season. Michael came back over the Col de Chavière to Modane,
with a party from Marseilles which included a little girl of ten, who
cheered on her nervous mother over the névé at the top.

Othon joined him at Saint-Michel de Maurienne, as usual on the day after the Guides' Feast; from the Commandraut chalets they did the Aiguille Méridionale d'Arves—'rock the worst I've ever met.' Then they climbed the Écrins from La Bérarde (eating a breakfast of strawberry jam and *petit beurre* biscuits in a corner of the bergschrund); and two days later traversed the Meije from the Promontoire hut to La Grave. It was very windy: Michael lost the large black hat that had so enraged the gendarme at Bellegarde, and they came off the rocks—seven hours from hut to hut—with their finger-tips full of cuts. It was Othon's first expedition to the Dauphiné, and on the Aiguilles d'Arves and the Meije they were the only party climbing. He led with all the assurance, speed, and precision that he had shown traversing the Rothorn the year before. There was a new apophthegm: 'Il n'y a rien de difficile pour nous.' The hardest work of the year, though, had probably been in the Caron hut under the Écrins, which they had found empty and disgraceful. Immediately Michael had been sent off to get water. 'By the time I had come back Othon had the tin table outside, the palliasses airing, the blankets spread on the roof, and the pots and pans out for me to scrub. The stove itself had been lugged out, and stood upside down to be cleaned. And when the obvious duties had been done, I was told off to scrape the candle-grease off the tables with an ice-axe.'

Next June we were climbing together again, in Skye. We had a good first day up Sgurr nan Gillean by the Pinnacle ridge, and then two days running we tried to do the Blaven Clach-Glas Garbh-bheinn ridge. The first day mist sent us down from Garbh-bheinn; the second, we tried from the other end, and only reached the top of Blaven by crawling much of the way on hands and knees, with occasional sharp rushes when the wind abated for a moment. On the way up, we had seen it whipping the waters of Loch Coire Uaigneich fifteen feet high; on the way down we saw it blow the water of the burn that goes down to Camasunary, *up* the slope towards the *bealach* at its head. We were blown up that slope too—by stretching out our arms like sails we had only to keep our balance, and allow the wind to do the work. The Mod at Portree was the objective of our third wet day, but the next day promised well, and we took the roomy car that acted as a bus for Glen Brittle. I led Michael up the north-west buttress of Sgurr Sgumain, a delightful climb on the best of rock, enhanced by my relief at discovering that, apparently, being a mother didn't spoil one's balance. We ate our pieces on top, and looked at the islands—Rum, Eigg, Canna, and Muck—so clear that it seemed you could toss your apple core on to them. Then we turned, and saw two men doing Collie's climb on Sgurr Alasdair; it was a pleasure to watch their easy movement up the sky-line. Nearer, another couple were in trouble on the only bad step between Sgumain and Alasdair; one of them fell off as we looked. When we reached them they allowed us to go first, and accepted our offer of a rope. We had looked at the ridge with the Alpine scale in our minds; it was startling to be on Alasdair in twenty minutes instead of the estimated hour. There one of the men who had come up Collie's climb hailed me as a fellow member of the C.A.F. on the strength of the badge on my wind-jacket. We talked about the Dauphiné and Mont Blanc, and the islands spread out on the sea at our feet. We all felt angry about Rum, and the owner who refused to let his tenants take in lodgers; not long ago, it appeared, the tax-collector had been stranded, and the only shelter he could find was the telephone box, in which he spent an upright night. Then off the other pair went with a final reminder: 'And if you *want* an island, Knight, Frank & Rutley have Rockall on their books.'

The couple from the bad step passed us as we sat, but we found them again on the slabs beyond Thearlach. Once more they were glad of a rope to see them down. We were glad to help, but it took a fair amount of time: our rope was not meant for four, so Michael had to descend half way down the pitch, see the party to the bottom, then throw the rope back to me. Coming last down the slabs I felt more sense of responsibility than leading up in the morning; it was pleasantly important. We gave the doubting couple a rope down two more pitches and across the gap watched the good pair in King's Chimney on Mhic Choinnich. The doubters had ideas about following them; tactfully but firmly we pointed to the gathering clouds, and urged them to go home by the stone shoot. We had to go down the other side of the ridge, for the long trek home to Sconser. The best of the day had gone, and the scene

was weird as well as grand when we looked down Loch Coruisk.
It was tedious scrambling down by boulders, grass, and reddish,
pock-marked rock, and worse pulling up again to the long ridge
of Druim nan Ramh.   Mist came down on the top; we luckily
struck the right place down to Harta Corrie, and the endless boggy
path down the Sligachan glen.

It was a good day, and the whole week was a happy prelude
to the Alps.   We were meeting Hughes again for a week in the
Tarentaise; we wanted to do some of the 'forbidden' passes into
Italy, such as the Col Perdu and the Col de Séa.   There was a
lot of bother about passports, and expensive telegrams to Rome,
with no better result than that the consular agent at Modane *might*
have permission for the *conjugi Roberti.*   Of course he never did.
Then on 15th August, the day of the Guides' Feast, we would go
up to Courmayeur, and next day be off with Othon.   'Je ferais
monter beaucoup de confiture au Torino pour Jeannette,' he had
written, 'et du tabac surtout.'   This year, at last, climbs on the
south side of Mont Blanc seemed possible.

Michael went out first, with the boys, leaving me precise instructions how to reach the Péclet-Polset hut from Modane in ten
days' time.   At Victoria he read the news which I had seen earlier
in that day's *Times.*   Othon had been killed.   'On the Col du
Géant' was all we could learn from the report.

On the surface the holiday began as usual.   The school party
went to Entre deux Eaux; Hughes joined them for the last few
days, and was with Michael at Modane to meet me.   In the café
in the square opposite the station they told me about the last
day's climb, a traverse of the Pointe de Vallonet and the Grand
Roc Noir.   They had gone straight up the ice-fall of the Glacier
de Vallonet, cutting up icy canyons, ridges, and turrets; there had
been a delicate traverse on the icy col between the peaks, and a
nice bit of rock to the summit of the Grand Roc Noir.   'An
interesting climb,' said Hughes, adding, with Fell and Rock precision,
'and six feet severe.'   Then, with a touch of bitterness: 'You always
take us up a first-class climb, Michael, but the trouble is that no
one's ever heard of it!'

Remembering the short commons of three years ago, we filled
our packs with supplementary rations to take up to the Averole

hut next day. We got off the bus at Bessans; our packs made us lazy up the valley. I was the worst, and Hughes carried my crampons most of the way. (To his all-purpose home-made trousers he had this year added a capacious wind-jacket with a monkish hood; this turned him at once into Brother Hughes.) We were still lazy next morning; but a clear sky offered no excuse, so we were off for the Charbonnel at 6.30. This time we knew better than to go down the valley to cross the Lombarde, as we had done on that ill-tempered day in 1935. There was a snow-bridge across the Ruisseau d'Arnes, and we expected to find one across the Lombarde. There was no sign of it, so we wandered upstream to the point where a big rock leans over and bridges the gorge—the Pas de la Mule. The climb up the Charbonnel was an uneventful succession of grass slopes and scree. We crossed a shoulder, looked into the desolate dun-coloured Vallon du Ribon that leads straight down to Bessans, passed behind the summit ridge, and found a respectable little chimney that brought us to the top, and a sight of Averole again. As we ate our second lunch, a little cairn along the ridge began to worry us—it *might* be a foot higher—so to lay the Charbonnel ghost once for all we put on the rope for the first time, solemnly trotted a hundred yards round the curved ridge to the indisputably highest point, reversed, and trotted back. We stopped once on the way down to have a good look at the Bessanese, where we hoped to go to-morrow. There was a thin white streak which seemed to stretch all the way from the summit ridge to the glacier, and might be worth looking at. The rest of the descent was a quick business of scree-sliding, glissading on névé, and loping down grass slopes to the valley.

When I, very unusually, got up first next morning and woke the others, there were more groans at the fine day. 'This is Doldenhorn weather, Fellenberg'—even our favourite Alpine quotation could not make us ambitious. Easy pastures, which demanded nothing of one except a sleepy plod, took us up to the Glacier d'Entre deux Ris; we didn't choose a very good way on to it, and spent some time cutting steps. On the other side we breakfasted on some rocks near the foot of the snow couloir that we had marked from the Charbonnel. Mercifully, on the spot it didn't look quite so steep as it had done from a distance, but it was quite steep enough for me. Hughes led up it, kicking or cutting steps that were usually directly above each other, about two feet apart. I forced myself to concentrate as I stood in my step—one foot square in, with my weight on it, the other toe nicked in beside it, the ice-axe driven in and my hands firm on the shaft—waiting my turn to move up: it is so fatally easy to fidget, to let one's fancy stray. But I could tell, almost without looking, that the clouds were massing low over the Charbonnel behind us to our right. There were one or two rock pitches, and once Hughes led us expertly into a wet cave and then out and over the icy bulge above. Snow began to fall lightly. After about two hours of the gully we came out on the main ridge of the Bessanese, north of the summit. The weather was frankly bad, and both Michael and Hughes had difficulty in seeing through their snowy spectacles. Just above us on the ridge was a sharp pinnacle, very like the Razor on the Zinalrothorn, which looked as if it might be a bit of trouble; and just below us, on the Italian side, was an open-work iron cross. We started up in properly sober mood, but soon we could not help enjoying the rocks in spite of the falling snow. We picked up human tracks—a guide's printed card, an old sardine tin, a piece of chocolate paper printed in Italian. The snow stopped, though mist still hid the rest of the ridge. We climbed up, still enjoying ourselves; then in one gust the mist parted, and showed us a cairn and a pole not far ahead. As we went towards it, the mist closed again; we reached one cairn, but with no pole; then a few yards further on we could see another, with a lightning conductor (the pole we had seen) and a Madonna. But between us and it was a cleft; we must be near the reputedly delicate summit traverse that we had read about in Gaillard. Hughes was let down on to the Italian face to prospect a way. He found a piton, and that looked promising, but when he started talking about crawling under an overhang we pulled him up, and Michael took his turn. He was just admitting that this desperate suggestion seemed to be the only possibility, when Hughes spied an absurdly easy ledge on the French side. We had missed it, because the obvious way on to it started a few yards back, when we had been still intent on following the ridge. The rock arête down from the top was perfectly simple—very like the ordinary way down

Sgurr nan Gillean—but thanks to the mist we complicated matters a little by going off on to a rocky spur instead of keeping to the true ridge. We came off the rocks just before they rise again to the Pointe Pareis, and after glissading down a small field of névé, had a most lovely walk in clearing weather round the grassy south-west shoulder of the Bessanese and down the pastures, using a sketchy track that nipped across boiler-plates and sidled along grassy ledges between crumbly cliffs. The air, after rain, was sweet and cool; the green of the pastures came with a rush of delight to eyes newly freed from dark glasses; and, with the familiar click in the ears, hearing also was renewed and sharpened. Climbing up in the early morning, our landmarks had been rocks and mountain-tops; now, the scale had shifted, and we marked our way down by the saxifrage in the rocks, yellow and white, the wavy yellow poppies, the fragile soldanelles, and the small starry gentians, so infinitely sweeter than the overrated flannelly edelweiss.

Michael and I dawdled slowly down, and reached the hut just as the herdsman who came up from the hamlet beneath was calling in the sheep and cattle. Hughes, who had arrived first, was exploiting our position as the hut's oldest inhabitants to ensure us a special dinner; and in due course the *gardienne* produced a very small chicken, for fifteen francs. Hughes's treatment of French reminded me of the jokes about Tommies in France: it was brutal but effective. One noun, naked of all clogging articles, unattended by any trailing phrases, would, when hurled at a waiter or shopkeeper, often produce far quicker results than our murmured idioms. But this effectiveness was matched by an exaggerated respect for our linguistic achievements. After we had sat through a hot afternoon at Aosta eating water-ices, 'I didn't know you knew Italian,' said Hughes with surprise to Michael, who had played every variation of tone on the single word *gelati*.

Next day Michael and Hughes went to have a look at the Baounet glacier, the Croce Rossa, and the Ouille d'Arbeyron. The hut filled up: a guide from Bessans, after asking what we'd done, described our sporting couloir of yesterday (not at all accurately) as 'the north-face climb' of the Bessanese, and made us feel impressive.

In the same misty sort of weather we started off next morning for the Évettes hut over the top of the Albaron. It was fiercely hot on the Glacier du Collerin, but as soon as we got to the top and started eating the sun went in. Mist seeped up as we came down the rock ridge to the Selle d'Albaron and started down the glacier. I fumbled the rope, let it drag, and asked angry questions about the route through the crevasses; in spite of provocations Michael took a very good line, and we were soon on the long path down under the cliffs of the Pic Regaud. It rained. Once, nearing the Évettes hut, we turned, and saw Hughes, his monkish hood up over his face, followed by a long string of black figures. We had seen no one on the mountain, nor on the lower Évettes glacier, and could only conclude that we were being overtaken by our sins. We hastened into the hut to escape them, and with anxiety watched the black dots stealing up on Hughes, who plodded on in ignorance. The path passed behind a rounded hillock; we waited breathlessly for the string to reappear. Then Brother Hughes came in sight again — alone! We had escaped our reckoning and ordered an extra omelette for supper on the strength of it.

New snow put the Pic Regaud out of action next morning: I had hankerings after the Cheminée Meade. We half-heartedly considered alternative plans, but in the end no one did anything. Robert Amiez, the young guide with whom Michael had done the Lepéna the year before, came up with two expansive Frenchmen; he was in high spirits because they were off to the Dauphiné, and he hoped to do the Meije. They were off in a minute, down the valley again, leaving us still puzzled as to why their Dauphiné trip had started with a call at the Évettes. Waking to rain next morning, we threw away our plans to do a high-level route from the Col de l'Iseran to Pralognan, and went down ourselves. We stopped at Bonneval for a gossip with the Cusinos. They had already built an extension to the Hôtel des Glaciers des Évettes, and my only fall of the year was in nailed boots on the bare stone staircase of the annexe, striking sparks as I skidded from top to bottom and most painfully grazing my elbow. Mme Cusino showed off her washing-machine, and was enthusiastic about the English who made such beautiful conveniences.

I hadn't the heart to tell her it was American. M. Cusino produced Asti, and talked politics: he was all for Mr. Eden—*he* knew *la politique*, and what Hitler was clearly up to. Various of Cusino's old friends from Turin and Milan had visited him this summer, from across the Mont Cenis. They thought he might well go back to Italy now; but he preferred to sit snug at the head of the valley.

The hotel was obviously prospering; Cusino (dealing out the Asti with generous hand) outlined further plans for attracting tourists to Bonneval. Other innkeepers in the valley were less sanguine, and doubts were heard in Bessans and Lanslebourg about the *congés payés* instituted by the Front Populaire which were beginning to have their full effect this year. The doubts seemed to arise, not from any wish to deny industrial workers their holiday, but from a deep-seated reluctance to make tourism too important a part of the economy of these Alpine valleys. Within the last two years, hotels had sprouted like mushrooms at Val d'Isère; but, in the opinion of many, there was no guarantee that before the mortgages were paid off the fickle stream of tourists would not have been diverted elsewhere, or that outside events would not have dried up the flow. It was wholly natural that Cusino, an outsider with a place to make for himself, should be exploiting the new tendencies; others in the valley, able to view the situation with a longer perspective, had their doubts. At Valloire, so Michael had learnt the year before, they had refused to sell land belonging to the commune for another ski-ing hotel. 'There were some who wanted to accept,' the mayor had told him: 'twenty thousand francs is a good round sum, you know, but I saw to it that we turned it down. It only means one cow more or less in the commune, perhaps, but that goes on, and that's our life. Whereas twenty thousand francs, what can you do with that? Put it in a bank, or speculate. And these new hotels: they get their provisions up from Albertville or Saint-Jean de Maurienne; they get servants from Lyons or Turin. If they buy milk from us, it's at the same price as the combine would buy it anyway. And the tourists spend their money in the little *boutique* run by the woman from Saint-Jean. Two or three dozen more tourists trapesing through our fields—it doesn't do much harm—I've nothing against tourism—but it doesn't do us any good either. So we've said no.'

Somehow Cusino procured a taxi to take us as far as Lanslebourg, and a protracted lunch, then there was the hard-seated tram to Modane. We dumped our things at the hotel by the station and trailed back up the long road by the marshalling yards to buy puttees in the town, and some provisions, on the chance that it might be fine next morning. But no, the mist was hanging low. We decided to cut our losses and find some sun, and after half an hour's brisk work consequent on this decision, ending with a hurdle race through the customs shed hallooed on by the bored Italian guards, we got the train for Turin. We came out of the Mont Cenis tunnel into blue sky; it had been the right choice.

Soon from the train windows we saw the smart cylindrical hotels, familiar to us from Othon's postcards; it was Sestrières, where he had spent his winters. So far, the holiday had followed a familiar pattern—the mild explorations and late returns of our Tarentaise expeditions, the welcomes from our friends in the mountain huts and village inns. It was hard to believe in the reality of that newspaper paragraph, or of that deeply-black-edged announcement from Courmayeur, sent on behalf of Brons and Olliers, Proments and Petigaxes. Now, travelling into Italy, we began to understand that all the pleasant days behind us had been in a sense a postponement of the moment when we should have to realize the greatness of our loss.

This was 14th August, and next morning the train up the valley from Aosta was crowded with holiday people going up to Courmayeur for the guides' feast. I had to sit with my arms round the white flowers I was taking to Mme Bron, to protect them from the shoving and the heat: it was impossible to get to the window for the first sight of Mont Blanc. The Droguerie had been sold the year before, but the Brons still had the house behind. We found Mme Bron in the back room where we had written in Othon's guide's book and laughed with him over the Samivel drawings. This is the story she told us.

Othon had been up at the Col du Géant for several days; about the 15th July he had come rushing down to Courmayeur, because he had dreamt that Horace was dead. On the 24th he did the Géant three times, meeting the second and third parties at the foot of the rock. That night he told his brother, now guardian of the Torino, that he wanted to settle his account; and next morning he started for the Montanvert with two young Italians. One was a young student of nineteen from Rome, the other was about twenty-four; neither had done much climbing before. There was some new snow on the Glacier du Géant, and the going was fairly tricky; twice Othon went into small crevasses up to his waist. They were near the séracs when he stopped and lit a pipe, saying there was just one more stretch, and the worst would be over. Almost immediately he stepped on to a snow-bridge (tested already with his axe), and it broke; he sprang for the further side, just failed to reach it (he had a heavy sack), and fell; his two clients tightened the rope, but while Othon was still swinging it was cut by a blade of ice in the crevasse itself. He fell forty metres. The two young men called for help; the Requin hut wasn't far off. For over an hour Othon lay there conscious, talking; the two men did not like to go near the lip of the crevasse, so they could not hear what he said, though at one moment it sounded as if he were praying. Men arrived from the hut; the first was a porter from Courmayeur. Othon heard his voice—'C'est toi, Henri?'—and asked him to take his pocket-book and watch to his wife. He told them not to try to lift him. 'Tu souffres, Othon?' 'Je souffre.' As they were bringing him up, he died.

The fall was at about 3.45; they did not reach the Torino hut till midnight. Léon Bron the guardian thought that Othon was only unconscious, he looked so calm. Early next morning Mme Bron was sweeping her front step when she saw her brother Octave Ollier. He was going to talk to her, but she spoke first: 'Othon is dead.' He tried to tell her that Othon was only badly hurt, thinking this would break it gently, but she wouldn't listen, saying she knew that he was dead. She went up to tell Horace, but could hardly get the words out. 'Oh, but I knew father was dead,' he said. 'I was told it in the night.'

They brought him down that day from the Torino, and two days later he was buried. Eight guides came over from Chamonix and walked behind the coffin with the Courmayeur men, in their guides' clothes, their ropes on their shoulders. There were appreciations in the French as well as in the Italian papers. 'Bron était un gars solide,' said one of the cuttings Mme Bron showed us, 'tel que la montagne sait les former. . . . Qui, à Chamonix, ne connaissait pas ce profil bronzé aux traits accentués et énergiques, toujours souriant, et, à la lèvre, toujours la blague. . . . C'était un Valdôtain, et l'on peut dire un gars de chez nous.'

Mme Bron, who had always been so silent when Othon was there, talked to us for a long time in the darkened room; Horace, a pale little boy of five with his fair hair curled into a beautiful sausage on the top of his head, wandered in and out from the sunny balcony or stood, looking gravely at us. We could not talk to him much, for he spoke Italian only; but he was clearly a precocious and intelligent child, and fine-drawn as such children often are. Mme Bron had not seen many like him; she found him small and frail compared with the village children, and was very worried. There were other problems too: the letting of a house they owned in the Val Ferret, the threatened widening of the main street of Courmayeur which would pull down the Droguerie. Mme Bron had always seemed older than Othon, more care-worn; now she looked anxiously at us as if we, because of our friendship with him, might somehow be able to transmit a little of his sanguine vigour. On one small point we could help: the transporting of two pairs of skis which belonged to the two English girls with whom Othon had made a long tour that spring in the Monte Rosa region, and who had been going to join him again next year. Mme Bron did not like to risk the skis unattended across frontiers.

In the afternoon she took us to the churchyard. Among the votive wreaths and twisted metal flowers was a temporary wooden cross: OTHON BRON, 27.5.97–25.7.38.

We went back to Aosta that evening, carrying the skis: the sun was off Mont Blanc, and our last sight of it was cold and white. Next day we crossed the Great St. Bernard.

II

We had no special plans, but shoved away in a pocket I had a letter with the name of a guide of whom a friend of mine spoke highly, but at second hand. 'A good young guide from St. Niklaus,' was my rather vague memory of her description. We had been told that he might be at the Riffel, so we got the hotel at Visp to ring him up. We were unexcited: he would probably not be there, and if he were would not be free. But Madame called us to the telephone, Michael spoke to him, and it was arranged to meet to-morrow. Then the name, Johann Brantschen, stirred memories: when I had finally placed him as having climbed with Geoffrey Young before the war, and again more recently, I felt like a woman who, having asked for the name of the little dressmaker round the corner, finds herself being fitted by Chanel. We met the Zermatt train next day, and there was a pleasant man of about fifty, ready to step at once into the train for Brigue when we suggested the Oberland. We went as far as Fiesch that night—a village which makes a charming picture in memory, perhaps because of the plates of fresh raspberries and blaeberries, topped with meringues and cream, that we had for dinner. Walking up to the Eggishorn next morning was like the first day in a new school. Actions that were usually automatic were to-day undertaken with consciousness and deliberation. I took care to walk with my heels as well as my toes; I did not want a stumbling rhythm, a trip over stone or branch, to give Hans Brantschen a bad impression. We drank great glasses of milk at the Hôtel Jungfrau and watched the *pensionnaires* settled on the windy terrace in curious hutch-like chairs. On the Aletsch glacier the Concordia hut kept on looking just about half an hour away: it was a long two and a half hours' plod. The hut seemed a paradise, with a wonderfully clean and efficient guardian, helped by a girl with flaxen pigtails.

It was mild and starry at 2.30 next morning when we started for the Finsteraarhorn: there was no need of the lantern once we were on the glacier, nor of gloves. Shooting stars streaked across the sky; I saw one clearly against the snow, which it appeared to hit about twenty yards in front of Hans. There had been new snow lately, and he tested with his axe for crevasses all the way up to the Grünhorn Lücke and down the other side. The way up the Finsteraarhorn was pleasant and uneventful. The snow slope beneath the Hugisattel looked steeper than it really was; only occasionally did Hans need to flick a groove with the pick end of his axe, or scoop out a hole with the shovel. We left our axes on the saddle, and enjoyed the easy scramble on good rock to the top. We breakfasted, gazed down the south-east face, with admiring thoughts of Gertrude Bell and her two days out in the storm, and looked at the peaks all round rising from a sea of clouds. We made sanguine plans: the Mittelegi ridge of the Eiger, the Jungfrau, the Aletschhorn, and Hans suggested that we should enjoy a day on the Fusshörner, whose rocky comb had attracted us as we walked up to the Concordia.

We took a more direct line down the lower snows than in coming up, trudged up to the Grünhorn Lücke, and sloshed down the far from 'dry' glacier to a late lunch at the Concordia. It wasn't fine enough for the Aletschhorn next morning, so we slept late, and over breakfast were entertained by a gentleman from Locarno who had come over the Simplon by train, missed the connection at Brigue, hired a taxi (which broke down) to Fiesch, finally reaching the Aletsch glacier at 9 p.m. and the Concordia at midnight. And his new boots hurt! We strolled up to the rocks behind the hut; they looked attractive, and we went up a bit. I came down and collected the rope and we had a nice little climb in rubbers up to point 3244. Meanwhile Hans had come out and, feeling responsible for us, climbed up too. It was fascinating to see him come up, without the least hurry, in a third of the time it had taken us—and we had thought it easy!

We had crossed one or two items off our list of hoped-for expeditions, and began to worry about provisions, when in came two English girls from the Bergli hut. The weather was driving them down to the valley, and they kindly gave us their spare food. One of their Grindelwald guides, a most likable weather-beaten character, had brought with him a pack of Tarot cards, and Hans joined them in a game. I dodged round, trying to get a good look at the Hanged Man and the others, so familiar from *The Waste Land*

I had forgotten that they really did exist. This guide, we were told, was a considerable Grindelwald capitalist. Every time he went up by rail to the Jungfraujoch, and the train stopped at Eigerwand to let the day-trippers gaze at the awful north face, he would whip out his telescope, train it on the Faulhorn, and count his cows.

To cheer up the day and spin out our provisions we lunched at the Pavillon Cathreen, the tiny hotel above the climbing hut. 'Ce n'est pas gai,' said the lady in charge, sadly shaking her head at the grey sky, grey mountains, and grey glacier. We were back there next day, which was worse, and had a long talk with her. She came from Saint-Luc in the Val d'Anniviers, where her father kept the Bella Tola Hotel; and fifteen years ago she had spent a year at Ditchling with Eric Gill's family. Had we ever heard of him? She was pleased when I told her that I had worked for four years just over one of his carvings. She spoke very warmly of her home at Saint-Luc, and the woods, and the haymaking, and the processions with her eldest boy singing in the choir. We wondered why she spent her summer on this platform of rock above a great sea of ice; but she assured us warmly that she loved this too, the view was always different, one felt so elevated, and yet so free.

The visitors' book helped to pass the time. I copied out three entries. The first, by an Englishman: 'Wife fell down only once.' A Frenchman was responsible for: 'Je suis très agité car ma mère a manqué de tomber dans les crevasses. Temps splendide. Bonne cuisine.' The third, dated 1899, was: 'G. W. Young and A. M. Mackay with guide Albrecht. Finsteraarhorn, up, 4 h. 10; down, 2 h. 50.'

We went back to the hut to find every one gone down, or over the Lötschenlücke or Grünhorn Lücke to another hut or valley, except for ourselves and two Japs with tight trousers. To our surprise, Hans woke us early next morning and said the Grünhorn would go. When we left the hut there was mist on the Aletsch glacier, but the peaks were clear above and we could see a light in the observatory at the Jungfraujoch. After a very careful descent on the icy path from the hut, we passed into the mist ourselves as we stepped on to the glacier, and could see nothing ahead or around. A few yards on and we were clear, with the gap of the

Grünhorn Lücke ahead, behind us a wonderful blue light over the Lötschenlücke, and in the sky the new moon, 'wi' the auld moon in her arm.'

It was bitterly cold, and the new snow was frosted over. We put on our crampons before starting up the glacier to the Grüneckhorn. Hans took a fairly steep line, and I found it hard work flexing the ankles, driving all ten spikes square into the slope, and keeping up his pace. The Japs had started just before us, for the Grünhorn too; but their two Grindelwald guides had gone further towards the pass before striking up. Hans turned and shouted advice about the best way of getting through the crevasses.

We came out on to a snowy ridge falling sharply on the left to the Ewig Schnee Feld ice-fall, and as the slope steepened there were horrid groans: Hans explained them as the new snow settling into the layer of old. From this point to the top the snow looked as if it might peel off at any moment, and Hans kept as near to the ridge as possible. It was a good way of looking at the Oberland, walking between the Ewig Schnee Feld and the Fiescher Firn, with every ridge and tooth of the Finsteraarhorn sharply outlined against a sea of cloud. As soon as we got to the top of the Grünhorn, the Schreckhorn put itself into the category of mountains that must be climbed. Going down on the snow was far less unpleasant than I had feared: by digging the heels well in one could usually get a good footing in the old snow beneath, and by the time we got to the Grüneckhorn I was thoroughly enjoying it. For the first time I had the confidence to put into full practice the lesson I had angrily taught myself that winter day after my tumble on skis down the back of the Grande Casse: to walk down as boldly and confidently as if it were steep grass or scree, with the same conviction that a slip could at once be controlled. It all seemed quite easy to-day, even on the slopes where the new snow was fairly shooting off the old; but perhaps this was the influence of Hans behind. Anyway it was very pleasant to translate a remembered action, and an imagined action, into the action itself. (I have still to learn if the stem-christies I have swung through in thought so often since 1937 will as readily be transmuted into the real thing on an icy slope.)

It was extremely hot and slushy on the last stage to the

Concordia, which we reached at 11.45, to find an English *course collective* in full possession, shouting down the indigenous sound of German-Swiss as they asked each other puzzles at the tops of their voices and made personal remarks. We sat about in the sun; in the evening Michael and Hans played dominoes with concentration and good humour, while the guardian did his nightly hook-up on the wireless telephone: 'Joch von Concordia, Hollandia von Concordia'—he made a pleasant musical phrase of it, on three notes. Our German was not very conversational, and Hans was strongest in the English needed on a mountain—we noticed that he laughed much more often when talking German—but we very much enjoyed our moderately silent hours with him. Casually, over a ham omelet at the Pavillon Cathreen that evening, he told us it was the first time he had been up the Grünhorn. We were surprised: not only had he taken an unhesitating line, but he had authoritatively shouted advice to the Japs' Grindelwald guides, in whose parish the mountain lay, and they had at once taken it. He smiled: it had been a good joke.

Our last mountain had to be crossed off: next morning was no day for the Aletschhorn or any other peak. We said good-bye very warmly on the glacier—Hans going down to Fiesch and St. Niklaus, we to the Jungfraujoch and the train at Grindelwald. We trudged up in mist, uneventfully on the dry glacier, but very delicately indeed once we were on the Jungfrau Firn. There was new snow everywhere; Michael was extremely cautious, testing every step. To give him a rest, I took the lead. There was a grey blur all round, and it was hard to see anything, though sometimes the Joch showed through a clearing. It was always difficult to judge if a snow hummock in front were two or twenty feet high. Sometimes, in the Alps, you walk on the top of the world, commanding vast prospects over far countries, using mountain ranges as your landmarks; and then, involved in the séracs of an ice-fall, or caught in mist, your world crumples and shrinks to five yards, in which each snow crystal claims your eye. Now in this mist on the deceitful new-white glacier, we were conscious only of the need to walk carefully, to test our steps. We should hardly have noticed if we had been wet or hungry, the fact would have been shelved, to be considered at a more convenient time.

It would have been the same on difficult rock, or in a storm high up: the greater preoccupation would drive out all the less, though cold and hunger would reassert themselves all the more imperiously when the major problem had been solved. As for the humdrum worries of our working lives—and one of the main points of holidays is to free you, even temporarily, from these—they do not reappear till long after cold and hunger have exacted their toll of attention, and I incline to think that one of the reasons for short tempers in the valleys after days on the tops is that we are once more vulnerable to the possibilities of losing luggage, missing letters, running short of money, and to the health of the baby left at home.

I was not, however, thinking these thoughts: I was trying to take a good line towards the Jungfraujoch. I prodded every doubtful place with my ice-axe, and followed very gingerly myself. Suddenly there was a shout behind me; there was Michael up to his shoulders in a crevasse over which I had passed unknowing a second before. Foolishly, I sat down to pull—I thought I would distribute my weight better that way. Michael's words soon had me on my feet; I pulled like a demon, and he clawed his way out with his axe and crawled on to the slightly solider stretch beside me. But it all looked bad now. In a minute or two we were just under the entrance to the Jungfraujoch station—but for the mist, our incident with the crevasse would have provided local colour for the trippers at the plate-glass window high on the rock. At the entrance to the tunnel which leads into this combination of troll's cave and Grand Babylon Hotel was a notice: ACHTUNG GLETSCHER SPALTEN! ATTENTION, CREVASSES!

We had a quick bowl of soup, and took the train down to the Scheidegg. I was glad to have linked up with my 1931 outing with Hans Graf, and glad, too, to have reached the Joch on my own legs. At Eigergletscher we burst into the sun, and a sight of the gleaming, graceful Silberhorn; from the streets of Interlaken that evening we looked up at the Jungfrau shining white and clear in the sky.

We left the great mountains behind, knowing it might be our last year together among them for some time. But this year, for all its heartbreaking loss, had brought a new extension to the happiness of our mountain holidays. We might have to give up ambitious hopes of the Brenva Ridge or the Grépon from the Mer de Glace (though we could confidently count on guiding any one up the Sassière, even if we should not see it for twenty years); but we could not feel cheated. The good years would start again, if not for us, then for our children. That splendid traverse of the Meije, Michael's last climb with Othon, had filled me with envy the year before. Now I could think about it with something like equanimity; and five years later the last shred of grievance vanished, as we walked down the fellside to Grisedale, Helvellyn behind us, and our son running down the path in front. An hour ago he had been on Striding Edge, in mist and bitter wind; now the sun had come through, the wind had dropped. He had the two moments in his hand, the battle and the sunlight, and he ran towards the valley, and the running water, as I had run off windy Goatfell on that April day twenty-nine years before.

INDEX

INDEX

A' CHLIABHAIN, Ben, 3, 7
Albaron, 33, 58, 59, 60, 62, 148,
  168, 175
Albertville, 176
Aletsch glacier, 180, 181, 182, 184
Aletschhorn, 181, 184
Alpe Nuova, 106-8
Amiez, Robert, 168, 175
Aosta, 70-2, 74, 121, 122, 174,
  177, 179
Arbeyron, Ouille d', 60, 174
Arc, Val d', 33, 35, 63, 138, 149
Arolla glacier, 75
Arran, Isle of, 1-8, 10, 13, 19, 37,
  116
Arves, Aig. Meridionale d', 169
Assynt, Ben More of, 29
Averole, 59, 60, 172
Averole hut, 59, 171, 174
Ayer, 129

Ball's Guide to the Western Alps,
  35, 58, 65, 103, 111
Baounet glacier, 174
Bartholomew, Ian, 6
Bates, Robert, 133-5
Bec de Pralognan, Grand, 101-3
Bell, Gertrude, 14, 16, 181
Bellecôte, Sommet de, 100, 101,
  166
Bellegarde, 92-4, 169
Benachie, 8, 13, 162
Béranger, Aig. de, 84, 86
Bérarde, La, 169
Bertol hut, 75, 117
Bertoli, Mme, 153-4
Bessanese, 60, 172-4
Bessans, 60, 138-42, 150, 172, 174,
  176
Bétemps hut, 79-81, 130
Bidean nam Bian, 136
Biener, Alphonse, 14, 15

Bionnassay, Aig. de, 84, 88, 89, 91
Black, Max, 99
Blanc, Mont, 13, 17, 32, 34, 40,
  43, 44, 47, 54, 57, 62, 67, 68,
  73, 78, 80, 83-5, 87-92, 99, 100,
  105, 121, 131, 135, 158, 160,
  166, 170, 171, 177, 179
Blanc, Pierre, le pape, 59, 96, 127,
  143
Blanford, Thomas, 154
Blaven, 169
Boch, M., 97, 150, 155
Bonhomme, Col du, 32, 99
Bonneval, 37, 38, 59, 96, 107, 127,
  139-147, 149, 150, 168, 175, 176
Bonnevie, Mme, 97, 150
Bossons glacier, 47, 48
Boswell, James, 56
Bourg Saint-Maurice, 32, 33, 37,
  39-41, 54, 55, 57, 70, 99, 100,
  103, 137, 152, 153, 161, 166
Bourg Saint-Pierre, 72
Bournassien, Camille, 82, 83, 129
Bozel, 102
Braemar, 19-21, 24
Braeriach, 10, 20, 23, 32
Brantschen, Johann, 180-4
Breithorn, 11, 14, 79, 123, 124
Brenner Pass, 16, 41
Brenva, Aig. de la, 41-3
Breuil, 123, 124, 130, 134
Brevières, Les, 66, 69, 152
Brevoort, Miss, 65, 66
Brockedon, William, 40 n, 74, 93
Brodick, 1, 3-5
Bron, Horace, 40, 72, 122, 178-9
Bron, Léon, 131, 178
Bron, Mme, 41, 54, 70, 122, 177-9
Bron, Othon, 40-54, 69-84,
  122-135, 169, 171, 177-9, 186
Buachaille Etive, 136
Butler, Jock, 41-5, 131

ILLUSTRATIONS

1.   CIR MHOR AND GLEN SANNOX, ISLAND OF ARRAN

GLEN TILT

Looking back down the glen.

3.

4b. MAGGIE GRUER

4a. W. P. KER

5.

SUILVEN

Taken from Canisp, in spring. The ill-advised summer descent, described in the text, was from ledge to ledge, a little this side of the right-hand skyline.

6.

MER DE GLACE: DRAWING BY FRANCIS TOWNE

It was this scene that looked so familiar as we came round the dark buttress on the right of the picture, on our way from the Col du Géant, and looked up to our right at the Taléfre basin and the rocks rising to the Grandes Jorasses (under the cloud).

7.

MONT POURRI: ENGRAVING BY WILLIAM BROCKEDON

Brockedon went up from Bourg Saint-Maurice to Val d'Isére in 1829. 'Towering over this sombre valley, rises one of the grandest mountains in the Alps from its magnitude, and one of the most beautiful from its form – its vast mass of snow and glaciers surmounted by

8.   CASCADE AT TIGNES

9.   FROM THE TOP OF THE GRANDE SASSIÈRE
Across the Val d'Isère can be seen the black triangle of the Grande Casse.

10.　GRANDE CASSE, FROM THE GRANDE MOTTE

The snowy peak on the left is the Pic Mathews. Between the Grande Casse and the Lepéna (rock peak in right fore-

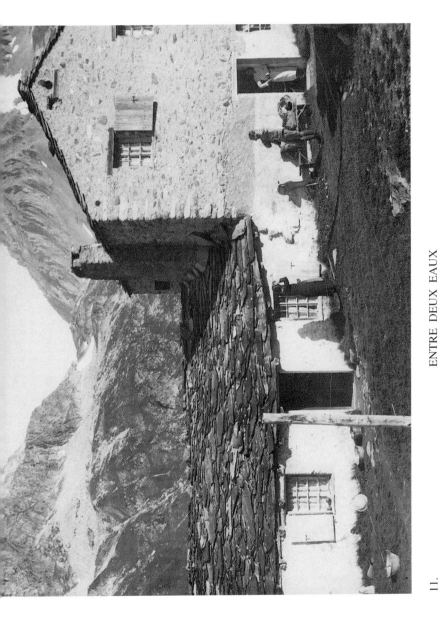

11.

ENTRE DEUX EAUX

Behind the farmhouse can be seen the eastern end of the Col de la Vanoise, a mile-long windy trough with the Refuge Félix-Faure at the further end. To the right of it rise the southern slopes of the Grande Casse.

12b.   SAINT-GRAT

A shrine at the foot of the Averole valley. Similar little wooden figures are found on the Italian side of the range, Saint-Grat being the patron saint of the diocese of Aosta.

12a.   AT THE TORINO HUT

Taken after our return from the Dent du Géant. The guardian is in the extreme background, then come Octave Ollier, Othon Bron, Janet Adam Smith, and Michael Roberts.

13.

AIGUILLE DE BIONNASSAY

Taken from the Dôme du Goûter. Our route went up the left-hand arête of the Bionnassay, over the black rocks on the skyline to the top, then along the snow ridge to the Dôme du Goûter.

ON THE WAY TO THE GRAND BEC DE PRALOGNAN

14.

CHAMPAGNY-LE-BOIS

15.

16.   CREVASSE ON THE GLACIER DU MULINET

17.   IN VALSAVARANCHE
The last hamlet, looking down the valley, with part of the Grivola visible on the right, behind the nearer ridge.

18. PIC DE LA GRIVOLA: ENGRAVED FROM A DRAWING BY S. W. KING

'Singularly beautiful as its wonderful outline had appeared at a distance, it was even far more extraordinary in close proximity. Towards the north its sharply defined slope cut the sky in a straight line, deeply and smoothly coated with snow, apparently far too steep for human foot to scale; while to the south it presented a bare rugged face, the protruding edges of unreared strata.' (THE REV. S. W. KING, 1858.)

19. GRIVOLA

The 'protruding edges' viewed from in front. The usual route, which we followed, goes up a rock rib in the middle of the face.

20.   SOURCE OF THE ARVEYRON: DRAWING BY FRANCIS
TOWNE (1781)

21. MATHON, IN THE GRISONS: DRAWING BY JAN HACKAERT (1656)

22a. MICHAEL ROBERTS AT TIGNES

22b. OTHON BRON

23.

GRÉPON AND GRANDS CHARMOZ

Taken from the top of the Requin, showing the great Mer de Glace face of the Grépon. The ordinary route comes up to the col between Grépon and Charmoz, from the far side, and then over the summits of the Grépon to the depression on the left of the picture.

24.   CARRO HUT, ABOVE BONNEVAL

25.　　　　　　BESSANS IN WINTER

W. EMPSON, ESQ.

On the way to the Col de la Leisse, which lies to the right, behind the sunlit slope.

26.

27.

ON THE ROAD TO TIGNES

Looking down the gorge between Val d'Isère and Tignes. In the sunlight is the Aiguille Percée and, to the right, the lower slopes of the Pourri.

28.

GRANDE CASSE

Taken from the Glacier de la Réchasse. On the right, connected by the snowy ridge, is the Grande Motte; from the

29.   NEAR ENTRE-DEUX-EAUX

30. H. V. HUGHES ON THE CROCE ROSSA

Looking down the Vallon de la Lombarde towards the Averole hut; on the left is the Charbonnel.

BESSANESE

Taken from a shoulder of the Charbonnel, with bad weather coming up from Italy.

31.

32.   OTHON BRON'S GRAVE
At Courmayeur, with plaque to the right: 'In memory of Michael Roberts 1902-1948
who climbed these mountains with Ottone Bron'.